The Student's **Shakespeare**

OTHELLO

THE MOOR OF VENICE

Introduction by Angela Sheehan

This edition published 2014 by Geddes & Grosset, an imprint of
The Gresham Publishing Company Ltd., Academy Park, Building 4000,
Gower Street, Glasgow, G51 1PR, Scotland, UK

ISBN: 978-1-84205-792-6

Printed and bound in Spain by Novoprint, SA.

 *Introduction*

William Shakespeare (1564–1616) had such a deep understanding of human nature that he was able to create characters and dramatic situations that have meanings beyond the time and place of his settings. *Othello* was probably written in 1604. It was first performed on 1 November 1604 at the court of the new king, James I, and then before the paying public at the Globe Theatre, London, and other theatres. It was published in 1622.

The play is set first in Venice, the centre of a once great trading empire, and then in Cyprus, an island ruled over by the powerful Venetian government. Shakespeare did not invent the story. As he so often did, he borrowed much of it from an earlier work, this time a tale in a collection called *Gli Hecatimmithi* by the Italian writer Giovanni Battista Giraldi Cinthio, which was published in 1566.

THE REPUBLIC OF VENICE

The full title of Shakespeare's play is *The Tragedy of Othello, the Moor of Venice*. Today the city of Venice on the Adriatic coast of northern Italy is a unique tourist destination, famed for the beauty of its art and architecture, and especially for its canals. The city is built on islands in a lagoon; the streets are canals, with bridges over them, and no cars are allowed. People travel in flat-bottomed boats called *gondolas* or in motorboat buses and taxis.

In medieval times Venice was a republic ruled by a council of senators led by a Doge, or Duke. The citizens had enlarged the islands and created new ones by driving wooden piles into the mud below the shallow waters. There was little land on which to grow crops, so the people turned to trade to support themselves.

Venetian ships sailed to far countries and brought back grain, spices, silks, carpets, precious stones and luxury goods that were prized in Europe. The port was a staging post for Christian pilgrims to the Holy

Lands and for Crusaders, who bought supplies and weapons for their journeys. As a result the city became wealthy, its warehouses full of foreign goods, and its coffers full of foreign cash.

To conquer new territories, protect their merchants and defend themselves against rival powers, such as Genoa and Turkey, the Venetians needed fighting ships and fighting men. There were no regular armies in medieval times. Nobles and rulers called on their peasants and workers to fight for them. They often hired trained professional soldiers called mercenaries, or 'soldiers of fortune', to recruit armies and lead them. Venice had a small population so its Doge needed to hire a foreign commander like Othello, the hero of Shakespeare's play.

The people of Venice

People visited Venice from three continents. In Venice today you can see a painting by Vittore Carpaccio called *The Healing of the Possessed Man* (1494). In the foreground of this busy scene we see a black gondolier rowing across the Grand Canal, and in the crowds beyond are people in a variety of oriental and African dress.

No one knows for sure where Othello is supposed to have come from. Originally the word 'Moor' applied to Muslims who conquered parts of Spain in the eighth century and settled there until they were driven out in the fifteenth century. More properly the word denotes the Muslim people of mixed Berber and Arab descent from North Africa, particularly from Mauritania and Morocco. Shakespeare would not have learned much geography in school and would not have known much about the vastness and variety of Africa and its peoples. He probably saw his Othello as a true black African from further south, and called him a Moor because the word was commonly used for any black person, as was the word 'blackamoor'.

Shakespeare lived and worked in London, a great port like Venice, with ships arriving daily from Africa and the Middle East via Portugal and Spain. Arab traders and scholars travelled widely in Africa, as far south as Zimbabwe, and sailed along its east and west coasts. As Europeans began to make contact with Africans and trade with them, they brought people back with them, some as crew and some as slaves to be sold. Black servants were a status symbol. Some Africans stayed on at sea as sailors, some married and settled down to other jobs on land. Some like Othello joined mercenary armies and fought for any ruler prepared to pay them – in Othello's case, a Christian state fighting a Muslim enemy.

Venice at war

In the late sixteenth century Venice was in conflict with Turkey, centre of the Ottoman Empire. Cyprus, the setting for most of *Othello*, was an important island in the Mediterranean, ruled by the Venetians. The Turks invaded the island in 1570. The Venetians defeated them in the naval battle of Lepanto in 1571 but the Turks rebuilt their fleet and Venice was forced to surrender the island to them in 1573. In the play, Othello has been ordered to Cyprus to fight the invading Turks, but when he arrives the Turkish fleet has been wrecked by a storm at sea. Beyond celebrating, there is nothing for his men to do. He himself has his new bride to keep him occupied.

For military men, lack of action is often dispiriting. Confined to their base, the characters have little to occupy their time, besides drunken revelries and personal rivalries and resentments. The atmosphere is fraught with danger: hotheaded soldiers, unrequited lovers, smouldering jealousies. Who has the ear of the commander? Who has been promoted? Who wants revenge?

Shakespeare's audience would have found the scene familiar. The court of Elizabeth I, who died the year before the play was written, was full of intrigue. Many of the audience would have served in armies fighting the Spanish or putting down rebellions in Ireland. All of them would have known of England's defeat of the Spanish Armada in 1588, and perhaps recognised the role heavy winds and high seas played in the wrecking of the fleet. Some may even have witnessed Queen Elizabeth's speech at Tilbury as her navy set sail.

It was not until Oliver Cromwell organised his troops to fight the English Civil War (1642–46) that the country had a proper army. Before then, the monarch paid for wars but local Lord Lieutenants (who represented the Crown) had to recruit, train and arm their men, pay them and hope to reclaim the money from the court. A good general like Othello, who had been commissioned by the Venetian state, would have seen that his men were well trained, well armed, well fed and well disciplined. But bad officers often neglected their troops, failing to pay them, forcing many to sell their weapons (often to the enemy) to avoid starvation or simply to turn to looting.

THE STORY OF *OTHELLO*

Shakespeare's tragedies and histories generally tell the stories of kings and queens and great figures of the past. *Othello* is different; its principal characters are army officers and their wives, from

Shakespeare's own day. The public events are a mere backdrop for the private tragedy brought about by one man's evil manipulation of another man's noble mind. It is a drama of love and hate, jealousy, revenge and murder, and outraged pride.

Act I Love and war

Othello, a career soldier and commander in the Venetian army, wins the confidence of the Duke (Doge), who sends him to defend Cyprus. He also wins the love of Desdemona, the daughter of Senator Brabantio. Though he admires him as a general, Brabantio thinks only sorcery could make his daughter love Othello, a man of a different colour and culture. Iago is the 'ancient' or ensign (flag bearer) and married to Emilia. Iago hates the Moor for making Cassio his lieutenant and leaving him a mere 'ancient'. He tells Brabantio that 'an old black ram/ Is tupping your white ewe.' (Act I Sc i), playing on the old man's racial prejudice and fears for his daughter's honour. Desdemona herself proclaims that the only magic Othello used was to tell her his thrilling war stories. He says, 'She loved me for the dangers I had passed/And I loved her that she did pity them./ This only is the witchcraft I have used:' (Act I Sc iii). Brabantio warns Othello, 'Look to her, Moor, if thou hast eyes to see./ She has deceived her father, and may thee.' (Act I Sc iii).

While he pretends loyalty, in reality Iago is set on destroying Othello, whom he suspects of making love to his wife, Emilia, who is Desdemona's maid. If he can persuade Othello that Desdemona has been unfaithful to him with Cassio, he can destroy Cassio at the same time. Roderigo, a Venetian gentleman, is in love with Desdemona, and Iago suggests to him that he can win her away from her new husband.

Act II Iago sets his traps

The Venetian party arrives in Cyprus to be greeted by the governor, Montano. Cassio has arrived first and greets Desdemona with compliments and courteously kisses her hand. Othello arrives and kisses Desdemona on the lips. Iago tells Roderigo that Desdemona encouraged Cassio to kiss her hand, so she must be tiring of Othello. He suggests that Roderigo pick a fight with Cassio, getting him into trouble and out of the way so that he can seduce Desdemona.

Iago plans to drive Othello mad with jealousy. As part of his scheme, during the celebrations to mark the naval victory and Othello's marriage, he will get Cassio drunk, despite the latter's reluctance to drink at all: 'Not tonight, good Iago. I have very poor and unhappy brains for drinking. I could well wish courtesy would invent some other custom of entertainment.' (Act II Sc iii). Iago prevails and soon everyone is singing drinking songs, clinking 'canakins' of wine, and Iago is pointing out Cassio's drunkeness to Montano, and setting Roderigo on him. A nasty brawl ensues, Montano intervenes, Othello is roused and Iago gives a damning account of the fighting, saying, 'I had rather have this tongue cut from my mouth/ Than it should do offence to Michael Cassio;' Othello, trusting Iago's every word, says 'Cassio, I love thee,/ But nevermore be officer of mine.' (Act II Sc iii).

Cassio, sobering up, asks Iago for advice. How can he restore his reputation? Iago suggests Cassio ask Desdemona to plead his cause with Othello who will refuse her nothing. But he might wonder why his wife is so keen to have him reinstated!

Act III The fateful handkerchief

Next day, Cassio entreats Emilia to intercede for him. Desdemona is easily persuaded and promises to help Cassio. As Cassio is leaving, Iago arrives with Othello. 'Was not that Cassio parted from my wife?' asks Othello. Iago says, surely not, 'I cannot think it/ That he would steal away so guilty-like,/ Seeing you coming.' (Act III Sc iii). Innocently, Desdemona begs Othello to forgive Cassio. 'Not now, sweet Desdemona – some other time,' he says, but she persists, and when Othello relents, she leaves, with him musing: 'Excellent wretch! Perdition catch my soul/ But I do love thee! And when I love thee not,/ Chaos is come again.' (Act III Sc iii).

Iago is standing by to plant more doubt in Othello's mind, while at the same time cunningly warning him against jealousy. 'It is the green-eyed monster which doth mock/ The meat it feeds on. That cuckold lives in bliss/ Who, certain of this fate, loves not his wronger.' (Act III Sc iii). Iago tells him to keep watch on Desdemona, and Othello is torn between believing his devious ensign or his faithful wife.

As she returns with Emilia, he cries out, 'If she be false, O, then heaven mocks itself!/ I'll not believe't.' (Act III Sc iii). Othello complains of a headache and Desdemona lovingly attempts to bind his brow with her embroidered handkerchief. But the handkerchief is too small and she lets it drop to the ground. Emilia retrieves it, pleased that she can pass it to her husband who has asked her many times to get hold of it. She has no idea that he plans to plant it in Cassio's rooms.

Othello is in turmoil. He does not want to believe that Desdemona has betrayed him. He must have proof. Iago lies: he has seen Cassio wipe his beard with Desdemona's handkerchief. Othello is distraught.

Iago is to kill Cassio. He says it will be done, but 'let her live', so planting a terrible idea in Othello's mind.

Pretending to have a cold, Othello asks to borrow Desdemona's handkerchief, but of course she has not got it, but is sure she has not 'lost' it. It was a precious wedding gift that once belonged to Othello's mother. Othello is furious 'To lose or give't away were such perdition/ As nothing else could match.' (Act III Sc iv). He becomes even more enraged and storms off when Desdemona tries to deflect his anger by talking about Cassio. She has no idea why he is so angry.

Desdemona tells Cassio that Othello will not listen to her, he must wait awhile. As she leaves, another woman comes to see Cassio. She is Bianca, a prostitute who is in love with him. She is upset that he has not been to see her. He begs her forgiveness and, to make amends, gives her Desdemona's handkerchief, which he has found in his house. He likes the embroidery, and asks her to sew him one like it. She assumes another woman has given it to him but agrees to meet him later.

Act IV Iago turns the screw

Othello is now in Iago's power. He is eaten up with jealousy, and self-doubt, and losing his grip on reality. He talks crazily about honour, lust, and the handkerchief, and eventually falls down with an epileptic seizure. While he is unconscious, Cassio comes in, but Iago tells him to go away and wait because he wants to talk with him.

When Othello recovers, Iago tells him to listen in secret to his conversation with Cassio. Their disrespectful talk is of Bianca, who 'gives it out that you shall marry her.' (Act IV Sc i), says Iago. Cassio laughs at the idea. Othello thinks they are speaking of Desdemona, and is completely convinced when suddenly Bianca arrives and thrusts Desdemona's handkerchief into Cassio's hand with the words: 'This is some minx's token – ' (Act IV Sc i). Iago could not have hoped for better luck. As Cassio departs, Othello's mind is set on murder: 'Ay, let her rot and perish, and be damned tonight, for she/ shall not live. No, my heart is turned to stone – ' (Act IV Sc i). He tells Iago to get him some poison, but Iago suggests strangling Desdemona instead, in their marriage bed.

Just then, a trumpet sounds, and Desdemona welcomes Lodovico, her noble Venetian relative. He brings a letter from the Duke, summoning Othello back to Venice. Cassio will take his office. As Othello reads the letter, Desdemona chats to Lodovico. But then Othello rounds on her, shouts at her, strikes her, and follows her back indoors. Lodovico cannot believe that this is the 'noble Moor' whom all the senate trusted. Was it the letter that made him angry? Are his wits safe? Iago hints that Othello may be mad.

At home, Othello questions Emilia about his wife's behaviour and sends her to fetch Desdemona. Despite Emilia's assurance that she would wager her own soul that her mistress is honest, when Othello is alone with Desdemona he accuses her at length of being a 'strumpet', a whore. She is naturally horrified but the more she defends herself the fiercer he becomes. After he has left, Desdemona asks Emilia and 'good' Iago if they have any idea what has made Othello so jealous. What can she do? She goes in to dinner with the Venetian visitors.

Roderigo now comes to see Iago. Why has Iago promised to win Desdemona for him and done nothing? He is tired of waiting. He has given him presents of jewels for her, but now he wants them back. Of course, Iago has kept them for himself, and never said a word to Desdemona. To retrieve the situation, Iago tells Roderigo about Othello's recall and Cassio's promotion. Only an unfortunate 'accident' happening to Cassio might make him stay. Roderigo will have an opportunity to kill Cassio as he leaves Bianca's house later that night. After Othello's supper guests have departed, Othello orders his wife to bed. Desdemona recalls a sad song her mother's maid sang about a girl whose beloved went mad and abandoned her. Emilia leaves her.

Act V Put out the light

Iago sees a way of being rid of Cassio and Roderigo. He can get them to kill each other, or one kill the other and the survivor be hanged for murder. He waits with Roderigo in the dark street, but Roderigo bungles his attempt to stab Cassio and is wounded by him. Iago then stabs Cassio. Othello, passing by, assumes that Iago has carried out his orders. Lodovico and a companion also pass by and hear Cassio and Roderigo, both half dead, calling for help. In the confusion, pretending that he is avenging Cassio, Iago kills Roderigo.

Othello enters Desdemona's bedroom, set on killing her, but he cannot bear to do it. 'Put out the light, and then put out the light.' (Act V Sc ii), the light of his life. Instead, he kisses her and she wakes. He asks if she has said her prayers, and tells her to pray for forgiveness. For what? she asks, and he accuses her of giving the handkerchief to Cassio. At last she realises that she has been the victim of a cruel plot. She begs Othello for time but it is 'too late'. He smothers her.

Emilia rushes in and tells Othello the news of Roderigo's death. Desdemona cries out with her dying breath, and Emilia gasps in horror,

'O, who has done this deed?' she asks. 'Nobody; I myself. O, farewell!' (Act V Sc ii), says Desdemona, and dies.

Emilia turns on Othello who confesses that he has killed Desdemona on Iago's evidence of her guilt. Iago arrives, and seeks to defend himself by saying that he told Othello only what he thought was true. When Othello mentions the handkerchief, Emilia realises what has happened and tells Othello that she gave the handkerchief to Iago.

Iago attacks Emilia and kills her and makes a run for it but he is arrested and brought back. At last Othello realises the dreadful truth. He takes his favourite sword and strikes Iago, but is prevented from killing him. While the others work out just what has happened, Othello is lost in thought. When Lodovico arrests him for his wife's murder, he asks to speak.

'When you shall these unlucky deeds relate,/ Speak of them as they are. Nothing extenuate,/ Nor set down aught in malice. Then must you speak/ Of one that loved not wisely, but too well;' (Act V Sc ii). Then he recalls a battle long ago when he killed a Turk; as he speaks of stabbing his enemy he stabs himself. He falls on the bed beside the lifeless Desdemona, and dies kissing her.

THE PLAY'S CHARACTERS

Othello

Othello is viewed in Venice as a noble character. He inspires trust and admiration but also jealousy and prejudice. He has impressed the Venetian senate enough to be given charge of Cyprus. But because he is not a Venetian, not a Christian and not white, he is not to be trusted with Desdemona. He is 'the Moor', an outsider, an alien. He has had to marry in secret. Despite provocation, he shows gentleness and restraint when he refuses to fight with his father-in-law, Brabantio. He calms him humorously but with respect. He is a powerful man, used to being obeyed, and a brave soldier with an adventurous past. In Cyprus, he shows his dislike of uncontrolled behaviour when Cassio gets drunk, but easily loses control of himself. He is gullible enough to trust everything Iago says, more willing to believe a fellow soldier than the woman he loves. Iago plays on his 'free and open' nature, and his deep insecurities: his fears that as a foreigner and a simple soldier the sophisticated Venetians will laugh at him, and his wife will be attracted by a younger man. Iago knows that Othello can 'be led by the nose', and driven mad with jealousy. He loves Desdemona, his 'soul's joy', so much that he cannot bear to lose her. When he realises he has been deceived he accepts his guilt, says he deserves to be 'roasted in sulphur', and honourably kills himself. He asks to be remembered in a good light but we must also remember that he was a murderer.

Desdemona

We are aware from the start that Desdemona is kind and clever and brave, with a mind of her own. Knowing her father would disapprove, she has married in secret a man she hardly knows, from a different culture, religion, class and colour. She is attracted by his bravery and excited by the stories he tells. She wants adventure herself, insisting on going to Cyprus where she may be in danger. Despite her privileged upbringing, she is strong-willed and immature. Young women in Venice had little experience of life outside the home. She is used to getting her own way, charming everyone with her beauty. She is relentless in her bid to help Cassio: 'If I do vow a friendship, I'll perform it/ To the last article;' (Act III Sc iii). But she cannot see how angry she is making her husband. She is so warm and loving herself that she has no idea that anyone might want to harm her. To the end, she trusts Iago and she is utterly loyal to Othello. She excuses his vile behaviour before the Venetian ambassadors, and even with her dying breath tries to take all the blame on herself.

Iago

Full of hate, Iago is a cold, cunning killer who presents a false face to the world: 'not I for love and duty,/ But seeming so for my peculiar end:' (Act I Sc i). He is a typical villain of 'revenge tragedy', a popular type of play in Shakespeare's time that dealt with evil deeds and deadly plots. But, instead of a stereotype, Shakespeare has made 'honest Iago' a real person: always ready with good advice, a helping hand, a drink or a joke. People trust him because he makes himself out to be an unsophisticated man of action. But the audience knows that he is a ruthless liar. He is highly intelligent, able to make devious plans and change them instantly. But with him, it is never a fair fight. We see him rob and later kill Roderigo, destroy Cassio, and drive Othello to murder. He is quick to spot other people's weaknesses: Roderigo's infatuation with Desdemona, Cassio's weak head for alcohol, Othello's insecurity. He has an eye for jealousy because he is jealous himself, even suspecting his own sweet wife of infidelity. And he is envious. He bears a grudge against Cassio because he feels he should have been promoted in his place. He is a brilliant strategist but he is also a coward, who kills his wife 'from behind' and then runs away.

Emilia

Unlike her husband, Emilia really is honest. She is kind and reassuring, and loves Desdemona dearly. Being married to Iago, she has a low opinion of men and admits that she might commit adultery. She tries to make Desdemona less trusting. But even she does not see what is going on. She will not steal to please her husband but when she comes across Desdemona's handkerchief, she gives it to him, without wondering why he wants it. When she does realise, she is fearless in establishing the truth. 'I care not for thy sword. I'll make thee known/ though I lost twenty lives.' (Act V Sc ii). She even screams at Othello: 'O murderous coxcomb, what should such a fool/ Do with so good a wife?' (Act V Sc ii).

Cassio

Also an outsider, a Florentine, Cassio knows the importance of good manners. He is a typical courtier: charming, intelligent and capable. He is also a thoughtful individual, who knows himself well. He has no head for drink and does not want to drink on duty but he does so to please Iago. He wishes to please Desdemona and Emilia and treats them with extravagant courtesy, which Iago mistakes for lust. When he is disgraced, he approaches Othello's wife in a proper manner without realising how his behaviour might appear to Othello. Most of all, he is loyal, never seeking revenge for being dismissed and staying with Othello to the end.

Roderigo

Why, we wonder, did Brabantio not wish Roderigo to marry his daughter? He has good manners, he is rich, he is handsome, what Brabantio calls a 'wealthy curled darling'. But he is pathetic. He hands his money to Iago and gives him jewels to give to Desdemona, even though he knows she is married, and to an extremely powerful man. He has no chance with her but vainly believes that she will turn to him when she tires of her husband. Like Brabantio he is prejudiced and refers to Othello as 'the thick-lips'. He believes what he wants to hear and is weak and self-centred. He knows it is wrong, but he goes along with Iago's plot to murder Cassio, and pays with his life.

Brabantio

Like the other Venetian nobles, Desdemona's father thought highly of Othello and treated him as a friend and peer. Othello says, he 'loved me, oft invited me,/ Still questioned me the story of my life' (Act I Sc iii). But Brabantio guards his daughter and her honour. He will not let Roderigo near her, and is horrified to know that she has left his house and run to 'the sooty bosom of such a thing as thou'. He publicly insults Othello and goes on to accuse him of witchcraft. Naively, Brabantio thinks that the Duke and the senators will back him, but he relents grudgingly when Desdemona admits that 'she was half the wooer'. He is enough of a politician to know when he must accept his fate.

THEMES AND LANGUAGE

Shakespeare wrote comedies, histories and tragedies, as well as sonnets. His greatest tragedies were written from 1600–08, and they are regarded as his finest plays. *Hamlet* (1600–01), is the story of a Danish prince who avenges the murder of his father. *King Lear* (1603–06) tells of an aged English king, who divides his kingdom between two of his three daughters, and goes mad when they ungratefully turn against him. *Macbeth* (1603–06) is a Scottish noble who murders his king and, following the prophecy of three witches, takes his place. As well as these, and *Othello*, Shakespeare wrote seven more great plays during this period. All of them contain memorable characters and speeches, and many expressions that we all use every day. You will find many examples of these in *Othello*. You will also find themes of good and evil and human nature in all his plays.

Jealousy and vengeance

The most important theme of *Othello* is the destructiveness of jealousy, how it arises, and how it can be sparked and inflamed. Iago knows from his own experience how envy of other people's good fortune (Cassio) and sexual jealousy (had Othello slept with his wife?) eats away at a person. He works on Othello's weaknesses, and plots how to make him mad with jealousy. He plants ideas and images of infidelity and revenge in Othello's head. He feeds them as they grow, and then slyly uses the handkerchief as 'proof'. Iago spurs on feeble Roderigo's jealousy, and even with no help from Iago, Bianca acts out of jealousy. Iago revels in the pain and misery he causes, as he coldly delights in his hated leader's decline into despair, and death.

Racism and sexism

Because we see the events of the play through modern eyes, issues arise that would not have occurred to Shakespeare's audience. We are appalled by the violence, the racism, and the sexism in the play but these would have seemed normal in Shakespeare's England, as they would to people in many cultures today.

Shakespeare exposes the inherent racism of some of his characters by the language he puts into their mouths. Goodness is 'fair', evil is 'black'. Nonetheless, he makes his hero black and his villain white. Iago has no respect for Othello despite his fine leadership, probably because he is black, and probably because he is jealous of him. He uses offensive language to describe him, and couples it with bestial sexual imagery guaranteed to terrify Brabantio: 'an old black ram/ Is tupping your white ewe.'; then 'you'll have your daughter covered with a Barbary/ horse. You'll have your nephews neigh to you – ' and 'your daughter and the/ Moor are now making the beast with two backs.' (Act I Sc i). No wonder Brabantio is worried. Iago has made Othello out to be nothing more than an animal with an unhealthy appetite for sex. Note, though, that Brabantio does call Iago a 'profane wretch' (Act 1, Sc i) for the language Iago uses about Othello.

The idea of a mixed marriage between a black man and a white woman would have shocked the audience, almost as much as it shocks Brabantio. Yet Shakespeare makes sure that we know that Desdemona and Othello are truly in love. It is Iago's malice, not their different cultures that comes between them.

Iago also calls Othello 'a devil', and Brabantio thinks that he must use 'black' magic, even though he is a Christian. In Elizabethan times, the devil was nearly always portrayed as black. People were said to practise witchcraft and were burnt for it. So it was a serious, unwarranted charge occasioned only by the colour of Othello's skin. Some critics in the past suggested Othello was a 'noble savage', but others argue Othello is not savage or barbaric. He is passionate and trusting, and says of himself: 'one not easily jealous, but, being wrought/Perplexed in the extreme;' (Act V, Sc ii). However, it is worth noting that he says this to explain his actions after he has strangled his wife.

Wives and daughters

Many young women today would find it hard to believe how subservient Desdemona is to her husband. But in Shakespeare's day, girls of the nobility were brought up to obey the men in their family, just as girls are in some cultures today. They had little education, besides learning how to sew and sing and maybe play a musical instrument. They had to dress modestly, and were not free to go out without an escort. They certainly could not meet men on their own.

Marriages were arranged and dowries paid. Once married, wives had to obey their husbands. They might be quite powerful in the home, directing the servants, but they had no freedom. Desdemona's elopement was a serious matter for her family. Brabantio is so upset that his friends think Desdemona is dead. 'Ay, to me', he says. For a new bride to flirt with a man, and pass on to him a precious love token like the handkerchief, would be unforgivable. To Othello it is evidence of adultery, the ultimate betrayal and cause of shame. He strikes her and, like so many battered wives today, she suffers his brutality and forgives him. Later, Othello feels that he has no choice but to kill her. Of course, he does have a choice. So-called honour killings in any age in any place are unacceptable.

Shakespeare's language

Shakespeare matches his language to his characters, so that their speech reflects their personality and helps create believable people and situations. He switches between verse and prose depending on the effect he wants to achieve. Othello's language is mostly prose, simple and direct, as befits a plain-speaking military man, but though he says he is 'rude' of speech, he does make two fine verse speeches at the beginning and the end of the play. Desdemona's speech is more poetic, the beauty of her nature revealed by the beauty of the verse. Cassio's flowery language marks him as a courtier, Emilia's is much coarser, especially when she speaks of men. Shakespeare's portrait of Iago is brilliantly achieved by the use of dramatic irony, monologues and asides that tell us what he's thinking. The audience hears and understands Iago but the other characters on stage do not. As Othello becomes stressed, his language becomes hesitant and almost incoherent, with numerous exclamations and heart-rending cries. His use of language betrays his state of mind.

EXAMINING THE PLAY

If you have to write an essay or answer an exam question on *Othello,* look carefully at the question or title. Think hard about it and gather the information you need before you begin. Answer only the question, even if you know more about some other topic. There are no marks for displaying your knowledge of some other aspect of the play.

For practice, look at some typical questions and try to answer them, for example: 'Is Iago the personification of evil?' From reading the play, you will know a lot about Iago, and you will have formed an opinion, probably that Iago does indeed embody evil. But it is not enough to assert that. You need to build an argument and support your view. You can start by describing Iago's character with evidence from the text, just as the author does in the introduction to this book. Find instances of Iago lying, betraying his friends, manipulating Othello and Roderigo, exploiting human frailty and being cruel and sadistic. Maybe you don't think Iago is totally evil. Can you find anything good to say about him? Do you feel that he has reason to be aggrieved because in some ways he may be more deserving of promotion than Cassio? Perhaps he is also envious of Desdemona, and wants more time with Othello. Where you can, use Shakespeare's own words, and give examples from the play.

Another question might be, 'Why is *Othello* relevant for our time?' This time you will have to think beyond the play. Do you recognise some of the feelings and behaviour of the characters? Can you give examples of people who get what they want by lying? Are they good talkers like Iago? Do you ever want to 'get your own back' when you have been unfairly treated? Is what happens in the play a timeless example of how human nature works? If you think *Othello* can teach us something about our own life and times, find parallels in newspapers or even in films and modern plays and television programmes. Are there still mercenary armies and commanders? How do modern soldiers cope with the boredom of waiting for combat? Think about racial prejudice. Would Othello suffer racial discrimination today? Think about women's liberation. Would a modern-day Desdemona be less subservient? Would Iago get away with his behaviour in a world of mobile phones and tweets, or would technology help him? Once again, think how the characters might communicate, and quote from the play to support your argument.

'For what reason is Iago *not* the main character in *Othello*?' is another question the examiners might ask, and it is difficult to answer. Perhaps you think Iago is the main character, and if you do, say why. He has more lines than the other characters, and spends more time on stage. He also drives the plot but you need to show how he does that. Think too about Shakespeare's audience. Did they want to see a play where the villain was more important than the hero? Consider the character of Othello. Is he not more interesting socially and psychologically, and a man with more depth, and better qualities than Iago? But then again, maybe you think that he wants to believe the lies that Iago tells him.

A favourite question is this: 'To what extent is this play a tragedy of a handkerchief?' Think of the role the handkerchief plays in the plot.

What does it symbolise? Read and quote Othello's description of the handkerchief's origin. When and why did he give it to Desdemona? What is the significance of the embroidery on it? Why is it an important love token? Is Othello justifiably upset that Desdemona has seemingly been careless with it? Does she treasure it enough? How often is it mentioned? Make sure you know what kind of an accessory a handkerchief was in Shakespeare's day, and how it differs from a modern-day one. Where would Desdemona have worn it? What was its use for her, and for Iago? What does it tell us about Iago and Emilia's relationship and their characters? Does the handkerchief demonstrate the importance of proof of loyalty and trust?

Whatever the question, you will need to discuss the language of the play. Show how Shakespeare uses it to achieve both beautiful and horrible ends. Think about other themes and questions too: Was Othello right to promote Cassio? Was Brabantio right to be wary of Othello? Why did Othello kill Desdemona? Why did Desdemona allow Othello to kill her? Think of your own questions, find the answers in the text and you will enjoy the play even more.

Angela Sheehan

Characters

OTHELLO: a Moor, general in the Venetian army
IAGO: Othello's ancient
CASSIO: Othello's lieutenant
DESDEMONA: Othello's wife
EMILIA: Iago's wife
BIANCA: a prostitute
RODERIGO: a Venetian gentleman
BRABANTIO: a Venetian senator and Desdemona's father
GRATIANO: Brabantio's brother
LODOVICO: a relative of Brabantio
MONTANO: Othello's predecessor as Governor of Cyprus
DUKE OF VENICE
CLOWN: servant to Othello
Senators of Venice, a Sailor, a Messenger, a Herald, Gentlemen of Cyprus, Musicians, Soldiers, Attendants and Servants

The pace and action of this dramatic first scene, with its opening wrangle between Iago and his dupe, Roderigo, and the hectic midnight arousing of Brabantio to the news of his daughter's elopement, set the tempo and manner of the whole play. It is odd to have a first scene that creates a false picture of the hero, but the correction of this, soon to come, strongly emphasizes the deceit of Iago, while the scene certainly establishes a fascinating, credible, and in many ways human, villain.

1–3   *Tush . . . this.* Shakespeare quite often begins scenes with the illusion of a conversation in progress. Roderigo is reproving Iago for withholding information, and 'this' probably refers to Othello's intended elopement with Desdemona.

4   *'Sblood,* by God's blood.

8–33   *Despise . . . ancient.* Always recall Bradley's warning: 'One must constantly remember not to believe a syllable that Iago utters . . . until one has tested his statement by comparing it with known facts and with other statements of his own or of other people, and by considering whether he had in the particular circumstances any reason for telling a lie or for telling the truth' (*Shakespearean Tragedy*, p. 211).

10   *Off-capped.* Respect was shown by doffing one's hat. The Quarto reads 'Oft capped'. [This and all following 'Quarto' references are to the first Quarto of 1622.]

13   *bombast circumstance,* padded-out circumlocution. 'Bombast' was cotton stuffing.

14   *epithets.* In the modern sense; or possibly, 'phrases'.

16   *Nonsuits,* (legal) utterly rejects, dismisses.   *Certes,* certainly.

19   *arithmetician.* A 'theorist'—one who can do the calculations.

20   *Florentine.* Contemptuous, since Florence was pre-eminently a place of merchants and bankers.

21   *A fellow . . . wife.* A slip: Cassio, a husband in Cinthio's story, is unmarried in Shakespeare's play. Granville-Barker's gloss may be the correct one: 'Cassio was "almost damned" because every fellow with a fair wife is, in Iago's estimation, a predestined cuckold' (*Preface to Shakespeare, Fourth Series*, p. 3). And note for future reference 'damned'.

22   *squadron.* A company of soldiers, not necessarily cavalry.

23   *division.* Might mean 'organization'.   *battle.* Either 'army' or 'fighting'.

24   *spinster.* Probably the modern meaning.   *unless . . . theoric,* except in a theoretical way.

25   *toged consuls.* Venetian senators in togas.   *propose.* Either 'talk' or 'lay down the law'.

26–7   *Mere . . . soldiership.* The heart of Iago's grievance—that Cassio lacks practical experience.

30   *lee'd.* As when a sailing ship has its wind intercepted by another ship. Cassio has checked Iago's advance.   *calmed,* becalmed.

Act One · Scene One

Venice · A street

Enter RODERIGO *and* IAGO

RODERIGO Tush—never tell me! I take it much unkindly
    That thou, Iago, who hast had my purse
    As if the strings were thine, shouldst know of this.

IAGO 'Sblood, but you will not hear me!
    If ever I did dream of such a matter,   5
    Abhor me.

RODERIGO Thou told'st me thou didst hold him in thy hate.

IAGO Despise me if I do not. Three great ones of the city,
    In personal suit to make me his lieutenant,
    Off-capped to him; and by the faith of man   10
    I know my price—I am worth no worse a place.
    But he, as loving his own pride and purposes,
    Evades them with a bombast circumstance,
    Horribly stuffed with epithets of war,
    And in conclusion   15
    Nonsuits my mediators. For 'Certes', says he,
    'I have already chose my officer.'
    And what was he?
    Forsooth, a great arithmetician,
    One Michael Cassio, a Florentine—   20
    A fellow almost damned in a fair wife—
    That never set a squadron in the field,
    Nor the division of a battle knows
    More than a spinster—unless the bookish theoric,
    Wherein the toged consuls can propose   25
    As masterly as he. Mere prattle without practice
    Is all his soldiership. But he, sir, had the election,
    And I, of whom his eyes had seen the proof
    At Rhodes, at Cyprus, and on other grounds
    Christian and heathen, must be lee'd and calmed   30

31   *debitor and creditor*, a mere account-book (or the man who keeps
         it).   *counter-caster*, literally, one who calculates with coun-
         ters. Both these abusive terms are roughly synonymous
         with 'arithmetician'.

33   *God . . . mark!* An exclamation indicating impatient scorn,
         indignation, etc. The 'mark' was probably the sign of the
         Cross.   *ancient*. Strictly speaking, an 'ensign' or 'standard-
         bearer'. Iago appears to be third-in-command to Othello or
         his A.D.C.

35   *there's no remedy*, there it is—there's nothing to be done about it.

36   *letter*. Probably the recommendation of some influential
         person.   *affection*, the feeling or inclination of the man
         making the appointment.

37   *old gradation*, seniority as followed in the old days.

39   *term*, relationship, way; or possibly 'sense'.   *affined*, bound,
         constrained.

42   *serve my turn*, further my own ends.

44   *truly*, faithfully.   *shall*. In the sense of 'are bound to'.

45   *knee-crooking*, bending the knee in a bow.   *knave*. Probably a
         mixture of the two meanings 'servant' and 'rascal'.

47   *ass*. The beginning of much animal imagery in the play.

48   *cashiered*, dismissed from service, discarded.

49   *me*. The old ethic dative commonly used for colloquial em-
         phasis.

50   *Who . . . duty*, who, dressed in a dutiful manner and appear-
         ance.

53   *lined*, strengthened. A modern version of 'lined their coats'
         might be 'feathered their nests'.

57   *Were . . . Iago.* A difficult line. Following what he has just said,
         Iago may be stating that if he were Othello (1) he would be
         doing homage to himself, not to others, or (2) that he would
         not have to put on a show of duty, etc. But it may be that
         Iago has a habit of mystifying his hearers with enigmatic, even
         meaningless, remarks.

59–60   *Heaven . . . end.* A possible paraphrase might be: 'As Heaven is
         my judge, I don't follow Othello out of love and duty. I
         merely pretend love and duty, for my private (*peculiar*) ends'.

61–3   *For . . . extern*, for when my action, an outward thing, shows my
         outside demeanour corresponding with the innate workings
         and character of my heart, etc.   *complement*, that which
         completes a character in external appearance or demeanour.

64   *I . . . sleeve*, i.e. I will fully expose my heart and its inner wor-
         kings.

65   *doves*. We may make a choice between the Folio 'daws' (jack-
         daws), signifying simpletons, or the Quarto 'doves', signi-
         fying particularly mild birds.   *I . . . am*. A memorable half
         line that epitomizes Iago's deceit and false appearance.

66–7   *What . . . thus.* All Roderigo can express is envy for the hand-
         some fortune Othello may gain if the marriage is accepted.
         He is so stupid that, in spite of Iago's frank confession, the
         thought never crosses his mind that Iago's attitude to him
         may be the same as Iago's attitude to Othello.   *full*, large,
         handsome.   *owe*, own.   *carry it*, pull it off.

By debitor and creditor, this counter-caster.
He in good time must his lieutenant be,
And I—God bless the mark!—his Moorship's ancient.

RODERIGO   By heaven, I rather would have been his hangman.

IAGO   But there's no remedy. 'Tis the curse of service—   35
Preferment goes by letter and affection,
Not by the old gradation, where each second
Stood heir to the first. Now sir, be judge yourself
Whether I in any just term am affined
To love the Moor.

RODERIGO   I would not follow him then.   40

IAGO   O sir, content you.
I follow him to serve my turn upon him.
We cannot all be masters, nor all masters
Cannot be truly followed. You shall mark
Many a duteous and knee-crooking knave   45
That, doting on his own obsequious bondage,
Wears out his time much like his master's ass,
For naught but provender; and when he's old—cashiered!
Whip me such honest knaves. Others there are
Who, trimmed in forms and visages of duty,   50
Keep yet their hearts attending on themselves,
And throwing but shows of service on their lords,
Do well thrive by them; and when they have lined their coats,
Do themselves homage. These fellows have some soul,
And such a one do I profess myself; for, sir,   55
It is as sure as you are Roderigo,
Were I the Moor, I would not be Iago.
In following him, I follow but myself:
Heaven is my judge, not I for love and duty,
But seeming so for my peculiar end,   60
For when my outward action doth demonstrate
The native act and figure of my heart
In complement extern, 'tis not long after
But I will wear my heart upon my sleeve
For doves to peck at. I am not what I am.   65

RODERIGO   What a full fortune does the thick-lips owe
If he can carry it thus!

68–71   *Rouse . . . flies.* The first part of this refers to Brabantio, the last to Othello. But it may be part of Iago's deliberate ambiguity that at least one of the early phrases 'poison his delight' could also refer to Othello.   *make after,* follow.

70   *fertile climate.* This presumably describes Othello's present state of prosperity, good-fortune, etc.

71–3   *Though . . . colour.* Othello is experiencing true joy, but let us change it a little and spoil it a little by vexing him. The Folio reads 'chances' for the Quarto 'changes'.   *As,* so that in consequence.

75   *timorous,* fearful in the sense, not of feeling fear, but creating it.

76   *negligence,* Possibly we have to understand 'caused by' in front of this word.

80   *bags,* money bags. Obviously Brabantio's fortune—his house and money—is involved in his daughter's marriage to Othello. Iago typically plays on all Brabantio's possible apprehensions.

81   *(stage direction).* In the Elizabethan theatre the balcony at the back of the stage would be used for Brabantio's appearance.

83   *What . . . there?* What do you want with me?

86   *Zounds,* (an oath) God's wounds.

88–9   *Even . . . ewe.* Both the lewdness of speech and the repugnant animal imagery are characteristic of Iago. 'In Iago's semantic sphere there stand out, as word-slogans, word-clues, evocative words—names of things and animals arousing abhorrence, fear, disgust' (Kott, *Shakespeare Our Contemporary*, p. 89).

89   *tupping,* copulating with.

90   *snorting,* snoring.

91   *devil . . . you.* The devil was represented as black in colour.

93   *Most reverend signior.* Though Roderigo tries a more respectful approach, he is to receive a dusty answer.

94   *what.* As commonly, in the sense of 'who'.

IAGO   Call up her father,
Rouse him, make after him, poison his delight,
Proclaim him in the streets, incense her kinsmen,
And, though he in a fertile climate dwell,   70
Plague him with flies. Though that his joy be joy,
Yet throw such changes of vexation on't
As it may lose some colour.

RODERIGO   Here is her father's house. I'll call aloud.

IAGO   Do—with like timorous accent and dire yell   75
As when, by night and negligence, the fire
Is spied in populous cities.

RODERIGO   What ho, Brabantio! Signor Brabantio, ho!

IAGO   Awake! What ho, Brabantio! Thieves, thieves!
Look to your house, your daughter, and your bags!   80
Thieves, thieves!

Enter BRABANTIO *at a window above*

BRABANTIO   What is the reason of this terrible summons?
What is the matter there?

RODERIGO   Signior, is all your family within?

IAGO   Are your doors locked?

BRABANTIO   Why, wherefore ask you this?   85

IAGO   Zounds, sir, you're robbed. For shame, put on your gown;
Your heart is burst—you have lost half your soul.
Even now, now, very now, an old black ram
Is tupping your white ewe. Arise, arise,
Awake the snorting citizens with the bell,   90
Or else the devil will make a grandsire of you.
Arise, I say!

BRABANTIO   What, have you lost your wits?

RODERIGO   Most reverend signior, do you know my voice?

BRABANTIO   Not I. What are you?

RODERIGO   My name is Roderigo.

BRABANTIO   The worser welcome!   95
I have charged thee not to haunt about my doors.
In honest plainness thou hast heard me say
My daughter is not for thee. And now in madness,

99   *distempering,* intoxicating.

100   *bravery,* bravado; acting in a boisterous, rude, provocative way. The Folio reads 'knavery', but 'malicious' would make this word rather tautologous.

101   *start,* startle, disturb.

103   *spirit . . . place,* anger and position.

106   *grange,* a farm, i.e. a lonely house in the country.

107   *In . . . soul,* with utterly sincere intentions. In spite of Brabantio's attitude to him, Roderigo persists in his respectful role as the honest well-wisher. This makes an effective contrast with the manner of Iago, whom Brabantio rightly describes as a 'profane wretch'.

108–13   *Zounds . . . germans.* Scholars are sometimes too ready to find reasons for Shakespeare's shifts between prose and verse. It might be said that this speech is in prose because of its 'low' context. But what of ll.86–91?

108–9   *if . . . you.* This, in reference to himself, has a truth that Iago does not intend. But the stress is on 'bid', not 'devil'.

110   *Barbary.* Loosely, an Arab horse. As a Moor, Othello (or his ancestors) may have come from Barbary, north and north west Africa.

111   *nephews,* grandsons.

112   *coursers,* chargers, or racehorses.   *cousins,* relatives.   *gennets,* (or jennets) small Spanish horses of *Moorish* origin. *germans,* blood relations.

113   *profane,* filthy-mouthed (not necessarily blasphemous).

116   *You . . . senator.* A very characteristic Iago remark. It could be taken as harmless enough—even a tribute to Brabantio's position. But the tribute and respect might be mocking; or, alternatively, Iago may be playing a game of tit for tat, with 'senator', as Iago utters the word, the equivalent of a 'villain'.

119   *wise.* Either in the sense of 'properly informed', or, perhaps, 'having fully considered'.

121   *At . . . night.* About midnight, in the indeterminate time between the beginning and end of night.   *dull,* sleepy, inactive, lifeless.

123   *knave . . . hire,* common hired servant.

124   *Moor.* There is a suspension of the sentence here. The 'If' construction is taken up again.

125   *your allowance,* (has) your permission.

126   *saucy,* (stronger than the modern word) insolent, impertinent.

127   *manners,* code of proper behaviour (synonymous with later 'civility').

129   *from,* contrary to, ignoring.

Being full of supper and distempering draughts,
Upon malicious bravery dost thou come   100
To start my quiet?

RODERIGO   Sir, sir, sir—

BRABANTIO   But thou must needs be sure
My spirit and my place have in them power
To make this bitter to thee.

RODERIGO   Patience, good sir.

BRABANTIO   What tell'st thou me of robbing? This is Venice: 105
My house is not a grange.

RODERIGO   Most grave Brabantio,
In simple and pure soul I come to you.

IAGO   Zounds, sir, you are one of those that will not serve God if the
devil bid you. Because we come to do you service, and you think
we are ruffians, you'll have your daughter covered with a Barbary   110
horse. You'll have your nephews neigh to you—you'll have
coursers for cousins and gennets for germans.

BRABANTIO   What profane wretch art thou?

IAGO   I am one, sir, that comes to tell you your daughter and the
Moor are now making the beast with two backs.   115

BRABANTIO   Thou art a villain.

IAGO   You are—a senator.

BRABANTIO   This thou shalt answer. I know thee, Roderigo.

RODERIGO   Sir, I will answer anything. But I beseech you,
If it be your pleasure and most wise consent,
As partly I find it is, that your fair daughter,   120
At this odd-even and dull watch o' the night,
Transported with no worse nor better guard
But with a knave of common hire, a gondolier,
To the gross clasps of a lascivious Moor—
If this be known to you, and your allowance,   125
We then have done you bold and saucy wrongs.
But if you know not this, my manners tell me
We have your wrong rebuke. Do not believe
That from the sense of all civility
I thus would play and trifle with your reverence.   130
Your daughter, if you have not given her leave,

133-4	*Tying . . . In*, giving (a stranger) complete control over.
133	*wit*, mind.
134-5	*extravagant . . . everywhere*. Othello was an alien mercenary without permanent roots in Venetian society. See his own words in the next scene, 1.26. *extravagant*, vagrant. *wheeling*, circuitously wandering (like an unfixed star?) *stranger*. Probably in the sense of 'foreigner'.
139	*taper*, a candle of tapering shape.
140	*This . . . dream*. One of the many touches of superstition in the play; and it prepares the way for Brabantio's idea of 'charms', etc. *accident*, event, happening.
146	*However . . . check*, however this may cause some galling reprimand (*check*) for him. *cast*, dismiss.
147-8	*for . . . wars*. Presumably Othello has already been appointed to the command. *embarked*, engaged.
148	*With . . . reason*, i.e. Othello is so obviously the man for the job. *loud*, obvious, forcible, urgent.
149	*stands in act*, are in progress.
150	*fathom*, calibre, capability.
154	*flag*. Synonymous with 'sign'.
156	*Saggitary*. The name (after the zodiacal sign) of some inn or house. *raised search*, the search party that has been aroused.
159	*despised*. Brabantio is probably referring to the dishonour that is now upon him.
160-5	*Now . . . you*. Brabantio is partly addressing Roderigo or the servants, partly speaking his thoughts.

I say again hath made a gross revolt,
Tying her duty, beauty, wit, and fortunes
In an extravagant and wheeling stranger
Of here and everywhere. Straight satisfy yourself.   135
If she be in her chamber or your house,
Let loose on me the justice of the state
For thus deluding you.

BRABANTIO   Strike on the tinder, ho!
Give me a taper! Call up all my people!
This accident is not unlike my dream.   140
Belief of it oppresses me already.
Light, I say, light!   [*Exit above*

IAGO   Farewell, for I must leave you.
It seems not meet nor wholesome to my place
To be produced (as if I stay, I shall)
Against the Moor. For I do know the state,   145
However this may gall him with some check,
Cannot with safety cast him; for he's embarked
With such loud reason to the Cyprus wars,
Which even now stands in act, that for their souls
Another of his fathom they have none   150
To lead their business. In which regard,
Though I do hate him as I do hell's pains,
Yet for necessity of present life
I must show out a flag and sign of love,
Which is indeed but sign. That you shall surely find him,   155
Lead to the Sagittary the raised search,
And there will I be with him. So farewell.   [*Exit*

Enter BRABANTIO *in his night-gown, and Servants with torches*

BRABANTIO It is too true an evil. Gone she is,
And what's to come of my despised time
Is naught but bitterness. Now, Roderigo,   160
Where didst thou see her? . . . O unhappy girl! . . .
With the Moor, say'st thou? . . . Who would be a father?
How didst thou know 'twas she? . . . O, she deceives me
Past thought! . . . What said she to you? . . . Get more tapers.
Raise all my kindred . . . Are they married, think you?   165

RODERIGO Truly I think they are.

167   *of the blood*, of one's own flesh and blood.

169   *Is.* 'Are' in modern grammar.   *charms.* See l.140.

170   *property*, nature.

171   *abused*, deceived, corrupted.

173   *O . . . her!* Note Brabantio's change, under stress, from ll.95-8.

176   *discover.* Not 'find' but in the sense of 'reveal', 'expose to view'.

179   *go*, come.

180   *special . . . night.* A precise reference to a certain kind of Venetian police officer.

181   *deserve*, repay.

Scene Two

The second scene, centering on the exciting encounter of Othello and Brabantio in the street at midnight, continues straight on from the first; and the swift-moving dramatic quality of the action is not only maintained but intensified. Comparatively short as the scene is and limited in scope, it memorably represents much of the true and essential nature of Othello. Iago emerges as a consummate actor.

1-11   *Though . . . married.* There is an immediately striking change in Iago's dutiful tone from that employed in the first scene. He is of course putting his own abuse of Othello into Roderigo's mouth.

2   *very stuff*, heart, essence.

3-4   *I . . . service.* A highly ironical line: 'I haven't the unscrupulousness I sometimes find I need.' It is possibly worth noting that 'Iniquity' was another name for the comic 'Vice' in old morality plays.

5   *yerked*, struck with a hard, swift blow.

10   *full hard*, with difficulty.   *forbear*, endure, tolerate.

12   *Magnifico.* A title given to the chief Venetian citizens.

13-14   *And . . . Duke's.* The general meaning is that Brabantio is as powerfully influential as the Duke. 'Voice' often means 'vote', and Shakespeare may have thought, wrongly, that the Duke had a double vote in government business.   *potential*, powerful, or, just possibly, the present meaning.

BRABANTIO O heaven! How got she out? O treason of the blood!
　　Fathers, from hence trust not your daughters' minds
　　By what you see them act. Is there not charms
　　By which the property of youth and maidhood   170
　　May be abused? Have you not read, Roderigo,
　　Of some such thing?

RODERIGO　　　　　　Yes, sir, I have indeed.

BRABANTIO Call up my brother . . . O would you had had her!
　　Some one way, some another! Do you know
　　Where we may apprehend her and the Moor?   175

RODERIGO I think I can discover him, if you please
　　To get good guard and go along with me.

BRABANTIO Pray you, lead on. At every house I'll call—
　　I may command at most. Get weapons, ho!
　　And raise some special officers of night.   180
　　On, good Roderigo—I'll deserve your pains.   [*Exeunt*

Scene Two

Venice · Another street

Enter OTHELLO · IAGO · *and Attendants with torches*

IAGO Though in the trade of war I have slain men,
　　Yet do I hold it very stuff of conscience
　　To do no contrived murder. I lack iniquity
　　Sometimes to do me service. Nine or ten times
　　I had thought to have yerked him here, under the ribs.   5

OTHELLO 'Tis better as it is.

IAGO　　　　　　　　Nay, but he prated
　　And spoke such scurvy and provoking terms
　　Against your honour
　　That, with the little godliness I have,
　　I did full hard forbear him. But I pray, sir,   10
　　Are you fast married? For be sure of this,
　　That the Magnifico is much beloved
　　And hath in his effect a voice potential

15   *grievance*, oppression, annoyance.

17   *cable*, scope. Another of Iago's nautical terms.

18–24   *My ... reached*. There is pride here, but most would find it just and dignified.

18   *signiory*. The Venetian government.

19   *'Tis ... know*, i.e. it is not public knowledge.

21   *provulgate*, make commonly known. The Folio has 'promulgate'.

22   *siege*, rank. (The Quarto reads 'height'.)

22–4   *my ... reached*. Othello is saying that his proud fortune, especially his marriage with Desdemona, is deserved. There seems to be a personification in which his 'demerits' (merits) are addressing 'fortune'. 'Unbonneted' (see Act1Sc.1,l.10) probably means with hat on, but it could possibly be the opposite.

26   *unhoused*, (literally) without house; not settled down.

27   *circumscription and confine*, confining limits; restriction.

28   *sea's worth*. As a source of sunken treasure, pearls, etc. See *Richard the Third*, Act1Sc.4,ll.26–7.

29   *raised*, rouse up.

31   *parts*, personal qualities.   *perfect soul*, clear conscience. 'Perfect' should not be misunderstood to turn this into a boastful utterance.

32   *Shall . . . rightly*, shall show me as I truly am, i.e. having the strength and support of these good qualities.

33   *Janus*. A two-faced Roman god. This oath has an unconscious appropriateness.

34–54   *The servants . . . you*. This meeting with Cassio, though it certainly furthers the action, probably heightens our suspense for the encounter with Brabantio.

37   *haste-post-haste*. An emphatic way of expressing 'haste'—immediate haste.

38   *matter*, business, concern.

40   *heat*, pressing urgency.

41   *sequent*, following one upon the other.

43   *consuls*, senators or counsellors (as in Act1Sc.1,l.25).

44   *hotly*, urgently. (See note on l.40 above.)

As double as the Duke's. He will divorce you,
Or put upon you what restraint and grievance   15
The law, with all his might to enforce it on,
Will give him cable.

OTHELLO   Let him do his spite.
My services which I have done the signiory
Shall out-tongue his complaints. 'Tis yet to know
(Which, when I know that boasting is an honour,   20
I shall provulgate) I fetch my life and being
From men of royal siege, and my demerits
May speak unbonneted to as proud a fortune
As this that I have reached. For know, Iago,
But that I love the gentle Desdemona,   25
I would not my unhoused free condition
Put into circumscription and confine
For the sea's worth. But look, what lights come yonder?

IAGO   These are the raised father and his friends—
You were best go in.

OTHELLO   Not I! I must be found.   30
My parts, my title, and my perfect soul
Shall manifest me rightly. Is it they?

IAGO   By Janus, I think no.

Enter CASSIO, *and Attendants with torches*

OTHELLO   The servants of the Duke and my lieutenant!
The goodness of the night upon you, friends.   35
What is the news?

CASSIO   The Duke does greet you, General,
And he requires your haste-post-haste appearance
Even on the instant.

OTHELLO   What is the matter, think you?

CASSIO   Something from Cyprus as I may divine—
It is a business of some heat. The galleys   40
Have sent a dozen sequent messengers
This very night at one another's heels,
And many of the consuls, raised and met,
Are at the Duke's already. You have been hotly called for.
When being not at your lodging to be found,   45

Notes &
Commentary

46   *about*, around the city.   *quests*, search-parties.

49   *makes*, does.

50-1   *Faith . . . ever.* More nautical (and bawdy) expression. *carack*, a ship, probably for treasure carrying; 'land' because of the reference to Desdemona.

51   *prize*, capture (as in war).

52   *I . . . understand.* We later learn that Cassio has been much involved in Othello's wooing of Desdemona and his ignorance here may seem odd. But perhaps for some good reason, like not betraying confidence, he is merely pretending ignorance. *To who?* 'to whom' in modern grammar.

53   *Marry, to.* A pun on the oath 'By the Virgin Mary' and 'marry' in the usual sense. Naturally Iago breaks off at Othello's re-entry. *Have with you*, I'll accompany you.

55   *advised*, take advice, or, be careful.

56   *He . . . intent*, he intends to do you harm. *to*, for the purpose of.

58   *Come . . . you.* Iago singles out Roderigo for mock attack because he does not wish this source of money to come to harm.

59   *Keep . . . them.* A wonderful, frequently quoted line. Its simplicity, force, and touch of irony (rare in Othello) express his controlled authority. A good example of the poetic effect Shakespeare so often gets from simple, monosyllabic, concrete language.

60-1   *you . . . weapons*, the respect due to your age will do more for you than this display of force.

64   *I'll . . . sense*, I'll submit my argument to all considerations (or people) of reason, good sense, etc. Virtually the same meaning as l.72 that follows.

67   *opposite*, opposed.

68   *wealthy curled darlings.* This expression mainly refers to the more superior husbands (in Brabantio's eyes) that Desdemona might have found. 'Curled' hair probably signifies aristocratic rank, and 'darlings' (without any contempt) 'favourites', 'loved ones'.

70   *guardage*, guardianship, i.e. of himself.

The senate sent about three several quests
To search you out.

OTHELLO   'Tis well I am found by you.
I will but spend a word here in the house
And go with you.   [*Exit*

CASSIO   Ancient, what makes he here?

IAGO   Faith, he tonight hath boarded a land carack.   50
If it prove lawful prize, he's made for ever.

CASSIO   I do not understand.

IAGO   He's married.

CASSIO   To who?

Re-enter OTHELLO

IAGO   Marry, to—Come, Captain, will you go?

OTHELLO   Have with you.

CASSIO   Here comes another troop to seek for you.

Enter BRABANTIO · RODERIGO · *and Attendants with torches and weapons*

IAGO   It is Brabantio. General, be advised—   55
He comes to bad intent.

OTHELLO   Holla, stand there!

RODERIGO   Signior, it is the Moor.

BRABANTIO   Down with him, thief! [*They
draw swords on both sides*]

IAGO   You, Roderigo? Come, sir, I am for you.

OTHELLO   Keep up your bright swords, for the dew will rust them.
Good signior, you shall more command with years   60
Than with your weapons.

BRABANTIO   O thou foul thief! Where hast thou stowed my daughter?
Damned as thou art, thou hast enchanted her,
For I'll refer me to all things of sense,
(If she in chains of magic were not bound)   65
Whether a maid, so tender, fair, and happy,
So opposite to marriage that she shunned
The wealthy curled darlings of our nation,
Would ever have, to incur a general mock,
Run from her guardage to the sooty bosom   70

71   *to . . . delight*, calculated to frighten, not delight her.

72   *Judge . . . world*, let the world judge.   *gross in sense*, obvious to reason.

73   *practised*, worked in an intriguing way for evil purposes.

74   *Abused*. See Act 1 Sc. 1, l. 171.   *minerals*, mineral (and poisonous) drugs. Medicines, drugs, poisons etc. constitute a small but characteristic group of images and references in the play.

75   *weaken motion*, impair the faculties.   *disputed*, thoroughly discussed, considered, examined.

77   *attach*, arrest.

78   *abuser of the world*, possibly something like 'enemy of society'.

79   *Of . . . warrant*, of forbidden and illegal (i.e. black) magic.

82   *inclining*, side, party.

83–4 *Were . . . prompter*. An interesting theatrical metaphor. As one might expect, such metaphors are not uncommon in Shakespeare's plays.

85–6 *till . . . session*, probably something like 'till the time when the court in its lawful and regular procedure'. In view of Brabantio's eagerness to punish Othello it is tempting—and possible —to take 'direct' to mean an immediate session of court. But 'fit time' seems to rule this out.

88   *therewith*, i.e. by my arrest and imprisonment.

90   *present*, immediate.

95   *idle*, trivial.

98–9 *For . . . be*. The common emphatic ending of a scene with a resounding, rhymed couplet. One of the likeliest meanings seems to be that if the senators freely permit such a marriage between coloured and white, then they will turn themselves (perhaps literally) into coloureds, who, in Brabantio's eyes, are essentially slaves and pagans.

Of such a thing as thou—to fear, not to delight.
Judge me the world, if 'tis not gross in sense
That thou hast practised on her with foul charms,
Abused her delicate youth with drugs or minerals
That weaken motion. I'll have't disputed on; 75
'Tis probable, and palpable to thinking.
I therefore apprehend and do attach thee
For an abuser of the world, a practiser
Of arts inhibited and out of warrant.
Lay hold upon him. If he do resist, 80
Subdue him at his peril.

OTHELLO   Hold your hands,
Both you of my inclining and the rest.
Were it my cue to fight, I should have known it
Without a prompter. Where will you that I go
To answer this your charge?

BRABANTIO   To prison, till fit time 85
Of law and course of direct session
Call thee to answer.

OTHELLO   What if I do obey?
How may the Duke be therewith satisfied,
Whose messengers are here about my side
Upon some present business of the state 90
To bring me to him?

ATTENDANT   'Tis true, most worthy signior.
The Duke's in council, and your noble self
I am sure is sent for.

BRABANTIO   How? The Duke in council?
In this time of the night? Bring him away.
Mine's not an idle cause. The Duke himself, 95
Or any of my brothers of the state,
Cannot but feel this wrong as 'twere their own;
For if such actions may have passage free,
Bondslaves and pagans shall our statesmen be.   [*Exeunt*

With this more static and formal, but substantial and dramatic, third scene in the Venetian Senate chamber, the first movement of the play, almost a kind of prologue, comes to an end. Othello is appointed to the Cyprus command, and, in spite of the protest of Brabantio, receives an official endorsement, as it were, of his marriage to Desdemona. The scene completes the exposition of the main characters, particularly of the heroic and romantic Othello, whose soldiership is so necessary to the Venetian state, and of the 'demi-devil' Iago. In his soliloquy at the end Iago gives the first clear indication of the tragedy to come.

1	*composition*, consistency. *news*, reports, tidings.
2	*gives them credit*, makes them credible. *disproportioned*, discrepant.
3	*galleys*, i.e. of the Turkish fleet.
5	*jump*, agree, coincide. *just account*, exact number or reckoning.
6-7	(*As . . . difference*), as in these cases where guesswork enters their reports there is often inconsistency. The Folio reading 'the aim reports' would seem to amount to the same meaning of reports based on conjecture.
10-12	*I . . . sense*, I don't build a false confidence on these inconsistencies (by assuming the whole report is false); on the contrary, I accept that the gist of the report is alarmingly true, i.e. that the Turkish fleet is making for Cyprus.
14	*preparation*, fleet equipped for war.
16	*Angelo*. No other mention. The commander of the Venetian ships at sea?
17	*by*, about.
18	*assay*, test. *pageant*, show, spectacle (literally of a theatrical kind).
19	*To . . . gaze*, to keep us looking the wrong way, to deceive us.
22	*it . . . Turk*, Cyprus is more important to the Turk.
23	*question*. Probably means 'fighting'. *bear it*, capture it.
24	*brace*. Probably 'readiness' or 'state of defence'.

Scene Three

Venice · A Council chamber

The DUKE and SENATORS sitting at a table, with lights · Attendants

DUKE There is no composition in these news
That gives them credit.

1 SENATOR   Indeed they are disproportioned.
My letters say a hundred and seven galleys.

DUKE And mine a hundred and forty.

2 SENATOR   And mine two hundred.
But though they jump not on a just account   5
(As in these cases where they aim reports
'Tis oft with difference) yet do they all confirm
A Turkish fleet, and bearing up to Cyprus.

DUKE Nay, it is possible enough to judgment.
I do not so secure me in the error,   10
But the main article I do approve
In fearful sense.

SAILOR [*within*]   What ho! What ho! What ho!

ATTENDANT A messenger from the galleys.

Enter SAILOR

DUKE   Now, what's the business?

SAILOR The Turkish preparation makes for Rhodes—
So was I bid report here to the state   15
By Signior Angelo.

DUKE How say you by this change?

1 SENATOR   This cannot be
By no assay of reason. 'Tis a pageant
To keep us in false gaze, when we consider
The importancy of Cyprus to the Turk.   20
And let ourselves again but understand
That as it more concerns the Turk than Rhodes,
So may he with more facile question bear it,
For that it stands not in such warlike brace,

25–6   *the abilities . . . in,* the (military) resources that Rhodes is equipped with.

28   *which . . . first.* Presumably because Cyprus represents 'ease and gain', and Rhodes 'danger profitless'.

30   *wage,* risk (with a suggestion of gambling).

33   *Ottomites,* Turks.

35   *injointed,* jointed, united.   *after,* later.

37   *re-stem,* retrace.

38–9   *bearing . . . Cyprus,* undisguisedly carrying out their plans against Cyprus.

39   *Montano.* The Governor of Cyprus at that time.

41   *With . . . thus.* Something like 'with all honourable dutiful respects informs you thus'. This is the formal style of a message to the Senate.

44   *Marcus Luccicos.* Another mysterious name like the unknown Angelo.

46   *post,* speed, go with haste (synonymous with 'dispatch').

47   *valiant.* Note that it is only Othello who gets a distinguishing epithet and that the word is immediately repeated by the Duke. Brabantio is merely Brabantio.

48–50   *Valiant . . . see you.* It is Othello who is the first to receive the Duke's attention. If anything, the Duke's later apologetic words to Brabantio would only increase Brabantio's sense of his secondary importance.

53   *place,* i.e. as Senator.

54   *general care,* public affair.

55   *particular,* personal, private.

56–8   *so . . . itself.* Perhaps the meaning of this rather tortured expression is that while Brabantio's grief at Desdemona's behaviour is so overwhelming that it swallows up all other distresses, it is in no way coloured or modified by those distresses: it remains its essential, unaltered self.

56   *flood gate.* When opened, the flood- or sluice-gate lets through the full torrent of water. 'Torrential' would be a suitable gloss.

57   *engluts.* Hardly distinguishable from the following 'swallows'.

But altogether lacks the abilities 25
That Rhodes is dressed in. If we make thought of this,
We must not think the Turk is so unskilful
To leave that latest which concerns him first,
Neglecting an attempt of ease and gain
To wake and wage a danger profitless. 30

DUKE   Nay, in all confidence he's not for Rhodes.

ATTENDANT   Here is more news.

Enter a MESSENGER

MESSENGER   The Ottomites, reverend and gracious,
Steering with due course toward the isle of Rhodes,
Have there injointed with an after fleet. 35

1 SENATOR   Ay, so I thought. How many, as you guess?

MESSENGER   Of thirty sail; and now they do re-stem
Their backward course, bearing with frank appearance
Their purposes toward Cyprus. Signior Montano,
Your trusty and most valiant servitor, 40
With his free duty recommends you thus
And prays you to believe him.

DUKE   'Tis certain then for Cyprus.
Marcus Luccicos, is not he in town?

1 SENATOR   He's now in Florence. 45

DUKE   Write from us to him; post post-haste; dispatch!

1 SENATOR   Here comes Brabantio and the valiant Moor.

Enter BRABANTIO · OTHELLO · IAGO · RODERIGO · *and Attendants*

DUKE   Valiant Othello, we must straight employ you
Against the general enemy Ottoman.
[*to* BRABANTIO] I did not see you. Welcome, gentle signior. 50
We lacked your counsel and your help tonight.

BRABANTIO   So did I yours. Good your grace, pardon me.
Neither my place nor aught I heard of business
Hath raised me from my bed, nor doth the general care
Take hold on me, for my particular grief 55
Is of so floodgate and o'erbearing nature
That it engluts and swallows other sorrows
And yet is still itself.

60   *abused.* Note Brabantio's fondness for this word.

61   *mountebanks,* quacks.

62   *nature,* i.e. in Desdemona. This important word is repeated
        many times in the play, but it has not the significance that it
        possesses in *King Lear.*   *preposterously.* Probably 'absurdly', but
        might mean 'unnaturally'.

63   *Being . . . sense.* One may take all three adjectives to indicate
        impairment of reason ('sense').

64   *sans,* without.

67–9   *the . . . sense.* From the phrases 'bloody book' and 'bitter letter'
        the Duke is clearly stating that the offender shall receive
        heavy, probably capital, punishment. Those who prefer the
        Quarto '*its* own sense' argue that the Venetians would not
        allow even a Senator to interpret the law as he pleased. But
        the earlier phrase 'You shall yourself read' would hardly have
        much point unless the Duke was in fact promising Brabantio
        something of the kind.

69   *proper,* own.

70   *Stood . . . action,* was the man named in your accusation.

74   *part,* defence, support, side.

80   *head and front.* C. T. Onions in his *Shakespeare Glossary* gives
        'summit', 'height'.

81–2   *Rude . . . peace.* A modesty untrue of the following speech.
        rude, unpolished, inexpert, etc.

82   *soft.* The Quarto has 'set', which could be understood as
        'conventional', 'accepted'.

83–5   *For . . . field.* Presumably in making this reference to his arms
        Othello is thinking of oratorical gestures.

83   *pith,* vigour, strength.

84   *Till . . . wasted,* i.e. till nine months ago.

85   *dearest,* what was closest and most important to them.

86–7   *little . . . battle.* Important lines in which Othello confesses his
        limited experience and lack of knowledge of the ways of the
        'world', as we should say.   *broil,* battle.

90   *round,* plain, straightforward, blunt.

DUKE   Why, what's the matter?

BRABANTIO   My daughter! O, my daughter!

SENATORS   Dead?

BRABANTIO   Ay, to me.
  She is abused, stolen from me, and corrupted   60
  By spells and medicines bought of mountebanks;
  For nature so preposterously to err,
  Being not deficient, blind, or lame of sense,
  Sans witchcraft could not.

DUKE   Whoe'er he be that in this foul proceeding   65
  Hath thus beguiled your daughter of herself
  And you of her, the bloody book of law
  You shall yourself read in the bitter letter
  After your own sense, yea, though our proper son
  Stood in your action.

BRABANTIO   Humbly I thank your grace.   70
  Here is the man, this Moor, whom now it seems
  Your special mandate for the state affairs
  Hath hither brought.

ALL   We are very sorry for it.

DUKE [*to* OTHELLO]   What in your own part can you say to this?

BRABANTIO   Nothing, but this is so.   75

OTHELLO   Most potent, grave and reverend signiors,
  My very noble and approved good masters,
  That I have ta'en away this old man's daughter,
  It is most true; true, I have married her.
  The very head and front of my offending   80
  Hath this extent, no more. Rude am I in my speech
  And little blessed with the soft phrase of peace,
  For since these arms of mine had seven years' pith
  Till now some nine moons wasted, they have used
  Their dearest action in the tented field,   85
  And little of this great world can I speak
  More than pertains to feats of broil and battle;
  And therefore little shall I grace my cause
  In speaking for myself. Yet, by your gracious patience,
  I will a round unvarnished tale deliver   90

91–2   *what . . . magic.* Perhaps another slight touch of irony from Othello.

92   *conjuration,* magic utterance, incantation.

94–5   *A maiden . . . motion.* The Quarto has a different (and to some, preferable) punctuation and lineation.

95   *still,* quiet. Possibly both 'still' and 'quiet' are synonymous as an antithesis to 'bold', i.e. with the meaning of 'quiescent'.

95–6   *her motion . . . herself.* The problems here are (1) the meaning of 'motion', (2) whether 'herself' refers to 'motion' or to Desdemona. There is much to be said for taking 'motion' as an impulse of heart, inclination, desire (almost our modern 'emotion'), and 'herself' (printed as 'her self' in both Quarto and Folio) as 'itself'. Any start of feeling etc. caused Desdemona to blush, and this confirms that she was never 'bold'.

96   *in . . . nature,* against all natural promptings.

97   *Of years,* i.e. the difference of age between Desdemona and Othello.   *credit,* honour, reputation.

101–3   *must . . . be,* to account for Desdemona's behaviour one is forced to the conclusion that cunning, hellish strategems ('practices') must have been used. Presumably the understood subject of 'must be driven' is 'one' or 'a sound judgment' or something like that.

105   *dram,* dose, small draught.   *conjured,* affected by magic spells.

107   *more wider,* extensive. (The Quarto reads 'more certain'.) *test,* testimony.

108–9   *Than . . . him,* than these poor, threadbare, commonplace suppositions level against him.   *thin habits.* A clothing metaphor.   *modern,* everyday, commonplace.

111   *indirect,* crooked.   *forced courses.* Possibly 'unnatural means'. But the sense of 'forced' is uncertain.

113   *it,* i.e. her love.   *fair question,* honest (or honourable) speaking.

115   *Send . . . Sagittary.* The sense is perhaps clear if we understand 'to . . . Sagittary' immediately after 'Send'.

117   *foul,* wicked, to be condemned.

Of my whole course of love—what drugs, what charms,
What conjuration and what mighty magic
(For such proceedings am I charged withal)
I won his daughter.

BRABANTIO   A maiden never bold,
  Of spirit so still and quiet that her motion   95
  Blushed at herself—and she, in spite of nature,
  Of years, of country, credit, everything,
  To fall in love with what she feared to look on?
  It is a judgment maimed and most imperfect
  That will confess perfection so could err   100
  Against all rules of nature, and must be driven
  To find out practices of cunning hell
  Why this should be. I therefore vouch again
  That with some mixtures powerful o'er the blood,
  Or with some dram conjured to this effect,   105
  He wrought upon her.

DUKE   To vouch this is no proof
  Without more wider and more overt test
  Than these thin habits and poor likelihoods
  Of modern seeming do prefer against him.

1 SENATOR   But, Othello, speak.   110
  Did you by indirect and forced courses
  Subdue and poison this young maid's affections?
  Or came it by request and such fair question
  As soul to soul affordeth?

OTHELLO   I do beseech you,
  Send for the lady to the Sagittary,   115
  And let her speak of me before her father.
  If you do find me foul in her report,
  The trust, the office I do hold of you
  Not only take away, but let your sentence
  Even fall upon my life.

DUKE   Fetch Desdemona hither. [*Some Attendants* 120
  move towards the door]

OTHELLO   Ancient, conduct them. You best know the place.
                                    [*Exit* IAGO, *with Attendants*

123   *vices of my blood*, mortal sins.

124   *justly*, truthfully.

128–70 *Her . . . it.* 'Othello radiates a world of romantic, heroic, and picturesque adventure. All about him is highly coloured' (Wilson Knight, *The Wheel of Fire*, p. 105). Knight goes on to say of Othello's speech generally: 'It has a certain exotic beauty, is a storied and romantic treasure house of rich, colourful experiences' (p. 106).

129   *Still*, continually.   *questioned me.* Probably 'talked with me about'.

134   *chances*, events, happenings (synonymous with 'accidents' in the next line).

135   *moving*, stirring, exciting.

136   *scapes*, escapes.   *in . . . breach*, in the highly dangerous moment when some fortification, etc. was just about to be breached.

139   *And . . . history.* In the Folio this line reads: 'And portance in my traveller's history'. ('portance' would mean 'behaviour'.)

140–5   *Wherein . . . shoulders.* No doubt Shakespeare owed many of the details here to the travellers' tales of his time, and also to Holland's much-read translation of Pliny's *Natural History*, from which there are several echoes in the play. See the Pontic Sea reference in Act3Sc.3, ll.460–3 and the mention of 'chrysolite' in Act5Sc.2, l.147.

140   *antres*, caves.   *idle*, barren, or uninhabited and empty.

141   *Rough quarries.* In Shakespeare's time, and long after, 'quarry' could mean a mass of rock in its natural state, before it was quarried. This seems to be the sense here.

142   *hint*, opportunity, occasion.   *the process*, my account, how I proceeded.

144   *Anthropophagi*, (literally) man-eaters, cannibals.

145–6   *This . . . incline*, Desdemona was drawn to listen intently to all this.

147   *still*, (as in l.129) continually.

151   *pliant*, suitable, auspicious.

152   *of earnest heart*, heart-felt.

153   *pilgrimage*, journey (in a general sense), or, 'course of life'. *dilate*, fully describe.

154   *parcels*, bits and pieces, or, possibly, details.

155   *intentively*, with full (and perhaps continuous) attention.

156   *beguile her of*, win from her.

159   *pains*, i.e. in telling the story of his life.

And till she come, as truly as to heaven
I do confess the vices of my blood,
So justly to your grave ears I'll present
How I did thrive in this fair lady's love   125
And she in mine.

DUKE   Say it, Othello.

OTHELLO   Her father loved me, oft invited me,
Still questioned me the story of my life
From year to year—the battles, sieges, fortunes,   130
That I have passed.
I ran it through, even from my boyish days
To the very moment that he bade me tell it,
Wherein I spake of most disastrous chances,
Of moving accidents by flood and field,   135
Of hair-breadth scapes in the imminent deadly breach,
Of being taken by the insolent foe
And sold to slavery, and my redemption thence;
And with it all my travels' history,
Wherein of antres vast and deserts idle,   140
Rough quarries, rocks and hills whose heads touch heaven,
It was my hint to speak (such was the process),
And of the Cannibals that each other eat,
And Anthropophagi, and men whose heads
Do grow beneath their shoulders. This to hear   145
Would Desdemona seriously incline;
But still the house affairs would draw her thence,
Which ever as she could with haste dispatch
She'd come again, and with a greedy ear
Devour up my discourse; which I observing,   150
Took once a pliant hour and found good means
To draw from her a prayer of earnest heart
That I would all my pilgrimage dilate,
Whereof by parcels she had something heard,
But not intentively. I did consent,   155
And often did beguile her of her tears
When I did speak of some distressful stroke
That my youth suffered. My story being done,
She gave me for my pains a world of sighs.
She swore, in faith 'twas strange, 'twas passing strange,   160

163   *her.* A nice point in interpretation of Desdemona's character is involved here. Is she wishing (1) that she could have been a man like Othello, or (2) that she could have such a husband?

166   *hint.* This word continues the above question of interpretation. Does 'hint' mean 'opportunity' as in l.142 or the more modern 'suggestion'?

173   *Take ... best,* make the best of a bad job.

174–5   *Men ... hands.* Some otiose writing? The metaphor, of doubtful appropriateness anyway, hardly adds much to the previous line.

177   *bad.* Perhaps in the sense of 'injurious', 'offensive'.

180–9   *My ... lord.* After Brabantio's description of his daughter in ll.94–6, Desdemona's boldness in front of the Senate, here and in the rest of the scene, must create some surprise. Her speech has some resemblance to that of Cordelia in the later *King Lear* (Act1 Sc.1, ll.97–106).

182   *education,* (in the widest sense of the word) upbringing, rearing, breeding.

183   *learn,* teach.

183   *You ... duty.* This Quarto reading seems preferable to the Folio 'You are the Lord of duty'. In view of the speech's theme of divided duty, 'all my duty' might seem contradictory. But Desdemona is probably using present-tense verbs because she is speaking of a very recent past. In that almost 'present' time of 'education' Brabantio did receive all Desdemona's duty. The intended fusion of the two times is clinched by 'am' (present) 'hitherto' (past).

188   *challenge,* claim.   *profess,* acknowledge, or claim.

191   *get,* beget.

'Twas pitiful, 'twas wondrous pitiful.
She wished she had not heard it, yet she wished
That heaven had made her such a man. She thanked me
And bade me, if I had a friend that loved her,
I should but teach him how to tell my story,   165
And that would woo her. Upon this hint I spake.
She loved me for the dangers I had passed,
And I loved her that she did pity them.
This only is the witchcraft I have used.
Here comes the lady. Let her witness it.   170

Enter DESDEMONA · IAGO · *and Attendants*

DUKE I think this tale would win my daughter too . . .
Good Brabantio,
Take up this mangled matter at the best.
Men do their broken weapons rather use
Than their bare hands.

BRABANTIO   I pray you hear her speak.   175
If she confess that she was half the wooer,
Destruction light on me if my bad blame
Light on the man! Come hither, gentle mistress.
Do you perceive in all this noble company
Where most you owe obedience?

DESDEMONA   My noble father,   180
I do perceive here a divided duty.
To you I am bound for life and education.
My life and education both do learn me
How to respect you. You are lord of all my duty;
I am hitherto your daughter. But here's my husband,   185
And so much duty as my mother showed
To you, preferring you before her father,
So much I challenge that I may profess
Due to the Moor, my lord.

BRABANTIO   God be with you! I have done.
Please it your Grace, on to the state affairs.   190
I had rather to adopt a child than get it.
Come hither, Moor.
I here do give thee that with all my heart
Which, but thou hast already, with all my heart

195   *For your sake*, because of you.   *jewel*. An ironical word.

197   *escape*, i.e. elopement.

198   *clogs*. Blocks of wood to restrict leg movement.

199   *yourself*. Probably the Duke means 'your better (or true) self'.
        lay a sentence, formulate (or express) a maxim.

200   *grise*. Synonymous with 'step'.

202–9   *When . . . grief*. This is the 'sentence; and, as is his usual prac-
        tice with sententious utterance, Shakespeare puts it in
        rhymed couplets. In ll.210-19 Brabantio is made to express
        himself in the same way. Iago's speeches in Act 2 Sc.1, ll.129-59,
        though not serious, are rhymed for a similar reason.

202–3   *When . . . depended*, distresses, in which hopes and expectations
        are involved, cease when, facing the worst, we know there is
        no cure for them.

204   *mischief*, misfortune, calamity.

207   *Patience . . . makes*, i.e. an exercise of patience makes a mock of
        any blows ('injury') of fortune.

208   *The . . . thief*. The ingenious thought here is that if one can
        smile at being robbed one is stealing from the robber in the
        sense that one is depriving him of his full possible effect!

209   *bootless*, profitless, vain.

210–17   *So . . . equivocal*. Brabantio's chief point is that the maxims
        can be variously interpreted—as 'sugar' or 'gall'.

210–11   *So . . . smile*. Brabantio immediately takes up the 'robbery'
        maxim to give it an ironically dismissive application.   *beguile*,
        here probably means 'cheat' or 'trick'.

212–15   *He . . . borrow*. Brabantio seems to be saying that the comfort in
        the Duke's maxims is all right so long as it does not demand
        the exercise of patience. The antithesis may be pointed by the
        contrast between 'free' and 'borrow', though 'free' could
        mean 'generous' (perhaps ironically spoken).

216   *gall*, bitterness.

219   *pierced*. A difficult word to gloss.   *through the ear*, i.e. by com-
        forting words.

221–7   *The . . . expedition*. There seems no very evident reason why the
        Duke's speech should be changed to prose.

222   *fortitude*, strength.

223   *substitute*, deputy, i.e. Montano.   *allowed sufficiency*, admitted
        competence, ability.

224–5   *yet . . . you*, yet public opinion, the final decider of purpose
        (or of what is to be done), has more confidence in you for the
        safety of the island.

225   *slubber*, sully, smear.

226   *stubborn*. Not 'obstinate' but 'rough' or 'inflexible'.   *boister-*
        ous, rough (as opposed to calm); or, possibly, unyielding.
        Both epithets come near to a mixed metaphor with 'gloss'.

229   *flinty and steel*. Besides 'hardness', do these words suggest
        firing-pieces and swords?

230   *thrice-driven*. In the production of down, winnowing would
        separate the light feathers from the heavy—hence, 'softest'.
        agnize, admit, recognize in oneself.

231–2   *A natural . . . hardness*. Something like 'a natural inclination and
        readiness for hardship'.

I would keep from thee. For your sake, jewel,   195
I am glad at soul I have no other child,
For thy escape would teach me tyranny
To hang clogs on them. I have done, my lord.

DUKE   Let me speak like yourself and lay a sentence
Which, as a grise or step, may help these lovers   200
Into your favour.
When remedies are past, the griefs are ended
By seeing the worst, which late on hopes depended.
To mourn a mischief that is past and gone
Is the next way to draw new mischief on.   205
What cannot be preserved when fortune takes,
Patience her injury a mockery makes.
The robbed that smiles steals something from the thief;
He robs himself that spends a bootless grief.

BRABANTIO   So let the Turk of Cyprus us beguile,   210
We lose it not so long as we can smile.
He bears the sentence well that nothing bears
But the free comfort which from thence he hears;
But he bears both the sentence and the sorrow
That to pay grief must of poor patience borrow.   215
These sentences, to sugar or to gall
Being strong on both sides, are equivocal.
But words are words; I never yet did hear
That the bruised heart was pierced through the ear.
Beseech you now, to the affairs of the state.   220

DUKE   The Turk with a most mighty preparation makes for Cyprus.
Othello, the fortitude of the place is best known to you; and
though we have there a substitute of most allowed sufficiency,
yet opinion, a more sovereign mistress of effects, throws a more
safer voice on you. You must therefore be content to slubber the 225
gloss of your new fortunes with this more stubborn and boisterous expedition.

OTHELLO   The tyrant, custom, most grave senators,
Hath made the flinty and steel couch of war
My thrice-driven bed of down. I do agnize   230
A natural and prompt alacrity
I find in hardness, and do undertake
This present war against the Ottomites.

234 *bending . . . state*, bowing to your authority (or position).

235 *disposition*, arrangements, disposal.

236 *Due . . . place*, proper regard for her rank. *exhibition*, (financial) maintenance.

237 *besort*, suitable company or attendance.

238 *As . . . breeding*, as is appropriate to her upbringing.

243 *unfolding*, proposal. *prosperous*, favourable.

244 *let . . . voice*, may I have your approval, or support ('voice') for a permission, or privilege ('charter'), i.e. of accompanying Othello to the wars.

245 *And . . . simpleness*. This unfinished sentence would indicate hesitation. But would Desdemona hesitate? The Folio reads 'I' assist my simpleness'.

247 *downright violence*, forthright, bold action. *storm*. This might mean much the same, with Desdemona saying that she boldly took fate etc. into her own hands. But the Quarto 'scorn' may be right, and 'fortunes' (used again in l.252) certainly has the sense of 'money', 'possessions', etc. in Act5 Sc.2, l.368.

248–9 *My . . . lord*. This would mean something like 'I'm utterly in love with the essential nature of Othello'. The Quarto reading 'Even to the utmost pleasure', like 'rites' in l.255, would refer to sexual relations—and this could be what Shakespeare intended. So many of the text problems of this speech hinge on our interpretation of Desdemona and of Shakespeare's women generally.

250 *I . . . mind*, i.e. for me it was Othello's disposition, etc. that mattered, not his appearance.

254 *moth*. Most editors gloss as 'idle', 'useless', etc. But the reference is not really clear.

256 *interim*, interval.

257 *By*, by reason of. *dear*. Not our vague meaning but 'mattering so much to me'.

260 *appetite*, i.e. sexual.

261–3 *Nor . . . mind*. The general sense of this difficult and much discussed passage seems to be that Othello supports Desdemona's accompanying him to Cyprus because he wants to indulge *her* wish (l.263), not—he protests—to gratify his own sexual desires. The problem (with a possibly corrupt text) is what exactly he is saying about himself. As punctuated opposite, the lines might be paraphrased—[I do not beg this] to satisfy animal lust—hot, youthful desires ('affects') of that kind now being dead in me, [nor do I beg it] for self-satisfaction (of a more reasonable, controlled sort) etc. 'proper', most common in the sense of 'self', etc., might carry the modern meaning of 'rightful', 'legitimate', etc.

264 *defend*, forbid,

266 *For*, because. *toys*, trifles.

267–8 *Of . . . instrument*. This is the Folio reading. The Quarto is different in several respects.

267 *seel*. This verb refers to the practice of sewing up a hawk's eyelids at one stage of its training. *wanton dullness*. Probably 'lassitude produced by sexual over-indulgence'.

Most humbly therefore, bending to your state,
I crave fit disposition for my wife,   235
Due reference of place and exhibition,
With such accommodation and besort
As levels with her breeding.

DUKE   If you please,
  Be't at her father's.

BRABANTIO   I'll not have it so.

OTHELLO   Nor I.

DESDEMONA   Nor I. I would not there reside   240
  To put my father in impatient thoughts
  By being in his eye. Most gracious Duke,
  To my unfolding lend your prosperous ear
  And let me find a charter in your voice;
  And if my simpleness—

DUKE   What would you? Speak.   245

DESDEMONA   That I did love the Moor to live with him,
  My downright violence and storm of fortunes
  May trumpet to the world. My heart's subdued
  Even to the very quality of my lord.
  I saw Othello's visage in his mind,   250
  And to his honours and his valiant parts
  Did I my soul and fortunes consecrate.
  So that, dear lords, if I be left behind
  A moth of peace, and he go to the war,
  The rites for which I love him are bereft me,   255
  And I a heavy interim shall support
  By his dear absence. Let me go with him.

OTHELLO   Let her have your voice.
  Vouch with me, heaven, I therefore beg it not
  To please the palate of my appetite,   260
  Nor to comply with heat (the young affects
  In me defunct) and proper satisfaction,
  But to be free and bounteous to her mind.
  And heaven defend your good souls that you think
  I will your serious and great business scant   265
  For she is with me. No, when light-winged toys
  Of feathered Cupid seel with wanton dullness

268   *My . . . instrument.* Interpretation of this line is complicated by
        the plural form of 'instrument' in the Quarto. Othello's
        'speculative instrument' would be primarily his mind, though
        'speculative', carrying on the association of 'seel' and 'dullness',
        might also imply eyes, observation, alertness. 'officed' refers
        to the duties laid upon him.

269   *disports*, pleasures, diversions (probably of a sexual kind).

270   *skillet*, saucepan or cooking-pot.

271–2   *all . . . estimation!* i.e. may I lose my reputation ('estimation')
        because of my ignoble, shameful ('indign') behaviour. In some
        sense 'make head' (a term for military attack) includes the
        meaning of 'adversities' (oppositions).

279   *commission.* The official document of Othello's appointment to
        the Cyprus command.

280–1   *With . . . you.* A wordy expression.   *quality*, nature.   *respect.*
        Probably means 'consideration'.

281   *my ancient*, i.e. this is the officer I leave behind as you request.

282   *A . . . trust.* This line clearly indicates Othello's complete faith
        in Iago. Even if there is any truth in Iago's account of the
        Cassio promotion, Othello never thinks that Iago may bear
        resentment. 'Honesty' and 'honest', words of multiple and
        changing meaning, used fifty-two times in the play, are the
        subject of Empson's study in *The Structure of Complex Words*, ch. 11.
        Though this analysis is sometimes over-subtle for poetry that
        has to be taken in swiftly, by ear, it contains much interesting
        general comment like: 'It is the two notions of being ready to
        blow the gaff on other people and frank to yourself about
        your desires that seem to me crucial about Iago' (p. 220).

283   *conveyance*, escort.

287   *If . . . lack.* This seems to mean 'if virtue is its own beauty'—
        i.e. needs no physical beauty to set it off.   *delighted*, delightful.

288   *fair.* A rich range of meanings; 'white' (as opposed to 'black'),
        'beautiful', 'pure', 'admirable', etc.

289–91 *Use . . . thee.* Ominous and resonant words, especially those of
        Brabantio. Othello has every reason to remember Brabantio's
        comment, and Iago certainly does remember it (Act3Sc.3,
        l.210).

292   *My . . . Iago.* Almost the entire essence of the play is in this line;
        and note the 'honest'. The bracketing of the two subjects of
        'faith' is highly ironical.

295   *in . . . advantage*, at the most suitable opportunity.

296–8   *I . . . thee.* Presumably Othello is saying that even the short
        'hour' at his disposal cannot be entirely devoted to love, but
        must be interrupted by the business of his command.
        worldly. Probably means 'public'.   *direction*, giving instructions,
        commands, etc.

298   *We . . . time*, we must just accept the present situation.

My speculative and officed instrument,
That my disports corrupt and taint my business,
Let housewives make a skillet of my helm,   270
And all indign and base adversities
Make head against my estimation!

DUKE Be it as you shall privately determine,
Either for her stay or going. The affair cries haste,
And speed must answer. You must hence tonight.   275

DESDEMONA Tonight, my lord?

DUKE   This night.

OTHELLO   With all my heart.

DUKE At nine in the morning here we'll meet again.
Othello, leave some officer behind,
And he shall our commission bring to you,
With such things else of quality and respect   280
As doth concern you.

OTHELLO   So please your grace, my ancient—
A man he is of honesty and trust.
To his conveyance I assign my wife,
With what else needful your good Grace shall think
To be sent after me.

DUKE   Let it be so.   285
Good night to everyone. [to BRABANTIO] And, noble signior,
If virtue no delighted beauty lack,
Your son-in-law is far more fair than black.

1 SENATOR Adieu, brave Moor. Use Desdemona well.

BRABANTIO Look to her, Moor, if thou hast eyes to see.   290
She has deceived her father, and may thee.
                              [Exeunt DUKE · SENATORS · and Attendants

OTHELLO My life upon her faith! Honest Iago,
My Desdemona must I leave to thee.
I prithee let thy wife attend on her,
And bring them after in the best advantage.   295
Come, Desdemona, I have but an hour
Of love, of worldly matters and direction,
To spend with thee. We must obey the time.
                              [Exeunt OTHELLO and DESDEMONA·

RODERIGO Iago.

300   *noble heart.* About as contemptuously ironical as any remark
       could be. As well as providing some comic relief, the Roderigo
       sub-plot, if it can be called that, reveals various facets of Iago
       that are not evident in the main action.

303   *incontinently*, immediately.

305   *silly.* Like 'silliness' in the next line a shade or two less pejora-
       tive than our modern word. Gloss as 'foolish', 'foolishness'.

307   *prescription*, a doctor's 'general' instructions, not the modern
       meaning. The word may also mean 'claim' or 'right'.

308–12 *I . . . baboon.* 'Iago's creed . . . is that absolute egoism is the only
       rational and proper attitude, and that conscience and honour
       or any kind of regard for others is an absurdity. He does not
       deny that this absurdity exists' (Bradley, *op. cit.*, p. 219).

311   *guinea-hen.* A disparaging term for a woman—possibly, but not
       certainly 'prostitute'. 'Guinea-hen' and 'baboon' are two more
       of the play's numerous animal references.

313   *fond*, loving; possibly, infatuated.

314   *virtue.* Here the word must mean something like 'moral power
       or scope', for Iago's retort is that everything depends on will.

315   *A fig!* A fairly common dismissive exclamation.

317–18 *if . . . thyme.* According to Elizabethan ideas, 'temperament is
       merely the resultant of a mixture of the qualities of hot and
       cold, moist and dry' (Hardin Craig, *The Enchanted Glass*, p. 121).
       Since all created things were supposed to have these qualities
       Shakespeare's choice of particular herbs may be dictated by
       this belief.   *set*, plant.   *weed up.* Usually glossed as 'pull
       out' etc.; but might it simply mean 'weed'?

318   *gender*, variety, kind.   *distract*, divide up; possibly, confuse.

319   *manured*, cultivated, tilled.

320   *corrigible*, able to correct or control.

321   *balance*, weighing apparatus—virtually, weighing.   *scale*,
       balance-pan.

322   *poise*, counterbalance.   *blood and baseness*, base passions
       ('blood').

324   *motions*, desires, emotions (see l.95 and note); near-synonymous
       with 'stings', though this word has more sexual association.

325   *unbitted*, without a controlling bit (as used with horses).
       sect, cutting. But something may be said for Johnson's emen-
       dation 'set', meaning 'a shoot'.

326   *scion*, shoot.

328   *It . . . will.* Repeating his essential view about love, Iago, with
       his phrase 'permission of the will', may be hinting the theme
       of his speech—that Desdemona can be easily corrupted and
       seduced.

330–1 *knit . . . deserving*, devoted to securing what you deserve.

331   *perdurable*, everlasting.

332   *stead*, assist, help.

333   *Defeat . . . beard*, you don't look courageous, but you can
       disguise your appearance ('favour') by growing a beard.
       Defeat, overcome, or disguise.   *usurped*, wrongfully assumed
       and/or disguising.

337   *answerable sequestration*, corresponding separation, or, possibly,
       ending.

IAGO What sayest thou, noble heart? 300

RODERIGO What will I do, thinkest thou?

IAGO Why, go to bed and sleep.

RODERIGO I will incontinently drown myself.

IAGO Well, if thou dost, I shall never love thee after it. Why, thou
silly gentleman? 305

RODERIGO It is silliness to live when to live is a torment: and then we
have a prescription to die when death is our physician.

IAGO O villainous! I have looked upon the world for four times
seven years, and since I could distinguish between a benefit and an
injury, I never found a man that knew how to love himself. Ere I 310
would say I would drown myself for the love of a guinea-hen, I
would change my humanity with a baboon.

RODERIGO What should I do? I confess it is my shame to be so fond,
but it is not in my virtue to amend it.

IAGO Virtue? A fig! 'Tis in ourselves that we are thus, or thus. Our 315
bodies are our gardens, to the which our wills are gardeners, so
that if we will plant nettles or sow lettuce, set hyssop and weed
up thyme, supply it with one gender of herbs or distract it with
many, either to have it sterile with idleness or manured with
industry, why, the power and corrigible authority of this lies in 320
our wills. If the balance of our lives had not one scale of reason
to poise another of sensuality, the blood and baseness of our
natures would conduct us to most preposterous conclusions. But
we have reason to cool our raging motions, our carnal stings, our
unbitted lusts—whereof I take this that you call love to be a sect 325
or scion.

RODERIGO It cannot be.

IAGO It is merely a lust of the blood and a permission of the will.
Come, be a man. Drown thyself? Drown cats and blind puppies!
I have professed me thy friend, and I confess me knit to thy de- 330
serving with cables of perdurable toughness. I could never better
stead thee than now . . . Put money in thy purse. Follow these
wars. Defeat thy favour with an usurped beard. I say, put money
in thy purse. It cannot be that Desdemona should long continue
her love unto the Moor—put money in thy purse—nor he his to 335
her. It was a violent commencement, and thou shalt see an
answerable sequestration—put but money in thy purse. These

338   *wills*, sexual desires.

339   *locusts*. Sweet cobs of the carob tree.

340   *acerb*, bitter.   *coloquinta*. Bitter-apple purgative.

344   *sanctimony*. Ironic—either as 'holiness' or 'wedding rites'.

345   *erring*, wandering, unsettled (with possibly a suggestion of 'sinful').   *subtle*. Probably 'refined', 'sophisticated', 'choosy'.

346   *all . . . hell*, i.e. devils. Perhaps a more revealing expression than Iago intends.

347   *make*, raise, get hold of.

347–8   *clean . . . way*, quite the wrong course.

348   *hanged*. Possibly a hint of peril for Roderigo even if he is successful; or perhaps merely sharing Desdemona's favours will drive him to despair.

350   *Wilt . . . issue?* Will you firmly support my hopes if I pin everything ('depend') on a fortunate outcome ('issue')?

353   *hearted*. Probably 'fixed in the heart', i.e. deeply felt.   *conjunctive*, joined. The Quarto 'communicative' would mean 'allied and in touch'.

356   *Traverse*. Perhaps something like the modern 'get moving'. But it might refer to a drill position for holding weapons.

360   *betimes*, early.

361   *farewell . . .* The dots allow for Iago's afterthought as Roderigo moves off.

364   *I'll . . . land*. For an aristocrat of Shakespeare's time the chief way to raise money.

366   *For . . . profane*. Iago is obviously proud of the knowledge he believes he has gained from experience.

367   *snipe*. Contemptuous—and more 'animal' imagery.

368–72   *I . . . surety*. These lines (and still more the soliloquy in the next scene, ll.269–95) sharply raise the question of the validity of Iago's *self-stated* motives. Many important critics have maintained that Iago's own account of his actions tells us little or nothing about his real motives. But before we dismiss his confessions we should remember (1) that it was a convention of the soliloquy that the speaker revealed the truth about himself, and (2) that because Iago does not repeat or elaborate a self-stated motive it does not necessarily follow that this motive is an extempore invention. Iago is a character in a short, swift-moving play, not in a novel.

372   *do*, act, behave.   *as . . . surety*. Usually glossed 'as though I were certain'. But 'surety' could mean 'security', and just possibly Iago means that he will act to protect himself against any chance of Othello seducing Emilia.   *He . . . well*, he has a high regard for me.

374   *proper*, handsome.

375–6   *To . . . knavery*. Bradley, in his search for the 'real' Iago motive, finds the vital clue in these lines: 'To "plume up the will", to heighten the sense of power or superiority—this seems to be the unconscious motive of many acts of cruelty which evidently do not spring chiefly from ill-will, and which therefore puzzle and sometimes horrify us most' (*op. cit.*, p. 229). *plume up*. Probably something like 'impressively display'—as a bird with its feathers. (The Quarto has 'make up'.)

Moors are changeable in their wills—fill thy purse with money.
The food that to him now is as luscious as locusts shall be to him
shortly as acerb as the coloquintida. She must change for youth. 340
When she is sated with his body she will find the error of her
choice. Therefore put money in thy purse. If thou wilt needs
damn thyself, do it a more delicate way than drowning. Make all
the money thou canst. If sanctimony and a frail vow betwixt an
erring barbarian and a super-subtle Venetian be not too hard for 345
my wits and all the tribe of hell, thou shalt enjoy her. Therefore
make money. A pox of drowning thyself! 'Tis clean out of the
way. Seek thou rather to be hanged in compassing thy joy than
to be drowned and go without her.

RODERIGO Wilt thou be fast to my hopes, if I depend on the issue? 350

IAGO   Thou art sure of me. Go make money. I have told thee often,
    and I tell thee again and again, I hate the Moor. My cause is
    hearted; thine hath no less reason. Let us be conjunctive in our
    revenge against him. If thou canst cuckold him, thou dost
    thyself a pleasure and me a sport. There are many events in the 355
    womb of time which will be delivered. Traverse! Go, provide thy
    money. We will have more of this tomorrow. Adieu.

RODERIGO Where shall we meet in the morning?

IAGO   At my lodging.

RODERIGO I'll be with thee betimes.   360

IAGO   Go to; farewell . . . Do you hear, Roderigo?

RODERIGO What say you?

IAGO   No more of drowning, do you hear?

RODERIGO I am changed. I'll go sell all my land.   [Exit

IAGO   Thus do I ever make my fool my purse,   365
    For I mine own gained knowledge should profane
    If I would time expend with such a snipe
    But for my sport and profit. I hate the Moor,
    And it is thought abroad that 'twixt my sheets
    He's done my office. I know not if't be true,   370
    But I, for mere suspicion in that kind,
    Will do as if for surety. He holds me well—
    The better shall my purpose work on him.
    Cassio's a proper man. Let me see now . . .
    To get his place and to plume up my will   375

376   *double,* i.e. against both Cassio and Othello.   *How? . . . see.*
       This gives an impression of Iago improvising his plot.

379   *person.* Probably 'personal appearance'; possibly, 'personality'.
       smooth, pleasant, agreeable (almost certainly without any
       pejorative suggestion).   *dispose,* disposition, or manner.

380   *To be suspected,* i.e. because Cassio is attractive to women, he is
       the sort of man one would naturally suspect of seduction.

381–2 *The . . . so.* Lines to be closely considered in any interpretation
       of Othello—especially as coming from Iago.

383   *tenderly,* i.e. without painful awareness.   *led . . . nose.* This
       phrase has both a literal sense and figurative meaning 'fooled'.

385–6 *Hell . . . light.* There is no missing Iago's diabolic identification
       here.

In double knavery. How? How? Let's see.
After some time, to abuse Othello's ear
That he is too familiar with his wife.
He hath a person and a smooth dispose
To be suspected, framed to make women false.   380
The Moor is of a free and open nature,
That thinks men honest that but seem to be so,
And will as tenderly be led by the nose
As asses are.
I have't. It is engendered. Hell and night   385
Must bring this monstrous birth to the world's light.   [*Exit*

If, after a sharp, unusual break in the action, the play now makes a second start, this restart is an exciting one, set initially in a storm, filled with suspense (and some lighter relief), and leading up to the climax of the striking reunion of Desdemona and Othello. Of this reunion Maud Bodkin wrote: 'The words of Othello greeting Desdemona communicate the experience of that high rapture which in the tragic world brings fear. We feel a poise of the spirit like that of the sun at its zenith, or of the wheel of fate, before the downward plunge' (from *Archetypal Patterns in Poetry*, reprinted in the Penguin *Shakespeare's Tragedies*, p. 100). The coda, provided by Iago, is a frightening threat of this 'downward plunge'.

1–17   *What . . . flood.* An excellent example of how Shakespeare, in spite of the bare, simple Elizabethan stage, was able to create setting and atmosphere through the vividness of his descriptive writing.

2   *flood*, sea.

7   *ruffianed*, violently stormed or blustered. Possibly an original verb-coinage.

8   *mountains*, i.e. of water.

9   *hold the mortise*, keep their carpentered joints (*mortise*) intact.

10   *segregation*, separation, scattering.

11   *banning*. Either 'chiding', 'cursing'; or, 'forbidding the sea's advance'. The Folio reads 'foaming', and also 'chidden' for 'chiding' in l.12.

12   *main*, the main body of water (sustaining the 'surge'). Some editors read this as 'mane'.

14   *burning Bear*, shining constellation of the Little Bear. An aid to navigation.

15   *guards*. Two stars, known as the Guardians, in the Little Bear constellation.   *Pole*, Pole star.

16   *molestation*, turmoil.

17   *enchafed*, furious, enraged.

18   *embayed*, sheltered in a bay.

21   *banged*. This word carries a stronger sense of violence than it usually bears today.

22   *designment*, enterprise or plan.   *halts*, is crippled (rather than 'stops').   *Another . . . Venice*. To make sense of 'Another', it may be that the other, or first, ship was the one that carried the news of ll.20–2. The Folio reads: 'A noble ship of Venice'. Choice between these variants is tied up with the problem of 'A Veronesa' in l.26.

23   *wrack*, wreck.   *sufferance*, damage.

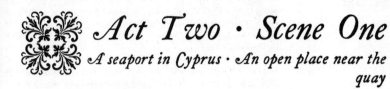

Act Two · Scene One

A seaport in Cyprus · An open place near the quay

Enter MONTANO *and two* GENTLEMEN

MONTANO What from the cape can you discern at sea?

1 GENTLEMAN Nothing at all. It is a high-wrought flood.
I cannot 'twixt the heaven and the main
Descry a sail.

MONTANO Methinks the wind does speak aloud at land; 5
A fuller blast ne'er shook our battlements.
If it hath ruffianed so upon the sea,
What ribs of oak, when mountains melt on them,
Can hold the mortise? What shall we hear of this?

2 GENTLEMAN A segregation of the Turkish fleet; 10
For do but stand upon the banning shore,
The chiding billow seems to pelt the clouds,
The wind-shaked surge, with high and monstrous main,
Seems to cast water on the burning Bear
And quench the guards of the ever-fixèd Pole. 15
I never did like molestation view
On the enchafèd flood.

MONTANO   If that the Turkish fleet
Be not ensheltered and embayed, they are drowned.
It is impossible they bear it out.

Enter a third GENTLEMAN

3 GENTLEMAN News, lords! Our wars are done. 20
The desperate tempest hath so banged the Turks
That their designment halts. Another ship of Venice
Hath seen a grievous wrack and sufferance
On most part of their fleet.

MONTANO How! Is this true?

Notes &
Commentary

26   *A Veronesa.* If this is Shakespeare's anglicization of the Italian *verrinessa* (cutter), there is no serious problem; and the reading 'A noble ship' in l.22 would probably be ruled out. The explanation that the ship was supplied by Verona, an inland city controlled by Venice, seems a little far-fetched.

31   *comfort,* pleasure, happiness.

32   *sadly,* gravely, very seriously.

35–6   *For . . . soldier.* Note Montano's tribute to Othello.

39–40 *Even . . . regard,* even till, through so much straining of our eyes, we can no longer distinguish the sea from the sky.

41–2   *For . . . arrivance,* for every minute we can expect the arrival of more ships.

43–4   *Thanks . . . Moor!* Cassio is judging by the evident signs of anxiety for Othello's safety that he has seen since landing.

45   *elements,* winds and seas.

48   *pilot.* Probably 'steersman' in a general sense.

49   *Of . . . allowance.* This might be paraphrased by something like 'regarded as well-tried and expert'.

50–1   *my . . . cure.* A rather involved expression. Because of Othello's well-built ship and excellent helmsman, Cassio has not excessively feared for his safety and so has not had to feed on his hopes so much that he has exhausted them. On the contrary, his hopes 'stand in bold cure'—i.e. are in an excellent state of health.

53   *brow,* edge—with probably some suggestion of height overlooking the sea.

55   *My . . . for,* I hope it is. Note again Cassio's elaborate turn of speech.

3 GENTLEMAN   The ship is here put in,   25
    A Veronesa. Michael Cassio,
    Lieutenant to the warlike Moor, Othello,
    Is come ashore. The Moor himself's at sea,
    And is in full commission here for Cyprus.

MONTANO   I am glad on't. 'Tis a worthy governor.   30

3 GENTLEMAN   But this same Cassio, though he speak of comfort
    Touching the Turkish loss, yet he looks sadly
    And prays the Moor be safe, for they were parted
    With foul and violent tempest.

MONTANO   Pray heaven he be,
    For I have served him, and the man commands   35
    Like a full soldier. Let's to the seaside, ho!
    As well to see the vessel that's come in,
    As to throw out our eyes for brave Othello,
    Even till we make the main and the aerial blue
    An indistinct regard.

3 GENTLEMAN   Come, let's do so,   40
    For every minute is expectancy
    Of more arrivance.

Enter CASSIO

CASSIO   Thanks, you the valiant of this warlike isle
    That so approve the Moor! O, let the heavens
    Give him defence against the elements,   45
    For I have lost him on a dangerous sea.

MONTANO   Is he well shipped?

CASSIO   His bark is stoutly timbered, and his pilot
    Of very expert and approved allowance;
    Therefore my hopes, not surfeited to death,   50
    Stand in bold cure.
    [*a cry within* 'A sail, a sail, a sail!']

Enter a fourth GENTLEMAN

CASSIO   What noise?

4 GENTLEMAN   The town is empty. On the brow o' the sea
    Stand ranks of people, and they cry 'A sail!'

CASSIO   My hopes do shape him for the Governor. [*A salvo is fired*]   55

56   *shot of courtesy*, a salvo of greeting.

60   *But . . . wived?* A most odd line, since Montano has had no
            means of learning about Othello's marriage. Either some
            earlier lines have been lost from the text or, more likely,
            Shakespeare has simply been careless.

61–5   *He . . . ingener.* Kott makes an interesting, if debatable, point
            when he writes: 'Desdemona is sexually obsessed with Othello,
            but all men—Iago, Cassio, Roderigo—are obsessed with
            Desdemona' (*op. cit.*, p. 94).

62   *paragons*, surpasses.   *wild.* Possibly means something like
            'fantastic', 'incredible'.

63   *quirks*, elaborate or ingenious phrases or figures of speech—
            'conceits' in the Elizabethan sense.   *blazoning*, praising,
            eulogizing.

64–5   *And . . . ingener.* M. R. Ridley in the *Arden* edition of the play has
            a brief and sensible paraphrase of l.64: 'just as God made her'.
            Ingener means 'inventor'. What Cassio seems to be saying is that
            any poet or painter would exhaust himself trying to create
            such a perfection of beauty and goodness as Desdemona is by
            nature. In the Quarto l.65 reads: 'Does bear all excellency'.

67   *speed.* This probably includes the idea of 'good fortune' as in
            'God-speed'.

69   *guttered rocks.* Several meanings have been suggested for
            'guttered': rocks that are worn away (and so jagged); rocks
            in channels; or possibly, submerged rocks.

70   *ensteeped.* This probably means 'hidden under water'.

71–2   *do . . . natures.* Whether we read the Folio 'mortal' or the
            Quarto 'common', and whether we take 'mortal' in the sense
            of 'deadly' or 'usual', the essential meaning is the same, i.e.
            that the rocks and sands have not been, as usual, perilous to
            life.

73   *The divine Desdemona.* Primarily this phrase is part of the poetic
            hyperbole of Cassio's speech: the rocks and sands have sub-
            mitted to the passage of a goddess. But 'divine' is to be noted as
            a key antithesis to Othello's later distorted vision of Desde-
            mona as a 'devil'.

76–7   *Whose . . . speed*, who has arrived a week earlier than we expected.
            footing, landing.

81   *extincted*, extinct, extinguished.

82   *comfort.* See a similar use of this word in l.31.

2 GENTLEMAN   They do discharge their shot of courtesy—
   Our friends at least.

CASSIO   I pray you, sir, go forth,
   And give us truth who 'tis that is arrived.

2 GENTLEMAN   I shall.   [*Exit*

MONTANO   But, good lieutenant, is your General wived?   60

CASSIO   Most fortunately. He hath achieved a maid
   That paragons description and wild fame—
   One that excels the quirks of blazoning pens,
   And in the essential vesture of creation
   Does tire the ingener.

Re-enter second GENTLEMAN

                 How now? Who has put in?   65

2 GENTLEMAN   'Tis one Iago, ancient to the General.

CASSIO   He's had most favourable and happy speed.
   Tempests themselves, high seas and howling winds,
   The guttered rocks and congregated sands,
   Traitors ensteeped to clog the guiltless keel,   70
   As having sense of beauty, do omit
   Their mortal natures, letting go safely by
   The divine Desdemona.

MONTANO   What is she?

CASSIO   She that I spake of, our great Captain's captain,
   Left in the conduct of the bold Iago,   75
   Whose footing here anticipates our thoughts
   A se'nnight's speed. Great Jove, Othello guard,
   And swell his sail with thine own powerful breath,
   That he may bless this bay with his tall ship,
   Make love's quick pants in Desdemona's arms,   80
   Give renewed fire to our extinct spirits,
   And bring all Cyprus comfort.

Enter DESDEMONA · EMILIA · IAGO · RODERIGO · *and Attendants*

                 O, behold,
   The riches of the ship is come ashore!
   Ye men of Cyprus, let her have your knees.
   Hail to thee, lady! And the grace of heaven,   85

87 *Enwheel*, encircle.

87–8 *I . . . lord?* Desdemona thanks Cassio for his courtesy. But notice how little he matters to her beside Othello.

94 *They . . . citadel.* This refers of course to the salvo of the cannon.

97–9 *Let . . . courtesy.* Possibly a fine point in our interpretation of Cassio is involved here. Since kissing was an accepted form of greeting, it would be wrong to see his behaviour as amorously gallant or flirtatious. But he himself uses the word 'bold', and with his repeated reference to 'manners', 'breeding', 'courtesy', he does seem to be excusing himself for something. Perhaps his kiss was unusually vigorous or prolonged!

   With reference to a famous nineteenth-century American actor of Iago, K. Muir writes: 'Booth was quite right to make Iago wince when Cassio kisses Emilia, for it leads on to the revelation in the second soliloquy that he fears Cassio with his night-cap too' (*New Penguin* ed., p. 18).

98 *extend.* This might mean 'stretch'—and to the full; or it might have the neutral meaning of 'show', 'display'.
   manners, forms of polite behaviour. *breeding*, i.e. good breeding.

104 *still*, continuously. *list*, wish, desire.

105–7 *Marry . . . thinking*, i.e. when Emilia is with Desdemona her nagging is unspoken, but it is still present in her heart and thoughts.

109–64 *Come on . . . scholar.* This long interchange between Iago and Desdemona may have been written as comic relief for the groundlings. But such an explanation does not justify the passage, and to some it may seem rather out of character that Desdemona should indulge in this cheap cross-talk rather than go to the harbour to make her own urgent inquiries about Othello. However, ll.123–14 present strong evidence that she is deliberately trying to divert herself from her anxiety. (For a defence of the passage see Granville-Barker, *op. cit.*, p. 18.)

109 *You . . . doors*, you present a fine—but illusory—appearance to the world.

110 *Bells*, i.e. noisily clamorous. *in your parlours ; in your kitchen*, at home.

111 *Saints . . . offended*, you do injuries under a saintly guise; you turn devils when you are offended.

112 *Players . . . beds.* The main antithetical gibe seems to be that women are seriously intent only when in bed. But some of the meaning is uncertain. 'Players' may mean 'those who merely play' (rather than 'stage-actors'), and 'housewives' may mean 'hussies'.

114 *Turk*, infidel.

Before, behind thee, and on every hand,
Enwheel thee round.

DESDEMONA   I thank you, valiant Cassio.
What tidings can you tell me of my lord?

CASSIO   He is not yet arrived; nor know I aught
But that he's well and will be shortly here.   90

DESDEMONA   O, but I fear! How lost you company?

CASSIO   The great contention of the sea and skies
Parted our fellowship.
[*a cry within* 'A sail, a sail, a sail!' *Another salvo*]
                                But hark, a sail!

2 GENTLEMAN   They give their greeting to the citadel.
This likewise is a friend.

CASSIO   See for the news.   95
                                [*Exit* SECOND GENTLEMAN
Good ancient, you are welcome. [*to* EMILIA] Welcome, mistress.
Let it not gall your patience, good Iago,
That I extend my manners. 'Tis my breeding
That gives me this bold show of courtesy. [*He kisses* EMILIA]

IAGO   Sir, would she give you so much of her lips   100
As of her tongue she oft bestows on me,
You'd have enough.

DESDEMONA   Alas, she has no speech.

IAGO   In faith, too much.
I find it still when I have list to sleep.
Marry, before your ladyship, I grant   105
She puts her tongue a little in her heart
And chides with thinking.

EMILIA   You have little cause to say so.

IAGO   Come on, come on. You are pictures out of doors,
Bells in your parlours, wild-cats in your kitchens,   110
Saints in your injuries, devils being offended,
Players in your housewifery, and housewives in your beds.

DESDEMONA   O, fie upon thee, slanderer!

IAGO   Nay, it is true, or else I am a Turk—
You rise to play and go to bed to work.   115

EMILIA   You shall not write my praise.

c

119   *critical*, censorious, carping.

120   *assay*, try, make an attempt.

122   *beguile*. This could mean 'disguise', but more probably 'distract attention from'.

123   *thing I am*, my true state (i.e. of distress, fearfulness, etc.).

125-7 *my invention . . . all*. In Iago's vivid, but characteristically unpleasant, image to describe the painful composition of his poem, 'frieze' (coarse woollen cloth) presumably refers to the bird-snarers' clothes. When they try to remove the highly glutinous birdlime that has got on to their garments they pull away the threads.

130   *The one's . . . it*. The obliquity of Iago's poem is not always easy to understand. In the first half of this line he appears to be echoing the very Shakespearean thought (see the *Sonnets*) that physical beauty is to be used, not hoarded. If a beautiful woman has 'wit' (intelligence, cleverness), she will use it to avoid a life of frustration, sterility, etc.

131   *black*, dark-haired.

133   *white*. A pun on 'wight' (man) and possible on the 'white' (or blank) at the target centre.

137   *folly*. A play on the double meaning—'foolishness' and 'wantonness'.

138   *old*, stale.   *fond*, foolish.   *paradoxes*, contradictions (especially to accepted beliefs).

139   *foul*, ugly, unattractive.

141   *thereunto*, in addition.

142   *foul pranks*, sinful promiscuities. (But of course Iago is not serious.)

145-6 *one . . . itself?* one whose merits were so unquestionable that she rightly compelled ('put on') the most malicious people to testify to them.   *vouch*, testimony, witness.

147-59 *She . . . beer*. These mainly closed heroic couplets, with their continued balance and antithesis, are remarkable for the Elizabethan period. Diction apart, they might almost come from the Augustan age.

148   *Had . . . loud*, had a ready tongue but did not abuse it.

IAGO   No, let me not.

DESDEMONA What wouldst thou write of me if thou shouldst
    praise me?

IAGO O, gentle lady, do not put me to't.
  For I am nothing if not critical.

DESDEMONA Come on, assay . . . There's one gone to the harbour? 120

IAGO Ay, madam.

DESDEMONA I am not merry, but I do beguile
  The thing I am by seeming otherwise.
  Come, how wouldst thou praise me?

IAGO I am about it, but indeed my invention   125
  Comes from my pate as birdlime does from frieze—
  It plucks out brains and all. But my muse labours,
  And thus she is delivered . . .
  If she be fair and wise, fairness and wit,
  The one's for use, the other useth it.   130

DESDEMONA Well praised! How if she be black and witty?

IAGO If she be black and thereto have a wit,
  She'll find a white that shall her blackness fit.

DESDEMONA Worse and worse.

EMILIA How if fair and foolish?   135

IAGO She never yet was foolish that was fair,
  For even her folly helped her to an heir.

DESDEMONA These are old fond paradoxes to make fools laugh i'the
  alehouse. What miserable praise hast thou for her that's foul and
  foolish?   140

IAGO There's none so foul and foolish thereunto,
  But does foul pranks which fair and wise ones do.

DESDEMONA O heavy ignorance! Thou praisest the worst best. But
  what praise couldst thou bestow on a deserving woman indeed,
  one that in the authority of her merit did justly put on the 145
  vouch of very malice itself?

IAGO She that was ever fair and never proud,
  Had tongue at will and yet was never loud;
  Never lacked gold and yet went never gay;
  Fled from her wish and yet said 'Now I may';   150
  She that being angered, her revenge being nigh,

152   *Bade ... stay*, decided to do nothing about the offence she had
       suffered.

154   *To ... tail*. An obscure line. The previous 'frail', in its sugges-
       tion of feminine weakness to sexual pressure and temptation
       ('Frailty, thy name is woman'), might indicate that the
       change is one of lovers. The 'cod's head' might be a dull, ugly
       husband, the 'salmon's tail' a lively lover.

159   *chronicle*. As we might say, 'chalk up'.   *small beer*, trivialities.

162   *profane*, wicked; or possibly, disrespectful, scurrilous.   *liberal*,
       free to the point of gross, licentious.

164   *home*. This is probably to be glossed as 'plainly', 'bluntly'. To
       read 'He speaks home' as 'he hits the mark' would identify
       Cassio too closely with Iago's attitude.

164-5 *You . . . scholar*. This might be rendered by something like:
       'You'll get a better impression of him as a soldier than as a
       philosopher'.   *in the*, in the role of.

165   *said*. As often in Shakespeare this probably means 'done'
       rather than 'spoken'.

167   *I ... courtesies*. The Folio reading: 'I will gyve thee in thine own
       courtship', may be preferred, but 'catch' seems more in
       keeping with the previous 'web' metaphor.

167-8 *You . . . indeed*. Presumably a mocking endorsement of what
       Desdemona and Cassio are saying.

169-70 *kissed . . . fingers*. This kissing of one's own hand was a common
       gentlemanly courtesy to a lady. (See, for example, *Twelfth
       Night*, Act3 Sc.4, ll.30-1).

170   *sir*, gentleman, gallant.

172-3 *clyster-pipes*. Tubes, or syringe, for anal injection. A typically
       gross expression from Iago.

174   *I . . . trumpet*. Men of importance had their own distinctive
       trumpet-call.

176   *my fair warrior*. Othello is saluting Desdemona's courage and
       resolution in accompanying him on the present campaign.

177-87 *It . . . fate*. This first speech of Othello, at what is to be the
       scene of his downfall and damnation, should be most closely
       noted. It is clear that his whole state of being depends, in a
       quite exceptional degree (and therefore with some potential
       danger), on his absolute love for Desdemona. Nothing less
       than his 'soul' is involved, and also his 'content' (twice men-
       tioned), which has a richer, more positive significance than
       today's word.
            The speech is also poignant with dramatic irony. Much of
       this is obvious, but there are some delicate touches, like the
       casual, simile allusion to heaven and hell. Further, the last
       lines of the speech strike a momentary note of chill, sombre
       premonition.

181   *hills of seas*. Cf. l.8 at the opening of this scene.

Bade her wrong stay and her displeasure fly;
She that in wisdom never was so frail
To change the cod's head for the salmon's tail;
She that could think and ne'er disclose her mind;   155
See suitors following and not look behind;
She was a wight, if ever such wight were—

DESDEMONA   To do what?

IAGO   To suckle fools and chronicle small beer.

DESDEMONA   O, most lame and impotent conclusion! Do not learn   160
of him, Emilia, though he be thy husband. How say you, Cassio?
Is he not a most profane and liberal counsellor?

CASSIO   He speaks home, madam. You may relish him more in the
soldier than in the scholar.

IAGO [*aside*]   He takes her by the palm. Ay, well said, whisper. With as   165
little a web as this will I ensnare as great a fly as Cassio. Ay, smile
upon her, do. I will catch you in your own courtesies . . . You say
true, 'tis so indeed . . . If such tricks as these strip you out of your
lieutenantry, it had been better you had not kissed your three
fingers so oft, which now again you are most apt to play the sir in.   170
Very good; well kissed, an excellent courtesy! . . . 'Tis so indeed . . .
Yet again your fingers to your lips? Would they were clyster-
pipes for your sake! [*trumpets within*]
[*aloud*] The Moor! I know his trumpet.

CASSIO   'Tis truly so.

DESDEMONA   Let's meet him and receive him.

CASSIO   Lo, where he comes!   175

Enter OTHELLO *and Attendants*

OTHELLO   O, my fair warrior!

DESDEMONA   My dear Othello!

OTHELLO   It gives me wonder great as my content
To see you here before me. O, my soul's joy!
If after every tempest come such calms,
May the winds blow till they have wakened death,   180
And let the labouring bark climb hills of seas,
Olympus-high, and duck again as low
As hell's from heaven. If it were now to die,
'Twere now to be most happy, for I fear

186   *comfort*. (See also ll.31, 82, and 188). In Elizabethan English this word has a richer—and less 'cosy'—significance than it bears today. It could imply 'delight', 'well-being', and 'content'. See a comparable use in the *Book of Common Prayer*: 'that we may receive the fruits of the earth to our comfort'.

187–9   *The . . . grow*. The expression of a more youthful optimism.

191   *here*. Othello might be referring to his voice or to his heart where his 'content' is centred. But the point is of no great consequence.

192–5   *And . . . music*. To appreciate the force of the expression here one must realize the significance the Elizabethans attached to the spirit of harmony and their idealization of music for that reason. Iago is saying a very wicked thing.

195   *set . . . pegs*, slacken the strings and so produce discord, or no music at all.

196   *As . . . am*. Probably 'as honest as men suppose me to be'. But Empson argues that in Iago's rejection of such romantic love he is, in one sense of the word, genuinely 'honest'.

199   *honey*. Interesting to find this term of endearment in Shakespeare. This is the only time Shakespeare uses the endearment as a noun.   *desired*, liked, beloved.

201   *out of fashion*, inappropriately, i.e. his mind should be on his business.

203   *coffers*, boxes, luggage, etc.

204   *master*, i.e. of the ship.

206   *challenge*, claim, demand, entitle to.

207   *well met*. A familiar form of greeting.

208–9   *presently*. Usually this means 'at once', but since Iago intends to have conversation with Roderigo, here the word may have its modern sense.

212   *court of guard*, guard room, or guard house.

215   *Lay . . . thus*. Possibly, in a sort of pantomime of exchanged secrets, Roderigo is to put his finger to his lips.

216   *but*, only, merely.

218   *discreet*, discerning, knowing.

My soul hath her content so absolute   185
That not another comfort like to this
Succeeds in unknown fate.

DESDEMONA   The heavens forbid
But that our loves and comforts should increase,
Even as our days do grow.

OTHELLO   Amen to that, sweet powers!
I cannot speak enough of this content;   190
It stops me here. It is too much of joy.
And this, and this, the greatest discords be [*kissing her*]
That e'er our hearts shall make.

IAGO [*aside*]   O, you are well tuned now!
But I'll set down the pegs that make this music,   195
As honest as I am.

OTHELLO   Come, let's to the castle.
News, friends—our wars are done, the Turks are drowned.
How do our old acquaintance of the isle?
Honey, you shall be well desired in Cyprus—
I have found great love amongst them. O my sweet,   200
I prattle out of fashion and I dote
In mine own comforts. I prithee, good Iago,
Go to the bay and disembark my coffers.
Bring thou the master to the citadel.
He is a good one, and his worthiness   205
Does challenge much respect. Come, Desdemona,
Once more well met at Cyprus!
                    [*Exeunt* OTHELLO · DESDEMONA · *and some Attendants*

IAGO [*to one remaining Attendant, who then leaves*]   Do thou meet me presently at the harbour. [*to* RODERIGO] Come hither. If thou be'st
valiant (as they say base men being in love have then a nobility 210
in their natures more than is native to them) list me. The lieutenant tonight watches on the court of guard. First, I will tell thee
this—Desdemona is directly in love with him.

RODERIGO   With him? Why, 'tis not possible!

IAGO   Lay thy finger thus, and let thy soul be instructed. Mark me 215
with what violence she first loved the Moor, but for bragging and
telling her fantastical lies. And will she love him still for prating?
Let not thy discreet heart think it. Her eye must be fed—and

219   *devil.* Note this key-word in the play, though Iago is here using it casually.

220   *act of sport,* copulation.

221   *favour,* external appearance and expression (not just 'face').

222   *sympathy,* correspondence, similarity.

223   *conveniences.* This probably carries the meaning of both 'desirable' and 'suitably harmonious' qualities.

224   *delicate tenderness.* In Iago's picture of Desdemona he is probably repeating what he had said when he described her as a 'super-subtle Venetian'. (See the note on Act1 Sc.3, l.345.)   *abused.* This word commonly has several close strands of meaning. Here it may mean 'disgusted' as well as 'deceived'.

225   *disrelish,* find distasteful.   *Very nature,* basic natural instincts.

227   *pregnant,* cogent, or obvious.   *position,* assumption, hypothesis.

227–8   *who . . . fortune.* This might be paraphrased: 'who stands so well placed to be next in the good fortune of Desdemona's love'.

229   *voluble,* glib, or facile.   *no . . . on.* A slightly obscure phrase that seems to mean something like 'whose only concession to conscience is assuming, etc.'

230   *humane,* courteous, polite (roughly synonymous with 'civil').

231   *salt,* lustful. (Cf. Act3 Sc.3, l.409.)

232   *slipper,* slippery.   *occasion,* opportunity.

233   *stamp,* coin (and so manufacture).   *advantages,* favourable (and possibly, profitable) opportunities. Though there may be some illogicality in Iago's remark, what he means, of course, is that Cassio can craftily create opportunities for himself out of nothing

236   *folly.* See note on l.137, page 27a.   *green,* inexperienced.

237   *found.* This verb follows naturally on 'look after' in the previous line.

239   *condition,* disposition, characteristics.

240   *Blessed fig's end!* blessed rubbish!

242   *Blessed pudding!* The particular force of this phrase is not quite clear. At the time 'pudding' chiefly meant a kind of sausage or sausage meat—and this might imply gross materiality. *paddle,* play fondly with.

245   *index,* (literally) a table of contents in a book; or, preface.

248–9   *When . . exercise.* Some effective alliteration.

248   *mutualities,* intimacies.

249   *incorporate,* physical, carnal.

254   *tainting,* saying something to discredit, etc.

255   *minister,* offer, provide.

what delight shall she have to look on the devil? When the blood
is made dull with the act of sport, there should be, again to 220
inflame it and give satiety a fresh appetite, loveliness in favour,
sympathy in years, manners and beauties—all which the Moor is
defective in. Now for want of these required conveniences, her
delicate tenderness will find itself abused, begin to heave the gorge,
disrelish and abhor the Moor. Very nature will instruct her in it 225
and compel her to some second choice. Now, sir, this granted
(as it is a most pregnant and unforced position) who stands so
eminently in the degree of this fortune as Cassio does—a knave
very voluble, no further conscionable than in putting on the
mere form of civil and humane seeming for the better compassing 230
of his salt and most hidden loose affection? Why, none; why,
none. A slipper and subtle knave, a finder of occasion, that has
an eye can stamp and counterfeit advantages, though true advantage never present itself—a devilish knave! Besides, the knave
is handsome, young, and hath all those requisites in him that 235
folly and green minds look after. A pestilent complete knave!
And the woman hath found him already.

RODERIGO I cannot believe that in her. She's full of most blessed
condition.

IAGO Blessed fig's end! The wine she drinks is made of grapes. If 240
she had been blessed, she would never have loved the Moor.
Blessed pudding! Didst thou not see her paddle with the palm
of his hand? Didst not mark that?

RODERIGO Yes, that I did, but that was but courtesy.

IAGO Lechery, by this hand—an index and obscure prologue to the 245
history of lust and foul thoughts. They met so near with their
lips that their breaths embraced together. Villainous thoughts,
Roderigo! When these mutualities so marshal the way, hard at
hand comes the master and main exercise, the incorporate conclusion. Pish! But, sir, be you ruled by me. I have brought you 250
from Venice. Watch you tonight. For the command, I'll lay't
upon you. Cassio knows you not; I'll not be far from you. Do you
find some occasion to anger Cassio, either by speaking too loud,
or tainting his discipline, or from what other course you please,
which the time shall more favourably minister.   255

RODERIGO Well.

256   *choler*, anger.

257   *truncheon.* This was carried by military officers.

259–60   *whose . . . but.* 'Qualification' is the most difficult word here.
         The clause can be roughly paraphrased: 'whose calming down
         (or appeasement) can only be properly guaranteed by'.

260   *displanting*, dismissal.

262   *prefer*, promote, advance.

263   *the which*, the removal of the impediment, Cassio.

264   *prosperity*, success, good fortune.

265   *if you can.* The Folio text. The Quarto reads: 'if I can'. A nice
         point of dramatic discrimination is involved here. Which
         seems preferable to you?   *if . . . opportunity*, if you can contrive
         the right sort of situation.

266   *I warrant thee*, my guarantee for that.

269–95   *That . . . used.* Iago now states that he wants revenge on Othello
         and Cassio because he believes that both have seduced Emilia.
         It is these changes that lead some critics to doubt his pro-
         fessed motives.

269–70   *That . . . credit.* These lines are often quoted to illustrate the
         limits of Iago's insight. But his belief about Cassio is not
         utterly impossible, and his comment on Desdemona may be
         more an opinion of what people, including Othello, may be
         tempted to think than his own conviction.

270   *apt*, natural, likely.   *of great credit*, highly credible.

271–2   *The . . . nature.* A tribute to be considered in any assessment of
         Othello.

274   *Now . . . too.* Iago's 'love' for Desdemona seems mainly enter-
         tained as a possible means of revenge. In Cinthio's story Iago's
         love for Desdemona was his chief motive.

276   *accountant*, accountable.

280   *poisonous mineral*, mineral poison. The intense simile suggests
         that Iago may be expressing a deep truth about himself.

285   *judgment.* Probably 'reason' or 'good sense'.

286   *this poor trash*, i.e. Roderigo.   *I trash.* Here 'trash' (in the sense
         of restraining fast hounds by means of weights on them) is
         the usual emendation for the Quarto 'crush' and the Folio
         'trace'. But, unless Iago is ironical, this meaning contradicts
         the situation.

287   *stand . . . on*, acts as I have incited him.   *putting on*, inciting
         (possibly with the pun of 'imposing on', which might support
         the 'trash' reading).

288   *on the hip*, just as I want him. The expression is from wrestling.

289   *Abuse*, malign.   *rank garb*, gross manner or fashion. In view
         of the next line this might refer to Cassio's alleged moral
         looseness, but it could describe Iago's manner of slander.

290   *nightcap*, wife.

292   *egregiously*, flagrantly.

293   *practising*, plotting.

294   *'Tis . . . confused.* At this stage Iago's plotting is improvised,
         not deeply laid.

295   *Knavery's . . . used.* Could this mean that the 'plain' (smooth,
         featureless) face of a knave gives nothing away—that the knave
         is not known till he does something knavish?

IAGO   Sir, he is rash and very sudden in choler, and haply with his
truncheon may strike at you. Provoke him that he may, for even
out of that will I cause these of Cyprus to mutiny, whose qualification shall come into no true trust again but by the displanting 260
of Cassio. So shall you have a shorter journey to your desires by
the means I shall then have to prefer them, and the impediment
most profitably removed, without the which there were no
expectation of our prosperity.

RODERIGO   I will do this, if you can bring it to any opportunity.   265

IAGO   I warrant thee. Meet me by and by at the citadel. I must fetch
his necessaries ashore. Farewell.

RODERIGO   Adieu.   [*Exit*

IAGO   That Cassio loves her, I do well believe't.
That she loves him, 'tis apt and of great credit.   270
The Moor, howbeit that I endure him not,
Is of a constant, noble, loving nature,
And, I dare think, he'll prove to Desdemona
A most dear husband. Now, I do love her too—
Not out of absolute lust (though peradventure   275
I stand accountant for as great a sin)
But partly led to diet my revenge,
For that I do suspect the lusty Moor
Hath leaped into my seat, the thought whereof
Doth like a poisonous mineral gnaw my inwards.   280
And nothing can or shall content my soul
Till I am evened with him, wife for wife,
Or failing so, yet that I put the Moor
At least into a jealousy so strong
That judgment cannot cure. Which thing to do,   285
If this poor trash of Venice, whom I trash
For his quick hunting, stand the putting on,
I'll have our Michael Cassio on the hip,
Abuse him to the Moor in the rank garb
(For I fear Cassio with my nightcap too)   290
Make the Moor thank me, love me and reward me
For making him egregiously an ass
And practising upon his peace and quiet
Even to madness. 'Tis here but yet confused.
Knavery's plain face is never seen till used.   [*Exit*295

This is an example of those very brief, 'extra' scenes, almost like momentary cinematic shots, that the Elizabethan theatre, without scene-shifting, curtains, etc., allowed Shakespeare to present. They would not produce any strong break in the continuously moving production.

2   *mere*, absolute, complete.   *perdition*, destruction. (Here the theological significance of the word is, at most, secondary.)
3   *triumph*, festivity, revelry.
5   *addiction*. The usual emendment of the Folio 'addition'. The Quarto reads 'mind'.
7   *offices*, the parts of the citadel from which food and drink could be obtained.

Scene Three

As well as forwarding the events of the plot, this scene of Cassio's disgrace and dismissal as Othello's second-in-command serves at least two other important functions. In its first part it provides the play's chief period of light, and at times comic, relief; it also, in preparation for the great central scene soon to come, builds up our belief both in Iago's masterly powers of intrigue and in Othello's instantaneous readiness to accept his 'honest' testimony. Once more Iago's coda to the scene stirs fearful expectations of worse to come.

1   *Michael*. This Christian name denotes some intimacy between Othello and Cassio.
3   *Not . . . discretion*, not to exceed discretion in our revelry.
7   *with your earliest*, at your earliest convenience.

Scene Two

Cyprus · A street in the same port

Enter a HERALD *reading a proclamation*

HERALD   It is Othéllo's pleasure, our noble and valiant General, that
   upon certain tidings now arrived importing the mere perdition
   of the Turkish fleet, every man put himself into triumph—some
   to dance, some to make bonfires, each man to what sport and
   revels his addiction leads him. For, besides these beneficial news,   5
   it is the celebration of his nuptial. So much was his pleasure
   should be proclaimed. All offices are open, and there is full liberty
   of feasting from this present hour of five till the bell have told
   eleven. Heaven bless the isle of Cyprus and our noble General
   Othello!   [*Exit* 10

Scene Three

Cyprus · A hall in the citadel

Enter OTHELLO · DESDEMONA · CASSIO · *and Attendants*

OTHELLO   Good Michael, look you to the guard tonight.
   Let's teach ourselves that honourable stop,
   Not to outsport discretion.

CASSIO   Iago hath direction what to do,
   But, notwithstanding, with my personal eye   5
   Will I look to't.

OTHELLO   Iago is most honest.
   Michael, good night. Tomorrow with your earliest
   Let me have speech with you. [*to* DESDEMONA] Come, my dear love,
   The purchase made, the fruits are to ensue;
   The profit's yet to come 'tween me and you.   10
   Good night.
                      [*Exeunt* OTHELLO · DESDEMONA · *and Attendants*

Enter IAGO

CASSIO   Welcome, Iago. We must to the watch.

13–24   *Not . . . perfection*. Note the contrasting ways in which Iago and Cassio speak of Desdemona.

14   *cast*, dismissed (as in Act1 Sc.1, l.147).

18   *game*. Synonymous with 'sport' in l.16.

20   *sounds . . . to*. Perhaps to be glossed by something like 'trumpets forth'. But the expression is odd since a 'parley' was sounded to bring a halt in fighting.

.23   *alarum*. A sound or cry to warn of imminent attack.

26   *stoup*, flagon or some kind of vessel for holding two quarts of drink.   *brace*. For what the point is worth, Iago refers to 'Three lads' in l.47.

27   *fain . . . measure*. Gladly drink a quantity.   *black*. The force of this calculated insult will depend to some extent on the actor's delivery.

32   *craftily*. Probably in the sense of 'wisely', 'prudently'.

33   *qualified*, diluted.   *innovation*, change for the worse, revolution.   *here*, i.e. in his head.

34   *Task*, test; or, put a strain on.

39   *dislikes*, displeases.

42   *offence*. This may mean readiness to take, rather than give, offence.

43   *As . . . dog*, as a quarrelsome dog. But the 'young mistress' reference is obscure.   *sick*. Several possible meanings— 'love-sick', 'sickly'.

44   *wrong side outward*, inside out, i.e. love has completely transformed Roderigo.

45–6   *caroused Potations*, tossed off full bumpers.   *pottle-deep*, to the bottom of a two-quart tankard.

47   *lads*. The Folio has 'else'.   *swelling*. Possibly 'proud'.

48   *That . . . distance*, who are touchy about anything concerning their honour.

IAGO   Not this hour, lieutenant; 'tis not yet ten o'clock. Our General
cast us thus early for the love of his Desdemona—who let us not
therefore blame. He hath not yet made wanton the night with her,   15
and she is sport for Jove.

CASSIO   She is a most exquisite lady.

IAGO   And, I'll warrant her, full of game.

CASSIO   Indeed, she is a most fresh and delicate creature.

IAGO   What an eye she has! Methinks it sounds a parley to provoca-   20
tion.

CASSIO   An inviting eye, and yet methinks right modest.

IAGO   And when she speaks, is it not an alarum to love?

CASSIO   She is indeed perfection.

IAGO   Well, happiness to their sheets! . . . Come, lieutenant, I have a   25
stoup of wine, and here without are a brace of Cyprus gallants
that would fain have a measure to the health of black Othello.

CASSIO   Not tonight, good Iago. I have very poor and unhappy brains
for drinking. I could well wish courtesy would invent some other
custom of entertainment.   30

IAGO   O, they are our friends! But one cup. I'll drink for you.

CASSIO   I have drunk but one cup tonight, and that was craftily
qualified too; and behold what innovation it makes here. I am
unfortunate in the infirmity and dare not task my weakness with
any more.   35

IAGO   What, man! 'Tis a night of revels. The gallants desire it.

CASSIO   Where are they?

IAGO   Here at the door. I pray you call them in.

CASSIO   I'll do't, but it dislikes me.   [*Exit*

IAGO   If I can fasten but one cup upon him,   40
With that which he hath drunk tonight already,
He'll be as full of quarrel and offence
As my young mistress' dog. Now my sick fool Roderigo,
Whom love hath turned almost the wrong side outward,
To Desdemona hath tonight caroused   45
Potations pottle-deep; and he's to watch.
Three lads of Cyprus, noble swelling spirits,
That hold their honours in a wary distance,

49   *very elements*, the quintessence (in fiery spirit).

51   *they.* The Quarto reads 'the'.

54   *consequence*, what follows.   *approve my dream*, confirm what I fancy.

55   *My . . . stream*, everything will be going splendidly for me. *stream*, current.

56   *a rouse*, a full draught.

59–63   *And . . . drink*. This was taken from an old song.   *cannikin*, small can.

62   *span*, short space of time.

67   *potting*, drinking. An admirable alliteration.   *swag-bellied*, with large, sagging belly; pot-bellied.

70   *drinks . . . facility*, has no difficulty in drinking.   *you.* The old ethic dative for colloquial emphasis.

71   *Almain*, German.

74   *I'll . . . justice*, fair enough for me too.

76–83   *King Stephen . . . thee*. From another old ballad.

79   *lown*, loon, rascal.

83   *auld*, old. Probably a sign of the ballad's north-country origin.

The very elements of this warlike isle,
Have I tonight flustered with flowing cups,   50
And they watch too. Now, 'mongst this flock of drunkards,
Am I to put our Cassio in some action
That may offend the isle.

Enter CASSIO · MONTANO · *and Gentlemen, also Servants with wine*

               But here they come.
If consequence do but approve my dream,
My boat sails freely both with wind and stream.   55

CASSIO   'Fore God, they have given me a rouse already.

MONTANO   Good faith, a little one. Not past a pint, as I am a soldier.

IAGO   Some wine, ho!
[*sings*]   And let me the canakin clink, clink;
               And let me the canakin clink;   60
                 A soldier's a man
                 A life's but a span;
               Why, then, let a soldier drink.
Some wine, boys!

CASSIO   'Fore God, an excellent song.   65

IAGO   I learned it in England, where indeed they are most potent in
potting. Your Dane, your German, and your swag-bellied
Hollander—drink, ho!—are nothing to your English.

CASSIO   Is your Englishman so expert in his drinking?

IAGO   Why, he drinks you with facility your Dane dead drunk; he   70
sweats not to overthrow your Almain; he gives your Hollander a
vomit ere the next pottle can be filled.

CASSIO   To the health of our General!

MONTANO   I am for it, lieutenant, and I'll do you justice.

IAGO   O, sweet England!   75
[*sings*]   King Stephen was a worthy peer,
               His breeches cost him but a crown;
               He held 'em sixpence all too dear;
               With that he called the tailor lown.
        He was a wight of high renown,   80
               And thou art but of low degree.
        'Tis pride that pulls the country down;
               Then take thine auld cloak about thee.

88-9 *there . . . saved.* Shakespeare might have taken a hundred and one topics for Cassio's drunken maunderings. In this play which concerns Othello's 'damnation' was it accident that Shakespeare chose here to exploit the subject of salvation?

94-5 *Ay . . . ancient.* In his drunkenness Cassio is unconsciously reminding Iago of the promotion grievance.

97-9 *This . . . enough.* It is not difficult to imagine Cassio's unconvincing attempt to demonstrate his sobriety.

103 *platform.* The citadel gun platform.   *set the watch,* mount the guard.

104 *fellow.* An insulting term in Shakespeare's usage, revealing Iago's true contempt, etc. for Cassio. Does it spurt out unconsciously, in an unguarded moment?

105 *stand by.* Probably in the sense of acting as Caesar's second-in-command.

107 *'Tis . . . equinox.* The 'equinox' is one of the two times in the year when the day and night are of equal length. Hence Iago is saying that Cassio's vice equally balances his virtue. The implication of course is that the vice is very serious.

108 *'Tis . . . him.* Something like 'most regrettable indeed'.

110 *some odd time,* some time or other.   *infirmity.* It may be typical of Iago that having firmly planted the word 'vice' he now substitutes this milder, more apologetic, term.

112 *'Tis . . . sleep,* the next thing is usually (or always) that he falls asleep. Once again Iago is artfully playing down the situation. Having hinted at dire consequences of Cassio's drunkenness, he now implies that it is harmless.

113 *He'll . . . set,* he'll watch the clock twice round.

117 *Prizes the virtue.* The Quarto reads 'Praises the virtues'. Here 'praises' would mean 'appraises', 'judges'.

Some wine, ho!

CASSIO 'Fore God, this is a more exquisite song than the other. 85

IAGO Will you hear't again?

CASSIO No, for I hold him unworthy of his place that does those things. Well, God's above all; and there be souls must be saved, and there be souls must not be saved.

IAGO It's true, good lieutenant. 90

CASSIO For mine own part (no offence to the General, nor any man of quality) I hope to be saved.

IAGO And so do I too, lieutenant.

CASSIO Ay, but, by your leave, not before me. The lieutenant is to be saved before the ancient. Let's have no more of this; let's to 95 our affairs. God forgive us our sins! Gentlemen, let's look to our business. Do not think, gentlemen, I am drunk. This is my ancient, this is my right hand, and this is my left hand. I am not drunk now. I can stand well enough and speak well enough.

ALL Excellent well. 100

CASSIO Why, very well then. You must not think then that I am drunk. *[Exit*

MONTANO To the platform, masters. Come, let's set the watch.

IAGO You see this fellow that is gone before—
He is a soldier fit to stand by Caesar 105
And give direction. And do but see his vice—
'Tis to his virtue a just equinox,
The one as long as t'other. 'Tis pity of him.
I fear the trust Othello puts in him,
On some odd time of his infirmity, 110
Will shake this island.

MONTANO   But is he often thus?

IAGO 'Tis evermore the prologue to his sleep.
He'll watch the horologe a double set
If drink rock not his cradle.

MONTANO   'Twere well
The General were put in mind of it. 115
Perhaps he sees it not, or his good nature
Prizes the virtue that appears in Cassio
And looks not on his evils. Is not this true?

121   *noble*. Note this so often repeated word.

122   *hazard*. 'Hazard' was a popular dice game of the time.

123   *ingraft*, ingrained, ingrafted.

130–1   *wicker-bottle*. A bottle cased in wicker-work. ('Twiggen', the word used in the Folio for 'wicker', means the same.) There is some doubt about the precise nature of the threat, but may it be that Cassio is talking of beating Roderigo down and across like wicker-work?

133   *prate*, talk, chatter (often in the sense of repeating).

135   *mazzard*, head.

136   *you're drunk*. Nothing was now more likely to enflame Cassio than this accusation.

137   *mutiny*, riot.

141   *watch*, keeping guard.

142   *Diablo*, the Devil.

Enter RODERIGO

IAGO [*aside*] How, now Roderigo!
  I pray you, after the lieutenant! Go!   [*Exit* RODERIGO 120

MONTANO And 'tis great pity that the noble Moor
  Should hazard such a place as his own second
  With one of an ingraft infirmity.
  It were an honest action to say so to the Moor.

IAGO Not I, for this fair island!   125
  I do love Cassio well and would do much
  To cure him of this evil.
  [*a cry within* 'Help! Help!']
                  But hark, what noise?

Re-enter CASSIO *driving in* RODERIGO

CASSIO Zounds, you rogue, you rascal!

MONTANO What's the matter, lieutenant?

CASSIO A knave teach me my duty! I'll beat the knave into a wicker 130
  bottle.

RODERIGO Beat me?

CASSIO Dost thou prate, rogue? [*striking* RODERIGO]

MONTANO Good lieutenant, pray sir, hold your hand!

CASSIO Let me go, sir, or I'll knock you o'er the mazzard.   135

MONTANO Come, come, you're drunk.

CASSIO Drunk! [CASSIO *and* MONTANO *fight*]

IAGO [*to* RODERIGO] Away, I say! Go out and cry a mutiny!
                                          [*Exit* RODERIGO
  Nay, good lieutenant ... God's will, gentleman!
  Help, ho! Lieutenant! Sir Montano! Sir!   140
  Help, masters! Here's a goodly watch indeed. [*A bell rings*]
  Who's that which rings the bell? Diablo, ho!
  The town will rise. God's will, lieutenant, hold!
  You will be shamed for ever.

Re-enter OTHELLO *and Attendants*

OTHELLO What is the matter here?
MONTANO   Zounds, I bleed still.
  I am hurt to the death.   145

148   *sense of place.* An emendation of Hanmer, an important eighteenth-century editor. Both Quarto and Folio read 'place of sense'.

151-2   *Are . . . Ottomites?* The phrase 'turn Turk' has several possible meanings. In the Arden edition M. R. Ridley paraphrases: 'Are we, in destroying ourselves, going to do the Turks' job for them, now that Heaven has prevented them doing it for themselves?' But might Othello simply be referring to the drinking of wine (and so getting drunk), which was forbidden by Mohammedan religious law?

154   *carve . . . rage,* use his sword in his fury.

155   *light,* i.e. in weight, of little worth.   *upon his motion,* the moment he moves.

157   *propriety,* proper state, i.e. of peace and quiet.

160   *all . . . now.* An emphatic way of saying 'a very short time ago'. Cf. *The Merchant of Venice,* Act 3 Sc.2, l.169.

161   *In quarter.* This obscure phrase has been variously glossed as 'in friendship' and 'on their proper station', i.e. in the guard room.   *in terms,* in relations, relationship.

162   *Devesting,* divesting.

163   *unwitted,* driven mad. A reference to the astrological belief that the planets could exercise a baneful influence on men. (See also Act 5 Sc.2, ll.111–13.)

166   *peevish odds,* senseless, or trivial, or perverse quarrel.

169   *Michael.* This is the last time Othello uses the intimate address. *you . . . forgot?* you thus forgot yourself?

171   *you . . . civil,* you have the reputation for conducting yourself properly.

172   *stillness,* sobriety.

174   *censure,* judgment.

175   *unlace,* undo, loosen.

176   *spend . . . opinion,* throw away your high reputation.

180   *offends,* hurts, distresses.

OTHELLO   Hold, for your lives!

IAGO   Hold, ho! Lieutenant! Sir Montano . . . Gentlemen!
Have you forgot all sense of place and duty?
Hold! The General speaks to you. Hold, hold for shame!

OTHELLO   Why, how now, ho! From whence arises this?   150
Are we turned Turks and to ourselves do that
Which heaven hath forbid the Ottomites?
For Christian shame, put by this barbarous brawl.
He that stirs next to carve for his own rage
Holds his soul light—he dies upon his motion.   155
Silence that dreadful bell. It frights the isle
From her propriety. What is the matter, masters?
Honest Iago, that looks dead with grieving,
Speak who began this. On thy love I charge thee.

IAGO   I do not know. Friends all but now, even now,   160
In quarter and in terms like bride and groom
Devesting them for bed—and then but now,
As if some planet had unwitted men,
Swords out and tilting one at others' breasts
In opposition bloody. I cannot speak   165
Any beginning to this peevish odds,
And would in action glorious I had lost
These legs that brought me to a part of it.

OTHELLO   How came it, Michael, you were thus forgot?

CASSIO   I pray you pardon me. I cannot speak.   170

OTHELLO   Worthy Montano, you were wont to be civil.
The gravity and stillness of your youth
The world hath noted, and your name is great
In mouths of wisest censure. What's the matter
That you unlace your reputation thus   175
And spend your rich opinion for the name
Of a night-brawler? Give me answer to it.

MONTANO   Worthy Othello, I am hurt to danger.
Your officer, Iago, can inform you,
While I spare speech, which something now offends me,   180
Of all that I do know. Nor know I aught
By me that's said or done amiss this night,
Unless self-charity be sometimes a vice,

183   *self-charity*, regard for one's self.

185–88   *Now . . . way.* What angers Othello is that he can get no straight answer to his question. There is a clear indication in these lines of the potential passion under Othello's self-control. See Bradley: 'for all his dignity and massive calm (and he has greater dignity than any other of Shakespeare's men) [Othello] is by nature full of the most vehement passion. Shakespeare emphasizes his self-control' (*op. cit.*, p. 190).

186   *blood.* Synonymous with the following 'passion'.   *safer guides*, rational faculties such as 'judgment'.

187   *collied*, darkened, clouded.

191   *rout*, riot, uproar.

192   *approved*, found guilty.

194   *Shall lose me*, i.e. my friendship and regard.

195   *wild*, unsettled.

196   *manage*, conduct.

197   *In*, at.   *on . . . safety?* In Act2Sc.1, l.212 Shakespeare speaks of the 'court of guard' (guard room), and there may be some corruption of text here. Presumably Othello is reproving his men either because the guard room was the scene of the disorder or because as members of the guard room or watch they were responsible for the safety of the town.

199   *partially affined*, made partial by any tie (e.g. of kinship). *leagued in office.* Could this difficult phrase refer to some kind of service loyalty—especially to superior officers?

201   *Touch . . . near.* The general sense of this is that Montano's words have put Iago in a difficult spot, and he may be saying something like 'don't press me so closely'. The two most likely meanings of 'Touch' are 'test' or 'hurt'.

208   *sword.* This seems to be an invention of Iago, for the Cassio who had threatened to beat Roderigo and hit Montano on the 'mazzard' is more likely to be using his truncheon than a sword.

209   *this gentleman*, i.e. Montano.

213   *fall in fright*, take alarm.

216   *high in oath*, loud with oaths and curses.

And to defend ourselves it be a sin
When violence assails us.

OTHELLO   Now, by heaven,   185
  My blood begins my safer guides to rule,
  And passion having my best judgment collied
  Assays to lead the way. Zounds, if I stir
  Or do but lift this arm, the best of you
  Shall sink in my rebuke. Give me to know   190
  How this foul rout began, who set it on,
  And he that is approved in this offence,
  Though he had twinned with me, both at a birth,
  Shall lose me. What! In a town of war
  Yet wild, the people's hearts brimful of fear,   195
  To manage private and domestic quarrel
  In night, and on the court and guard of safety!
  'Tis monstrous . . . Iago, who began't?

MONTANO   If partially affined or leagued in office,
  Thou dost deliver more or less than truth,   200
  Thou art no soldier.

IAGO   Touch me not so near.
  I had rather have this tongue cut from my mouth
  Than it should do offence to Michael Cassio.
  Yet I persuade myself, to speak the truth
  Shall nothing wrong him. Thus it is, General.   205
  Montano and myself being in speech,
  There comes a fellow crying out for help,
  And Cassio following him with determined sword
  To execute upon him. Sir, this gentleman
  Steps in to Cassio and entreats his pause.   210
  Myself the crying fellow did pursue
  Lest by his clamour (as it so fell out)
  The town might fall in fright. He, swift of foot,
  Outran my purpose, and I returned the rather
  For that I heard the clink and fall of swords   215
  And Cassio high in oath, which till tonight
  I ne'er might see before. When I came back
  (For this was brief) I found them close together
  At blow and thrust, even as again they were
  When you yourself did part them.   220

226 *strange*. Perhaps in the sense of 'exceptional', 'unusual'.

227 *pass*, ignore.

227–9 *I . . . Cassio.* These lines are most significant for the great central scene of the play, soon to follow, in which Iago persuades Othello of Desdemona's infidelity. Not only do they reveal Othello's absolute faith, with no further questions asked, in the 'honesty' of Iago's testimony. Othello also believes that Iago has been deliberately 'mincing' matters so as not to incriminate Cassio too seriously. He will therefore be the more ready to think the same when Iago begins to hint at an illicit affair between Cassio and Desdemona, namely that this honest creature 'Sees and knows more, much more, than he unfolds' (Act 3 Sc.3, l.247).

228 *honesty*. Obviously as used here (and again in Act3 Sc.3, l.156) 'honesty' does not mean a strict and absolute regard for truth.
   mince, extenuate, tone down.

232 *I'll . . . example.* It has been suggested that this threat has reference to the previous line, i.e. that an additional reason for Cassio's punishment is his disturbance of Desdemona. But it seems better to take l.232 as a kind of parenthesis or aside.

236 *Lead him off.* Though both the Quarto and Folio give these words to Othello, they may be a stage direction that has crept into the dialogue.

241 *lieutenant*. While on the surface this word shows a sympathetic deference to Cassio, after Othello's dismissal of him it is really rubbing salt into his wound.

246 *bestial*. This is perhaps not to be taken quite literally but as a rhetorical antithesis to 'immortal part'.

248 *offence*, hurt. The Folio has 'sense', and (with the meaning of 'feeling') this may have been Shakespeare's word.

249–51 *Reputation . . . loser.* When it suits him Iago says the opposite (see Act3 Sc.3, ll.158–9).

249 *imposition*, a burden (and forced upon one involuntarily). Just possibly the word is taking on the later meaning of 'imposture'.

250–1 *You . . . loser*, if you don't yourself think you have lost your reputation, you haven't, i.e. reputation is a subjective thing.

252 *recover*, win back the regard or friendship of. *cast*, dismissed.

253 *mood*, anger, displeasure. *policy*, conduct of political and administrative affairs (with a suggestion of 'prudence').
   malice, enmity (not implying 'spite').

254–5 *beat . . . lion.* A proverbial expression generally meaning to punish an insignificant (or innocent) man in the hope of deterring a much more powerful one.

More of this matter can I not report.
But men are men. The best sometimes forget.
Though Cassio did some little wrong to him,
As men in rage strike those that wish them best,
Yet surely Cassio, I believe, received   225
From him that fled some strange indignity
Which patience could not pass.

OTHELLO   I know, Iago,
Thy honesty and love doth mince this matter,
Making it light to Cassio. Cassio, I love thee,
But nevermore be officer of mine.   230

Enter DESDEMONA *with Attendants*

Look, if my gentle love be not raised up.
I'll make thee an example.

DESDEMONA   What is the matter, dear?

OTHELLO   All's well now, sweeting. Come away to bed.
Sir, for your hurts myself will be your surgeon.   235
Lead him off. [MONTANO *is led off*]
Iago, look with care about the town
And silence those whom this vile brawl distracted.
Come, Desdemona. 'Tis the soldiers' life
To have their balmy slumbers waked with strife.   240
                  [*Exeunt all except* IAGO *and* CASSIO

IAGO   What, are you hurt, lieutenant?

CASSIO   Ay, past all surgery.

IAGO   Marry, God forbid!

CASSIO   Reputation, reputation, reputation! O, I have lost my
reputation! I have lost the immortal part of myself, and what   245
remains is bestial. My reputation, Iago, my reputation!

IAGO   As I am an honest man I thought you had received some bodily
wound. There is more of offence in that than in reputation.
Reputation is an idle and most false imposition—oft got without
merit and lost without deserving. You have lost no reputation   250
at all, unless you repute yourself such a loser. What, man! There
are ways to recover the General again. You are but now cast in
his mood (a punishment more in policy than in malice) even so
as one would beat his offenceless dog to affright an imperious

256   *I . . . deceive*, if I sue to Othello I may be despised for it, but that is preferable to the thought of deceiving, etc.

257   *light*, irresponsible.

258   *speak parrot*, talk senselessly.

259   *fustian*, nonsense or bombast.

262   *sword*. Possibly because he remembers 'nothing distinctly' Cassio does not deny Iago's story about the pursuit with the sword.

274   *the devil wrath*. Presumably Cassio means anger with himself for his behaviour.

276   *moraller*, moralizer.

278–9   *mend . . . good*, for your own sake set about rectifying matters.

281   *Hydra*. The many-headed monster killed by Hercules.

282   *sensible*. Here the word is near its modern meaning: 'rational'.

283   *inordinate*, immoderate, excessive.

284   *ingredient*, chief component; perhaps simply, contents.

285   *familiar*, friendly. Perhaps, in reply to Cassio's 'devil', there is a punning reference to a good 'familiar spirit'.

288   *approved*, proved, tested.

289–90   *I'll . . . do*. As the following soliloquy in ll.308–34 makes clear, Iago immediately seizes this refusal of Cassio to approach Othello directly as a means of involving him with Desdemona. The reason for implicating Desdemona is made clear in the soliloquy.

291   *I . . . respect*, I may speak in these terms.   *for that*, because.

lion. Sue to him again, and he's yours.   255

CASSIO I will rather sue to be despised than to deceive so good a
commander with so light, so drunken, and so indiscreet an
officer. Drunk! And speak parrot! And squabble, swagger, swear!
And discourse fustian with one's own shadow! O, thou invisible
spirit of wine, if thou hast no name to be known by, let us call 260
thee devil.

IAGO What was he that you followed with your sword?
What had he done to you?

CASSIO I know not.

IAGO Is't possible?   265

CASSIO I remember a mass of things, but nothing distinctly—a
quarrel, but nothing wherefore. O God, that men should put an
enemy in their mouths to steal away their brains! That we should
with joy, revel, pleasure, and applause transform ourselves into
beasts!   270

IAGO Why, but you are now well enough. How came you thus
recovered?

CASSIO It hath pleased the devil drunkenness to give place to the
devil wrath. One unperfectness shows me another, to make me
frankly despise myself.   275

IAGO Come, you are too severe a moraller. As the time, the place,
and the condition of this country stands, I could heartily wish
this had not so befallen; but since it is as it is, mend it for your own
good.

CASSIO I will ask him for my place again. He shall tell me I am a 280
drunkard. Had I as many mouths as Hydra, such an answer
would stop them all. To be now a sensible man, by and by a fool,
and presently a beast! O, strange! Every inordinate cup is un-
blessed, and the ingredient is a devil.

IAGO Come, come. Good wine is a good familiar creature if it be 285
well used. Exclaim no more against it. And, good lieutenant, I
think you think I love you.

CASSIO I have well approved it, sir . . . I drunk!

IAGO You or any man living may be drunk at some time. I'll tell
you what you shall do. Our General's wife is now the General. 290
I may say so in this respect, for that he hath devoted and given

292   *denotement.* Though the usual meaning of 'denotement' is 'indication', here it must mean 'noting down'.

293   *parts,* qualities.

294   *free,* generous, magnanimous.   *kind,* well-disposed.

295   *apt,* willing.   *vice.* More in the sense of 'shortcoming'.

296   *brawl.* The Folio reads 'broken joint'.

297   *splinter,* put splints on.

298   *lay,* wager.   *crack,* breach. (Possibly some connection with the 'splinter' metaphor).

301   *protest,* (not in the modern sense) vow, assent.   *kindness,* fellow-feeling, humanity.

302   *I . . . freely,* I readily (or unreservedly) believe that.   *betimes,* early.

303   *undertake,* act as spokesman or advocate.

308–34   *And . . . all.* Iago's plotting is no longer 'confused' but much more clear and precise. And consider Granville-Barker's comment: 'Until now [Iago] has been a mere self-seeking scoundrel, and Cassio's lieutenancy is surely in sight. But how will Desdemona's ruin profit him? It is evil for its own sake that he starts pursuing now' (*op. cit.*, p. 28).

308–11   *And . . . again?* All heavily ironical of course.

308   *what's,* who is.

309   *free.* See gloss on l.294.

310   *Probal to thinking,* sure to be approved by reason, i.e. reasonable.

311–14   *For . . . elements.* Possibly an admission of Desdemona's goodness, but because of the preceding irony and the suggestion of sexual laxity in several of the words (notably 'fruitful' and 'free') Empson is probably right when he speaks of Iago turning 'the ironical admission of her virtue into a positive insult against her' (*op. cit.*, p. 223). (See Othello's similar use of 'fruitfulness' in Act 3 Sc.4, l.32.) 'Elements' may refer to 'Nature' generally or to the 'four elements' in Elizabethan scientific thinking, in which case Hardin Craig's observation is relevant: 'Man was formed of the four elements . . . and subject to their rare harmonies and never-ending discords' (*op. cit.*, p. 78). *inclining,* compliant, susceptible.   *subdue,* persuade.

316   *All . . . sin.* Christian observances, etc.   *seals,* authenticating signs or symbols.

317   *His . . . love.* All too true, though it comes from Iago. See note on Act 2 Sc.1, ll.177–87.

318   *make, unmake, do.* 'Him' or 'his soul' the understood object. *list,* pleases.

319–20   *her appetite,* his desire for her.

320   *function.* Probably 'rational faculties', 'reason'.

321   *parallel.* This probably means 'in keeping with my plot'.

322–5   *Divinity . . . now.* Besides establishing the 'demi-devil' quality of Iago, the implicit reversal of values in these lines preludes the centre of the play: the 'divine' Desdemona is to become, in Othello's eyes, a devil of hell.

323   *put on,* incite to.

324   *suggest.* The word carries a hint of tempting, seducing.

325   *honest.* Note Iago's transfer of this ironical word to Cassio.

329   *that,* namely that.   *repeals,* tries to get restored to favour.

up himself to the contemplation, mark, and denotement of her
parts and graces. Confess yourself freely to her. Importune her
help to put you in your place again. She is of so free, so kind, so
apt, so blessed a disposition, that she holds it a vice in her goodness 295
not to do more than she is requested. This brawl between you and
her husband, entreat her to splinter, and my fortunes against
any lay worth naming, this crack of your love shall grow stronger
than it was before.

CASSIO   You advise me well.   300

IAGO   I protest, in the sincerity of love and honest kindness.

CASSIO   I think it freely, and betimes in the morning I will beseech the
virtuous Desdemona to undertake for me. I am desperate of my
fortunes if they check me here.

IAGO   You are in the right. Good night, lieutenant; I must to the 305
watch.

CASSIO   Good night, honest Iago.   [*Exit*

IAGO   And what's he then that says I play the villain,
When this advice is free I give and honest,
Probal to thinking, and indeed the course   310
To win the Moor again? For 'tis most easy
The inclining Desdemona to subdue
In any honest suit. She's framed as fruitful
As the free elements; and then for her
To win the Moor, were't to renounce his baptism,   315
All seals and symbols of redeemed sin,
His soul is so enfettered to her love,
That she may make, unmake, do what she list,
Even as her appetite shall play the god
With his weak function. How am I then a villain   320
To counsel Cassio to this parallel course
Directly to his good? Divinity of hell!
When devils will their blackest sins put on,
They do suggest at first with heavenly shows
As I do now. For while this honest fool   325
Plies Desdemona to repair his fortunes,
And she for him pleads strongly to the Moor,
I'll pour this pestilence into his ear,
That she repeals him for her body's lust;

332   *pitch.* For its foul, black, and possibly sticky, associations.

336   *cry,* i.e. the pack that merely follows.

339   *wit,* intelligence, understanding of things. (In l.343 'clever-ness', 'intelligence'.)

347–8   *Though . . . ripe.* Perhaps the meaning of these enigmatic lines is that while all growing things develop, given favourable con-ditions, the first to ripen are those that blossom first. The Cassio business is 'blossoming', with his dismissal; and, with this rival out of the way, Roderigo can soon expect the 'ripe fruit'—Desdemona's love.

349   *By the mass,* an oath.

354   *move for,* plead for.

356   *Myself . . . apart.* Though the sense is clear there is no main verb here. Perhaps something of the force of 'I'll set' is carried over.

357   *jump,* exactly on time.

359   *device,* a plot or plan.

And by how much she strives to do him good,   330
She shall undo her credit with the Moor.
So will I turn her virtue into pitch,
And out of her own goodness make the net
That shall enmesh them all.

Enter RODERIGO

How, now, Roderigo?

RODERIGO I do follow here in the chase—not like a hound that 335
hunts, but one that fills up the cry. My money is almost spent;
I have been tonight exceedingly well cudgelled; and I think the
issue will be, I shall have so much experience for my pains; and
so, with no money at all, and a little more wit, return again to
Venice.   340

IAGO How poor are they that have not patience!
What wound did ever heal but by degrees?
Thou know'st we work by wit, and not by witchcraft,
And wit depends on dilatory time.
Does't not go well? Cassio hath beaten thee,   345
And thou by that small hurt hath cashiered Cassio.
Though other things grow fair against the sun,
Yet fruits that blossom first will first be ripe.
Content thyself awhile. By the mass, 'tis morning!
Pleasure and action make the hours seem short.   350
Retire thee; go where thou art billeted.
Away, I say, thou shalt know more hereafter.
Nay, get thee gone.   [*Exit* RODERIGO
                    Two things are to be done.
My wife must move for Cassio to her mistress—
I'll set her on.   355
Myself the while to draw the Moor apart,
And bring him jump when he may Cassio find
Soliciting his wife. Ay, that's the way.
Dull not device by coldness and delay.   [*Exit*

D

Most of this scene is clearly designed for relief between the high tension of the last scene and that of the third scene of this Act, soon to come. Such slackening of tension is justifiable, and the right sort of aubade serenade—fresh, joyous, (preferably Elizabethan?)—before the bridal window might produce some effectively ironic contrast with Iago's last words. But apropos of the Clown we can hardly avoid recalling Bradley's caustic comment, 'I believe most readers of Shakespeare, if asked whether there is a clown in *Othello* would answer No' (*op. cit.*, p. 177).

1	*I . . . pains.* I will reward your efforts.
3–4	*Why . . . thus?* Venereal disease was commonly called the 'Neapolitan disease', and there is almost certainly an obscure, and obscene, reference to it here. *speak i' the nose.* Presumably (among other things) a reference to the droning quality of the music. 'Pipes' are mentioned in l.18.
8	*tail.* Colloquial for 'penis'.
18	*for I'll away.* An apparently pointless remark since the Clown does not exit. It may be a misprint, or perhaps it is a snatch from some song serving to emphasize the Clown's point.
22	*quillets,* quibbles.
26–7	*shall . . . unto,* possibly something like 'I shall see to it that I inform her'. A clownish elaboration of speech.

Act Three · Scene One

Cyprus · Before the citadel

Enter CASSIO · CLOWN · *and Musicians*

CASSIO Masters, play here: I will content your pains.
Something that's brief; and bid 'Good morrow, General'. [*They play*]

CLOWN Why, masters, have your instruments been in Naples, that
they speak i'the nose thus?

1 MUSICIAN How, sir, how?   5

CLOWN Are these, I pray you, wind instruments?

1 MUSICIAN Ay, marry are they, sir.

CLOWN O, thereby hangs a tail.

1 MUSICIAN Whereby hangs a tale, sir?

CLOWN Marry, sir, by many a wind instrument that I know. But,   10
masters, here's money for you. And the General so likes your
music that he desires you, for love's sake, to make no more noise
with it.

1 MUSICIAN Well, sir, we will not.

CLOWN If you have any music that may not be heard, to't again.   15
But, as they say, to hear music the General does not greatly care.

1 MUSICIAN We have none such, sir.

CLOWN Then put up your pipes in your bag, for I'll away. Go, vanish
into air! Away!   [*Exeunt* MUSICIANS

CASSIO Dost thou hear, my honest friend?   20

CLOWN No, I hear not your honest friend. I hear you.

CASSIO Prithee keep up thy quillets—there's a poor piece of gold
for thee. If the gentlewoman that attends the General's wife be
stirring, tell her there's one Cassio entreats her a little favour of
speech. Wilt thou do this?   25

CLOWN She is stirring, sir. If she will stir hither, I shall seem to
notify unto her.

28 *In happy time*, luckily met. 'Happy' still carried some sense of 'hap' (luck, chance).

34 *presently*, immediately (the usual meaning).

35 *a mean*, means.

37 *free*, unimpeded. Here used in a modern sense.

39 *Florentine*, i.e. one of Cassio's fellow countrymen.

40 *lieutenant*. Compare Desdemona's use of Cassio's lost title with Iago's in l.241 of the previous scene.

41 *displeasure*, being out of favour.

45 *great affinity*, having relatives of importance.

48 *To . . . front*, once it is really safe, to seize the first opportunity, etc. Behind this line is the emblem of Opportunity, bald behind, who has to be seized by the forelock.

49 *bring you in*, restore you to favour.

51 *advantage*, the favourable opportunity.

54 *bosom*, heart.

CASSIO, Do good my friend.   [*Exit* CLOWN
Enter IAGO

                              In happy time, Iago.

IAGO   You have not been abed then?

CASSIO   Why, no. The day had broke before we parted.   30
    I have made bold, Iago,
    To send in to your wife. My suit to her
    Is that she will to virtuous Desdemona
    Procure me some access.

IAGO   I'll send her to you presently,
    And I'll devise a mean to draw the Moor   35
    Out of the way, that your converse and business
    May be more free.

CASSIO   I humbly thank you for it. [*Exit* IAGO] I never knew
    A Florentine more kind and honest.

Enter EMILIA

EMILIA   Good morrow, good lieutenant. I am sorry   40
    For your displeasure, but all will soon be well.
    The General and his wife are talking of it,
    And she speaks for you stoutly. The Moor replies
    That he you hurt is of great fame in Cyprus
    And great affinity, and that in wholesome wisdom   45
    He might not but refuse you. But he protests he loves you
    And needs no other suitor but his likings
    To take the safest occasion by the front
    To bring you in again.

CASSIO   Yet I beseech you,
    If you think fit or that it may be done,   50
    Give me advantage of some brief discourse
    With Desdemona alone.

EMILIA   Pray you, come in.
    I will bestow you where you shall have time
    To speak your bosom freely.

CASSIO   I am much bound to you.   [*Exeunt*

This is another fragment of a scene, mainly used by Shakespeare to effect a convenient entry of Othello and Iago together in the next scene.

2   *do*, convey.
3   *works*, i.e. the fortification.

Scene Three

Judged purely for dramatic artistry, this great scene, in which Othello is deceived into believing Desdemona's infidelity, must unquestionably rank among the most impressive in all Shakespeare's work. Our intellects are as intensely engaged as our emotions, for besides being deeply moved and horrified by what is taking place, we are closely involved in all the subtle, intricate interplay between Iago and Othello—in all Iago's diabolically clever manipulation of the hero. In less than five hundred lines, all irrelevancies of 'real' time obliterated, and with the utmost economy and concentration, Shakespeare achieves an utterly convincing transformation of Othello.

1   *do*, exert, perform.
7   *bounteous*. This links with Iago's tribute in Act2Sc.3, ll.313–14.
12   *strangeness*, aloofness, remoteness.
13   *Than . . . distance*, than as far as purely political considerations dictate.
14–16 *That . . . circumstances*. The first line seems fairly clear—that Cassio's 'banishment' may last too long. The second may mean that Othello will base his ideas of what constitutes public safety (the reason for his policy) on very thin grounds. Could the third mean that this policy of exclusion will develop further and the original circumstances that justified it (i.e. public safety) be forgotten?   *nice*, unsubstantial, trivial.

Scene Two

Cyprus · The citadel

Enter OTHELLO · IAGO · *and* GENTLEMEN

OTHELLO   These letters give, Iago, to the pilot,
    And by him do my duties to the state.
    That done, I will be walking on the works.
    Repair there to me.

IAGO   Well, my good lord, I'll do't.   [*Exit*
OTHELLO   This fortification, gentlemen, shall we see't?   5
GENTLEMEN   We wait upon your lordship.   [*Exeunt*

Scene Three

Cyprus · The garden of the citadel

Enter DESDEMONA · CASSIO · *and* EMILIA

DESDEMONA   Be thou assured, good Cassio, I will do
    All my abilities in thy behalf.

EMILIA   Good madam, do. I know it grieves my husband
    As if the case were his.

DESDEMONA   O, that's an honest fellow! Do not doubt, Cassio,   5
    But I will have my lord and you again
    As friendly as you were.

CASSIO   Bounteous madam,
    Whatever shall become of Michael Cassio,
    He's never anything but your true servant.

DESDEMONA   I know't; I thank you. You do love my lord.   10
    You have known him long, and be you well assured
    He shall in strangeness stand no further off
    Than in a politic distance.

CASSIO   Ay, but, lady,
    That policy may either last so long,
    Or feed upon such nice and waterish diet,   15

17   *supplied*, filled.

19   *doubt*, fear.

20   *warrant of thy place*, guarantee of restoration to your position.

22   *article*, clause or item in agreement, contract, etc.

23   *watch him*, keep him awake. Hawks were tamed in this way.
        out of patience. Presumably this means Othello will be unable to
        endure Desdemona's onslaught any longer.

24   *his . . . shrift*, his table a place of confessional.

27-8   *For . . . away*. Ironic in unconscious prophecy.

27   *solicitor*, (literally) one who is soliciting for you; advocate.

28   *Than . . . away*, than abandon your cause.

34   *do your discretion*, do as you think best.

35   *Ha! . . . that*. Iago strikes instantly, like a snake. His words regis-
        ter with Othello as we learn from ll.112-13 later.

38-40   *No . . . coming*. Though Iago's description of Cassio's departure
        is heavily coloured, at this moment Othello could still think
        that the 'guilty-like' etc. referred to the drunken brawl. Iago
        is not overplaying his hand.

47   *His . . . take*, reconcile yourself with him at once ('present').
        But 'reconciliation' perhaps mainly signifies the submission
        or repentance that precedes it.

Or breed itself so out of circumstance,
That I being absent and my place supplied,
My General will forget my love and service.

DESDEMONA Do not doubt that. Before Emilia here
    I give thee warrant of thy place. Assure thee,   20
    If I do vow a friendship I'll perform it
    To the last article. My lord shall never rest.
    I'll watch him tame and talk him out of patience.
    His bed shall seem a school, his board a shrift—
    I'll intermingle everything he does   25
    With Cassio's suit. Therefore be merry, Cassio,
    For thy solicitor shall rather die
    Than give thy cause away.

Enter OTHELLO *and* IAGO

EMILIA Madam, here comes my lord.

CASSIO Madam, I'll take my leave.   30

DESDEMONA Why, stay and hear me speak.

CASSIO Madam, not now. I am very ill at ease,
    Unfit for mine own purposes.

DESDEMONA Well, do your discretion.   [*Exit* CASSIO

IAGO Ha! I like not that.

OTHELLO   What dost thou say?   35

IAGO Nothing, my lord; or if—I know not what.

OTHELLO Was not that Cassio parted from my wife?

IAGO Cassio, my lord? No, sure, I cannot think it
    That he would sneak away so guilty-like,
    Seeing you coming.

OTHELLO   I do believe 'twas he.   40

DESDEMONA How now, my lord?
    I have been talking with a suitor here,
    A man that languishes in your displeasure.

OTHELLO Who is't you mean?

DESDEMONA Why, your lieutenant, Cassio. Good my lord,   45
    If I have any grace or power to move you,
    His present reconciliation take,
    For if he be not one that truly loves you,

49   *in cunning*. This might be glossed as 'deliberately' or 'knowingly'. 'Cunning' has its old meaning of 'knowledge', etc., not the modern one.

54   *call him back*. This almost certainly means 'restore him to his position'.

58   *dinner*. A mid-day meal.

64   *trespass*, offence, wrong-doing (as used in the *Lord's Prayer*). *in . . . reason*, as usually considered.

65–6   (*Save . . . best*) except that in war, so they say, even the most high-ranking officers must be made an example of, if necessary.

66–7   *not . . . check*, is a fault that hardly deserves so much as a private reprimand ('check').   *not almost*, hardly. This unfamiliar Elizabethan idiom has the sense of 'scarcely fault enough to, etc.'.

69   *you, me*. These words of course carry a heavy stress to make Desdemona's point.

70   *Or . . . on?* or that would cause me to stammer and hesitate.

70–1   *What! . . . you*. This first indication of Cassio's part in the wooing hardly squares with Othello's account in Act1 Sc.3. However, it gives Iago another lead which he takes up in ll.94–5.

74   *To . . . in?* Probably 'to get himself reinstated'.

76   *this . . . boon*, this is not a prayer for some exceptional favour. ('Boon' could mean 'a request'.)

79   *peculiar*, personal, individual. (Cf. Act1 Sc.1, l.60 and Act4 Sc.1, l.69.)

That errs in ignorance and not in cunning,
I have no judgment in an honest face.   50
I prithee call him back.

OTHELLO   Went he hence now?

DESDEMONA   Yes, faith, so humbled
   That he hath left part of his grief with me
   To suffer with him. Good love, call him back.

OTHELLO   Not now, sweet Desdemona—some other time.   55

DESDEMONA   But shall't be shortly?

OTHELLO   The sooner, sweet, for you.

DESDEMONA   Shall't be tonight, at supper?

OTHELLO   No, not tonight.

DESDEMONA   Tomorrow dinner then?

OTHELLO   I shall not dine at home.
   I meet the captains at the citadel.

DESDEMONA   Why, then, tomorrow night, or Tuesday morn,   60
   On Tuesday noon, or night? . . . On Wednesday morn?
   I prithee name the time, but let it not
   Exceed three days. In faith, he's penitent,
   And yet his trespass in our common reason
   (Save that, they say, the wars must make example   65
   Out of their best) is not almost a fault
   To incur a private check. When shall he come?
   Tell me, Othello. I wonder in my soul
   What you could ask me that I should deny
   Or stand so mammering on? What! Michael Cassio,   70
   That came a-wooing with you, and so many a time,
   When I have spoke of you dispraisingly,
   Hath ta'en your part, to have so much to do
   To bring him in? By'r Lady, I could do much—

OTHELLO   Prithee, no more. Let him come when he will;   75
   I will deny thee nothing.

DESDEMONA   Why, this is not a boon.
   'Tis as I should entreat you wear your gloves,
   Or feed on nourishing dishes, or keep you warm,
   Or sue to you to do a peculiar profit

81 *touch . . . indeed*, really test your love.

82 *full . . . weight.* 'Poise' is partly synonymous with 'weight', but, supported by 'difficult', it also carries the idea of a hard decision involved.

83 *fearful,* causing apprehension or agitation.

88 *Be . . . you,* be in whatever mood you please. Some strong dramatic irony here.

90–2 *Excellent . . . again.* Much might be said about these key-lines. Othello's words epitomize the depth and supreme 'soul' importance of his love: he would love Desdemona, he suggests, even if he were to suffer damnation for it. All the order and purpose of his world depends on his love, for its loss would mean (literally) 'chaos'. But what is now utterly unthinkable to him is to happen: he is to experience the loss of love, the chaos, the perdition. *wretch.* A term of endearment here. *Perdition.* Damnation of soul in the theological sense.

91 *But I do,* if I do not.

91–2 *And . . . again.* Othello is merely positing a possible, but quite unthinkable, state.

92 *My noble lord.* It is impossible in these notes to demonstrate all the diabolic manoeuvrings and mastery of Iago's persuasion of Othello that now begins. (See Granville-Barker's acute analysis, *Prefaces to Shakespeare, Fourth Series,* pp. 39–55 and 58–67.)

98 *further.* This implies that there is *some* harm in Iago's thought.

103 *Is . . . honest?* On the play with 'honest' that follows Empson writes: 'I think a queer kind of honesty is maintained in Iago through all the puzzles he contrives . . . The point of his riddles is to get "not hypocritical"—"frank about his own nature" accepted as the relevant sense; Iago will readily call him honest on that basis, and Othello cannot be reassured.' (*op. cit.,* pp. 221 and 222.) Othello cannot be reassured because 'honest' in this sense would mean that Cassio is easy-going and without scruples of conscience in his dealings with women.

109–19 *Think . . . thought.* The first effect of Iago's questions, hints, and pretended reluctance, is to work Othello to a pitch of curiosity and suspense and so to give momentum to his business.

To your own person. Nay, when I have a suit   80
Wherein I mean to touch your love indeed,
It shall be full of poise and difficult weight
And fearful to be granted.

OTHELLO   I will deny thee nothing,
Whereon, I do beseech thee, grant me this,
To leave me but a little to myself.   85

DESDEMONA   Shall I deny you? No; farewell, my lord.

OTHELLO   Farewell, my Desdemona, I'll come to thee straight.

DESDEMONA   Emilia, come. Be as your fancies teach you.
Whate'er you be, I am obedient.

                         [*Exeunt* DESDEMONA *and* EMILIA

OTHELLO   Excellent wretch! Perdition catch my soul   90
But I do love thee! And when I love thee not,
Chaos is come again.

IAGO   My noble lord—

OTHELLO   What dost thou say, Iago?

IAGO   Did Michael Cassio, when he wooed my lady,
Know of your love?   95

OTHELLO   He did, from first to last. Why dost thou ask?

IAGO   But for a satisfaction of my thought—
No further harm.

OTHELLO   Why of thy thought, Iago?

IAGO   I did not think he had been acquainted with her.

OTHELLO   O yes, and went between us very oft.   100

IAGO   Indeed!

OTHELLO   Indeed? Ay, indeed. Discern'st thou aught in that?
Is he not honest?

IAGO   Honest, my lord?

OTHELLO   Honest? Ay, honest.   105

IAGO   My lord, for aught I know.

OTHELLO   What dost thou think?

IAGO   Think, my lord?

OTHELLO   Think, my lord! By heaven, he echoes me
As if there were some monster in his thought   110
Too hideous to be shown. Thou dost mean something.

114   *of my counsel*, in my confidence—with possibly a suggestion of 'advisor'.

116   *purse*, draw together, wrinkle.

118   *conceit*, idea, notion.

123   *stops*, pauses, hesitations.

125   *of custom*, usual, habitual.   *just.* Probably 'upright', 'honourable'.

.126-7 *They . . . rule.* Two very difficult lines. 'Working' (did Shakespeare really intend the plural?) signifies intense activity, especially of a psychological kind; and 'heart...rule' probably describes someone able to control his feelings and so not blurt everything out. 'dilations' might suggest a swelling of heart under such strain. Alternatively, the Quarto reading 'denotements' (in place of 'dilations') could mean that Iago's pauses were 'indications' of some secret knowledge that his control of his feelings would not allow him to utter.   *close*, secret, inward, shut in, hidden.

128   *think.* This word (perhaps in a contrast with 'sworn') can be spoken with the most suggestively charged hesitation. Granville-Barker calls it 'the most provocative stroke yet' (*op. cit.*, p. 44).

130   *Or . . . none.* Talking 'none' as 'no men' and 'seem' in inverted commas to indicate play on the word, we might perhaps very literally paraphrase this line as—'Or those that are not (what they seem), would they might "seem" no men at all!' (i.e. die, or be non-existent). But this is a very doubtful rendering, and 'seem' or 'none' may be text corruptions.

134   *as . . . thinkings*, about your thoughts. Othello is probably catching up the word 'think' (l.132) that Iago has just used in a casual way. What Othello wants is Iago's deeply considered thoughts—hence 'ruminate'.

138   *free to*, free in regard to, i.e. even slaves are free to speak their thoughts or not.

140   *palace.* A somewhat odd word unless Shakespeare was already thinking of the following reference to 'leets', 'law-days', etc.

141-4 *Who . . . lawful.* This legal term of expression, if unexpected from Iago, is not uncommon in Shakespeare. Iago is saying that the best of us when trying to judge some possibly reprehensible issue in a rational way are never free from improper, discreditable surmises of guilt ('uncleanly apprehensions').   *leets.* District courts for non-capital offences.

145   *conspire.* Rather in the sense of behaving in a dishonest, harmful way.

I heard thee say but now, thou lik'st not that,
When Cassio left my wife. What didst not like?
And when I told thee he was of my counsel
In my whole course of wooing, thou criedst 'Indeed!'   115
And didst contract and purse thy brow together
As if thou then hadst shut up in thy brain
Some horrible conceit. If thou dost love me,
Show me thy thought.

IAGO   My lord, you know I love you.

OTHELLO   I think thou dost.   120
And for I know thou art full of love and honesty,
And weigh'st thy words before thou giv'st them breath,
Therefore these stops of thine fright me the more;
For such things in a false disloyal knave
Are tricks of custom, but in a man that's just   125
They are close dilations, working from the heart
That passion cannot rule.

IAGO   For Michael Cassio,
I dare be sworn I think that he is honest.

OTHELLO   I think so too.

IAGO   Men should be what they seem,
Or those that be not, would they might seem none!   130

OTHELLO   Certain, men should be what they seem.

IAGO   Why then, I think Cassio's an honest man.

OTHELLO   Nay, yet there's more in this.
I prithee speak to me as to thy thinkings
As thou dost ruminate, and give thy worst of thoughts   135
The worst of words.

IAGO   Good my lord, pardon me.
Though I am bound to every act of duty,
I am not bound to that all slaves are free to.
Utter my thoughts! Why, say they are vile and false?
As where's that palace whereinto foul things   140
Sometimes intrude not? Who has a breast so pure
But some uncleanly apprehensions
Keep leets and law-days and in session sit
With meditations lawful?

OTHELLO   Thou dost conspire against thy friend, Iago,   145

147–54   *I . . . observance.* Possibly some broken syntax, and the Quarto reads 'I entreat you then' for 'that your wisdom yet'. (In the reading given 'do beseech' has as its object 'that your wisdom', etc.) However, the general meaning is clear: Iago is pretending to confess reasons (his nose for misdemeanours, for instance) why Othello should not take his observations too seriously.

148   *vicious.* A masterly ambiguity: it could be taken as deprecatory self-reprobation of Iago's guesses, or it could refer to the enormity of the offence he is guessing about.

149–51   *As . . . not.* Another cunning stroke: in one breath Iago is saying that he is drawn to investigation of real wrong-doings ('abuses') and also that he imagines them.

150   *jealousy.* This word, which had not settled to its modern meanings, must always be considered most carefully. Here it means 'suspicious (or mistrustful) attitude in general'.

152   *conjects,* surmises, guesses. The Folio has 'conceits'.

154   *scattering.* Probably something like 'unconnected'.

155   *for,* befitting, right for.

156   *manhood,* courage, i.e. it would be cowardly to be enforced to speak his thoughts.   *honesty.* Empson takes the word here to mean—at least in part—'loyalty to one's friends'.

158–9   *Good . . . souls.* Proverbial. (And see note on Act2 Sc.3, ll.249–51.) By the inclusion of 'and woman' Iago may, just possibly, be making his first delicate move to bring Desdemona into the discussion.

159   *immediate,* of closest concern.

160   *purse,* i.e. money.

169   *jealousy.* Here means 'suspicion of sexual infidelity'. But still not the modern meaning of a continuous fear of losing (or having to share) someone's love. Othello is not jealous in that sense.

170–1   *It . . . on.* The five pages of commentary in the *New Variorum* edition hardly clarify this. The only certainty is that 'green-eyed jealousy' also occurs in *The Merchant of Venice* (Act3 Sc.2, l.110). The 'meat' may be the victim of the monster jealousy.

172   *his wronger,* i.e. his unfaithful wife.

175   *O misery!* Othello is here commenting on the second type of cuckold, not on his own feelings.

176–8   *Poor . . . poor.* The general sense of these proverbial remarks is that one is happier without possessions than having rich possessions and fearing to lose them.   *fineless,* unlimited.

179   *my tribe,* my kind. That Iago is pretending to confess an inclination to 'jealousy' seems to be confirmed by Othello's following words.

If thou but think'st him wronged, and mak'st his ear
  A stranger to thy thoughts.

IAGO   I do beseech you
  (Though I perchance am vicious in my guess,
  As I confess it is my nature's plague
  To spy into abuses, and oft my jealousy   150
  Shapes faults that are not) that your wisdom yet,
  From one that so imperfectly conjects,
  Would take no notice, nor build yourself a trouble
  Out of his scattering and unsure observance.
  It were not for your quiet nor your good,   155
  Nor for my manhood, honesty or wisdom,
  To let you know my thoughts.

OTHELLO   Zounds!

IAGO Good name in man and woman, dear my lord,
  Is the immediate jewel of their souls.
  Who steals my purse, steals trash: 'tis something, nothing;   160
  'Twas mine, 'tis his, and has been slave to thousands.
  But he that filches from me my good name
  Robs me of that which not enriches him
  And makes me poor indeed.

OTHELLO By heaven, I'll know thy thoughts.   165

IAGO You cannot, if my heart were in your hand,
  Nor shall not, whilst 'tis in my custody.

OTHELLO Ha!

IAGO O, beware, my lord, of jealousy!
  It is the green-eyed monster which doth mock   170
  The meat it feeds on. That cuckold lives in bliss
  Who, certain of this fate, loves not his wronger.
  But O, what damned minutes tells he o'er
  Who dotes yet doubts, suspects yet strongly loves!

OTHELLO O misery!   175

IAGO Poor and content is rich, and rich enough;
  But riches fineless is as poor as winter
  To him that ever fears he shall be poor.
  Good God, the souls of all my tribe defend
  From jealousy!

OTHELLO   Why, why is this?   180

182–3   *To . . . suspicions.* This may mean 'to wax and wane like the moon with ever-renewed suspicions'.

183–4   *to . . . resolved,* if I am ever in doubt, I shall want my doubts completely and immediately settled.

184   *goat.* More animal imagery. Presumably the goat stands—as usual—for a creature of lust. But the point of such a reference here is not entirely clear.

186   *exsufflicate and blown.* Usually glossed, synonymously, as 'inflated', 'windy', etc. But 'exsufflicate' is uncertain, and it may, like 'blown' also, mean 'fly-blown'.

187   *inference,* suggestion.

187–9   *'Tis . . . well.* Though Othello is using 'jealous' in the sense already given, what he is talking about would here fit in with the main modern meaning. At all events he is speaking the truth about himself.

189   *free.* This may signify 'open', 'generous', and so 'likely to elicit a friendly response'.

191   *from . . . merits,* on the grounds that I am myself undeserving of her.

192   *doubt,* suspicion, or, apprehension.   *revolt,* disloyalty.

193   *For . . . me.* This is the reason for Othello's previous confidence in his 'merits'.

197–208   *I . . . unknown.* Iago now judges it opportune to come out with an open charge.

202   *secure,* unsuspicious. Iago is advising a mean between too much and too little suspicion.

203   *free.* Here certainly in the sense of 'generous'.

204   *self-bounty,* innate magnanimity.

205–8   *I . . . unknown.* The first of two devilish masterstrokes. This comment is calculated to undermine Othello's confidence by reminding him that he is a foreigner and that he is totally ignorant of the ways of Venetian women. Also, as several commentators have pointed out, Iago's words could be the reason why Othello never cross-examines Desdemona.

206   *pranks,* adulteries, promiscuities, etc. (Cf. Act2Sc.1, l.142.)

207–8   *Their . . . unknown,* it's not their immoralities that worry them, but being found out.

210–12   *She . . . most.* The second devastating blow at Othello's confidence and faith in Desdemona, partly because Iago is speaking unchallengeable truth, and partly because his first words must recall Brabantio's warning (Act1 Sc.3, ll.290–1).

212   *Why . . . then!* Well, there you are!

213–15   *She . . . witchcraft.* Another difficult passage. However punctuated (possibly with an exclamation mark after 'oak') these lines as they stand must contain some broken or incomplete construction. For 'seel' see the note on Act1Sc3, l.267. (The Quarto reads 'seal' for 'seel'.) The 'oak' reference is commonly explained in terms of the close grain of this wood, but the simile appears to make little sense. The suggested emendation of 'hawk' for 'oak' is certainly tempting.

213   *give . . . seeming,* put on such an act.

Think'st thou I'd make a life of jealousy,
To follow still the changes of the moon
With fresh suspicions? No, to be once in doubt
Is once to be resolved. Exchange me for a goat,
When I shall turn the business of my soul   185
To such exsufflicate and blown surmises,
Matching thy inference. 'Tis not to make me jealous
To say my wife is fair, feeds well, loves company,
Is free of speech, sings, plays, and dances well.
Where virtue is, these are more virtuous.   190
Nor from mine own weak merits will I draw
The smallest fear or doubt of her revolt,
For she had eyes and chose me. No, Iago,
I'll see before I doubt; when I doubt, prove,
And on the proof there is no more but this—   195
Away at once with love or jealousy!

IAGO   I am glad of this, for now I shall have reason
To show the love and duty that I bear you
With franker spirit. Therefore, as I am bound
Receive it from me. I speak not yet of proof.   200
Look to your wife. Observe her well with Cassio.
Wear your eye thus, not jealous, nor secure.
I would not have your free and noble nature,
Out of self-bounty, be abused. Look to't.
I know our country disposition well.   205
In Venice they do let God see the pranks
They dare not show their husbands. Their best conscience
Is not to leave't undone but keep't unknown.

OTHELLO   Dost thou say so?

IAGO   She did deceive her father marrying you,   210
And when she seemed to shake and fear your looks,
She loved them most.

OTHELLO   And so she did.

IAGO   Why, go to, then!
She that so young could give out such a seeming,
To seel her father's eyes up close as oak . . .
He thought 'twas witchcraft. But I am much to blame;   215
I humbly do beseech you of your pardon
For too much loving you.

217 *I . . . ever.* These words are more terribly and deeply true than Othello realizes.

223–4 *To . . . suspicion.* An involved way of saying 'beyond the bounds of suspicion'. *issues,* conclusions. *reach,* extent, range.

226 *My . . . success,* my speech would produce a kind of unfortunate result ('success').

228 *I . . . moved.* This repeated phrase has the effect of fastening Othello's distress on him, as it were.

229 *honest.* Probably here more in the sense of 'chaste'.

232–7 *Ay . . . unnatural.* Notice how promptly Iago takes up and elaborates the new consideration that begins to cross Othello's mind.

233 *affect,* regard favourably, be inclined towards.

234 *clime,* country. *complexion.* Probably 'colour'. *degree,* social rank.

236 *will,* sexual appetite, lust. Iago is of course indirectly referring to Desdemona's perverted choice of a black lover rather than one of her kind and colour.

237 *disproportion,* want of fitness, unnaturalness; almost perhaps, perversion.

238–9 *I . . . her,* I am not positively ('in position') and particularly ('Distinctly') referring to her.

240 *recoiling to,* returning to.

241 *fall to match,* start (or come) to compare or measure against. *country,* country's. *forms,* ways of behaviour (here probably in sex relations).

242 *happily,* haply.

249 *scan,* consider. *Leave . . . time.* Just the opposite of what Iago really wishes.

OTHELLO   I am bound to thee for ever.

IAGO   I see this hath a little dashed your spirits.

OTHELLO   Not a jot, not a jot.

IAGO   I'faith, I fear it has.
  I hope you will consider what is spoke   220
  Comes from my love. But I do see you are moved.
  I am to pray you not to strain my speech
  To grosser issues nor to larger reach
  Than to suspicion.

OTHELLO   I will not.

IAGO   Should you do so, my lord,   225
  My speech should fall into such vile success
  As my thoughts aim not at. Cassio's my trusty friend.
  My lord, I see you're moved.

OTHELLO   No, not much moved.
  I do not think but Desdemona's honest.

IAGO   Long live she so! And long live you to think so!   230

OTHELLO   And yet, how nature erring from itself—

IAGO   Ay, there's the point—as, to be bold with you,
  Not to affect many proposed matches
  Of her own clime, complexion and degree,
  Whereto we see in all things nature tends.   235
  Fie! We may smell in such a will most rank,
  Foul disproportion, thoughts unnatural.
  But, pardon me, I do not in position
  Distinctly speak of her, though I may fear
  Her will, recoiling to her better judgment,   240
  May fall to match you with her country forms,
  And happily repent.

OTHELLO   Farewell, farewell.
  If more thou dost perceive, let me know more.
  Set on thy wife to observe. Leave me, Iago.

IAGO [going]   My lord, I take my leave.   245

OTHELLO   Why did I marry? This honest creature doubtless
  Sees and knows more, much more, than he unfolds.

IAGO [returning]   My lord, I would I might entreat your honour
  To scan this thing no farther. Leave it to time.

253   *means*, ways of getting his post back.

254   *strain his entertainment*, urge his reinstatement (or possibly, reception).

257   *busy*, meddlesome, interfering.

259   *free*, innocent.

260   *government*, proper conduct, self-control.

261–80 *This... quicken*. Appropriately, for an unintrospective character, Othello is given only this one true soliloquy.

261–3 *This ... dealing*. Notice Othello's respect for Iago's insight into human relations. Whatever the limitations of this insight, in so far as he is himself the unconscious object of it Othello's tribute is all too justified, ironically so. 'Iago seems to Othello so honest, so wise beyond himself in human dealings .. . because into what he speaks are projected the half truths that Othello's romantic vision ignored, but of which his mind held secret knowledge' (M. Bodkin, *Archetypal Patterns in Poetry*, reprinted in Penguin *Shakespeare's Tragedies*, p. 104).

263–6 *If ... fortune*. The meaning of this hawking metaphor is that, if Othello finds proof of Desdemona's infidelity, he will sever all ties with her, however painful to himself, and cast her off to prey on others. These lines suggest that at first Othello does not intend to kill Desdemona.

263   *haggard*, a wild, untrained hawk.

264   *jesses*. Straps on the hawk's legs for securing.

266   *at fortune*, at random, or, as chance will have it.

266–8 *Haply ... have*. These references show how Iago's arguments have gone home.

266   *Haply*, maybe, perhaps.

267   *soft ... conversation*, pleasing (or easy) graces of social intercourse ('conversation').

268   *chamberers*, gallants, 'social types', as we might say.

270   *abused*, deceived.

272   *delicate*, refined, exquisite.

273–6 *I ... uses*. Two points to notice: (1) evidence of jealousy in the main modern sense; (2) Othello is taking over Iago's characteristic animal imagery. 'Not only shall Othello crawl at Iago's feet; he shall talk his language' (Kott, *op. cit.*, p. 90).

277   *Prerogatived*, privileged. Possibly there is some corruption in this line. From the context Othello can hardly be saying that the great are more likely to be cuckolded than the base.

279   *forked plague*, the cuckhold's horns.

280   *do quicken*, are conceived, or born.   *Desdemona comes*. See Granville Barker's comment: 'The soliloquy and this brief passage between the two form a trough in the waves of the action, allowing us a survey of Othello as Iago's first attack has left him; passions not yet fired, but mind and imagination bewildered and warped, confidence gone' (*op. cit.*, pp. 54–5).

281–2 *If ... believe 't*. Othello momentarily recovers his faith in Desdemona.

283   *generous*, noble.

284   *attend*, await.

Though it be fit that Cassio have his place   250
(For sure he fills it up with great ability)
Yet if you please to hold him off awhile,
You shall by that perceive him and his means;
Note if your lady strain his entertainment
With any strong or vehement importunity.   255
Much will be seen in that. In the meantime,
Let me be thought too busy in my fears
(As worthy cause I have to fear I am)
And hold her free, I do beseech your honour.

OTHELLO   Fear not my government.

IAGO   I once more take my leave [*Exit* 260

OTHELLO   This fellow's of exceeding honesty,
And knows all qualities, with a learned spirit,
Of human dealing. If I do prove her haggard,
Though that her jesses were my dear heart-strings,
I'd whistle her off, and let her down the wind   265
To prey at fortune. Haply, for I am black
And have not those soft parts of conversation
That chamberers have, or for I am declined
Into the vale of years (yet that's not much),
She's gone. I am abused, and my relief   270
Must be to loathe her. O, curse of marriage,
That we can call these delicate creatures ours
And not their appetites! I had rather be a toad
And live upon the vapour of a dungeon
Than keep a corner in the thing I love   275
For others' uses. Yet 'tis the plague of great ones:
Prerogatived are they less than the base.
'Tis destiny unshunnable, like death.
Even then this forked plague is fated to us
When we do quicken. Desdemona comes: 280

Re-enter DESDEMONA *and* EMILIA

If she be false, O, then heaven mocks itself!
I'll not believe't.

DESDEMONA   How now, my dear Othello!
Your dinner, and the generous islanders
By you invited, do attend your presence.

287   *I . . . here.* Supported to some extent by Othello's next remark, this is probably a reference to the cuckhold's horns. Such Iago-like obliquity is new for the Othello we have so far known.

288   *watching*, sleeplessness.

290   *napkin*, handkerchief.

291   *it.* Since the preceding stage direction is editorial, not Shakespeare's, 'it' must refer to Othello's forehead. There is no reason for Othello insisting that the handkerchief, which neither recognize for the magic keepsake he had once given Desdemona, should stay on the ground.

293   *I . . . napkin.* In the original Cinthio story Emilia steals the handkerchief.

294   *remembrance*, keepsake.

295   *wayward.* Possibly 'perverse', but though this is obviously an important word, its meaning is not certain.

297   *conjured*, solemnly implored (perhaps insisting on an oath).

299   *ta'en out*, copied.

302   *I . . . fantasy*, I know nothing about the matter; I'm merely satisfying his whim ('fantasy').

315   *to the advantage*, at the stroke of luck; or, seizing my chance.

OTHELLO   I am to blame.   285

DESDEMONA   Why is your speech so faint? Are you not well?

OTHELLO   I have a pain upon my forehead here.

DESDEMONA   Faith, that's with watching; 'twill away again.
      Let me but bind it hard, within this hour
      It will be well.

OTHELLO   Your napkin is too little.   290
      [*He pushes the handkerchief away;* DESDEMONA *drops it*]
      Let it alone. Come, I'll go in with you.

DESDEMONA   I am very sorry that you are not well.
                              [*Exeunt* OTHELLO *and* DESDEMONA

EMILIA   I am glad I have found this napkin.
      This was her first remembrance from the Moor.
      My wayward husband hath a hundred times   295
      Wooed me to steal it; but she so loves the token
      (For he conjured her she should ever keep it)
      That she reserves it evermore about her
      To kiss and talk to. I'll have the work ta'en out
      And give it Iago. What he will do with it   300
      Heaven knows, not I;
      I nothing, but to please his fantasy.

Enter IAGO

IAGO   How now? What do you here alone?

EMILIA   Do not you chide. I have a thing for you.

IAGO   A thing for me? It is a common thing—   305

EMILIA   Ha?

IAGO   To have a foolish wife.

EMILIA   O, is that all? What will you give me now
      For that same handkerchief?

IAGO   What handkerchief?

EMILIA   What handkerchief!   310
      Why, that the Moor first gave to Desdemona,
      That which so often you did bid me steal.

IAGO   Hast stole it from her?

EMILIA   No, faith, she let it drop by negligence,
      And to the advantage, I being here took't up.   315

320   *import*, importance.

323   *Be . . . on't.* Possibly, 'Don't say you know anything about it',
           taking 'acknown' in the sense of 'admitting knowledge of'.

326–8   *Trifles . . . writ.* Often quoted lines.   *proofs . . . writ.* Bible words
           and therefore unquestionable truth.

329–33   *The . . . so.* These lines help to prepare us for the Othello, much
           further gone in suspicion, fury, and abandon, who is about to
           reappear.

330   *Dangerous.* Probably in the old sense of 'having power to harm'.
           conceits, ideas, notions.

331   *to distaste*, to be unpleasant to taste.

332   *act*, action.

333   *Burn . . . sulphur.* Presumably for Shakespeare a sulphur mine
           was a place of exceptionally tormenting heat. There may also
           be a faint suggestion of hell torment.   *I . . . so.* This is
           generally taken to mean that Othello's appearance on his re-
           entry confirms what Iago has just been saying.

333   (*stage direction*). This follows the Folio placing. But perhaps in
           stage production the right moment for Othello's reappearance
           is after 'mines of sulphur'.

334–7   *Not . . . yesterday.* Some of the most famous lines in the whole
           of Shakespeare. If we think there is any inconsistency be-
           tween this magnificent poetry and Iago's character, that is
           only because we make the mistake of thinking that Shake-
           speare (and the other Elizabethan dramatists) were intent ˌn
           thorough-going psychological realism.

334   *poppy*, opium.   *mandragora.* A narcotic from the plant of that
           name.

335   *drowsy syrups*, soporific drugs or medicines.

337   *owed'st*, didst own or enjoy.

338   *Ha . . . me!* How far are we to take this opening line as signi-
           ficant—as evidence of an excessive egocentricity or sense of
           self-importance?

340   *on the rack.* This expression would of course not have been a
           stale cliché for Shakespeare's audience.

341–2   *I . . . little.* These words come close to echoing what Iago had
           said earlier (ll.171–4).

343   *What . . . lust?* A radical change has occurred in Othello since
           we last saw him: he now seems convinced of Desdemona's
           infidelity. But this is a play, not real life: strict time is unim-
           portant, and we do not have to worry much about *reasons* for
           the change. All that concerns an audience is Othello's state
           now.   *sense*, awareness.

345   *free.* Probably with some sense like 'unconcerned', 'without
           worries'.

347   *wanting*, missing.

348   *Let . . . know't*, so long as he doesn't realize (that he has been
           robbed).

Look, here it is.

IAGO A good wench! Give it me.

EMILIA What will you do with it, that you have been
So earnest to have me filch it?

IAGO [*snatching it*] Why, what is that to you?

EMILIA If it be not for some purpose of import,   320
Give't me again. Poor lady, she'll run mad
When she shall lack it.

IAGO Be not acknown on't. I have use for it.
Go, leave me.   [*Exit* EMILIA
I will in Cassio's lodging lose this napkin,   325
And let him find it. Trifles light as air
Are to the jealous confirmations strong
As proofs of holy writ. This may do something.
The Moor already changes with my poison.
Dangerous conceits are in their natures poisons,   330
Which at the first are scarce found to distaste,
But, with a little act upon the blood,
Burn like the mines of sulphur. I did say so.

Re-enter OTHELLO

Look where he comes! Not poppy, nor mandragora,
Nor all the drowsy syrups of the world,   335
Shall ever medicine thee to that sweet sleep
Which thou owedst yesterday.

OTHELLO Ha, ha, false to me, to me!

IAGO Why, how now, General! No more of that.

OTHELLO Avaunt! Be gone! Thou hast set me on the rack.   340
I swear 'tis better to be much abused
Than but to know't a little.

IAGO How now, my lord?

OTHELLO What sense had I of her stolen hours of lust?
I saw't not, thought it not; it harmed not me.
I slept the next night well, was free and merry;   345
I found not Cassio's kisses on her lips.
He that is robbed, not wanting what is stolen,
Let him not know't, and he's not robbed at all.

IAGO I am sorry to hear this.

350–62　*I . . . gone.* This is one of Othello's speeches that those commentators who try to represent him as a rhetorical, self-dramatizing figure fasten on. But if his love for Desdemona has gone, it is truly a matter of 'farewell content'—in the fullest sense of the word 'content'; and in the apparent shattering of his world, it is right that he should lament the end of its other chief constituent, his soldiership. Further, whatever our legitimate modern objections, we must recognize that Othello has a sense of the poetry of war. A 'noble apostrophe' Wilson Knight calls this speech (*op. cit.*, p. 107).

351　*Pioners,* sappers or diggers. Regarded as the lowest kind of soldier.

352　*So,* provided that.

359　*pomp, circumstances.* Virtually synonymous for 'ceremonial', 'pageantry'.

360　*mortal,* deadly.

361　*Jove's dread clamours,* i.e. thunder.

362　*Othello's occupation's gone.* The simple, terrible truth, not exaggerated rhetoric.

364　*prove.* The main stress of the line is of course on this word.

366　*man's eternal soul.* In this tragedy concerning the damnation of Othello's 'soul', note this reference.

367　*dog.* A word of general, contemptuous abuse.

370　*probation,* proof.　*hinge . . . loop.* In Shakespeare's image it is easy to think of hanging something on a 'loop', which may also carry a suggestion of 'circuitous' or 'twisted'. But the 'hinge' reference is much less clear.

372　*My noble lord.* It is fairly certain that just before, or just after these words, Othello lays hands on Iago for the first time.

374　*Never . . . remorse.* 'Remorse' here has always been a problem word, but the whole line probably refers to that 'damnation' which Othello mentions at the end of the speech, in which case 'remorse' might mean God's compassion (and therefore mercy). Othello goes on, rhetorically, to invite Iago to commit further deeds of horror, since he is already sufficiently damned himself, if he has slandered Desdemona.

378–85　*O . . . offence.* Behind this calculated, hypocritical outburst there may be some genuine alarm at consequences Iago has not expected—the risk of violence to himself, and Othello's insistence on proof.

378　*grace.* A theological term—divine influence that helps one to endure ordeal, etc.

380　*take mine office.* This probably means 'take away my position as ancient'.

381　*vice.* Hardly 'sin'. Probably 'failing', 'fault'.

384　*profit,* profitable lesson.

385　*offence.* Probably 'harm', 'injury' (to the one showing love).

OTHELLO I had been happy if the general camp,   350
    Pioners and all, had tasted her sweet body,
    So I had nothing known. O, now for ever
    Farewell the tranquil mind! Farewell content!
    Farewell the plumed troop and the big wars
    That make ambition virtue—O, farewell!   355
    Farewell the neighing steed and the shrill trump,
    The spirit-stirring drum, the ear-piercing fife,
    The royal banner, and all quality,
    Pride, pomp and circumstance of glorious war!
    And, O ye mortal engines, whose rude throats   360
    The immortal Jove's dread clamours counterfeit,
    Farewell! Othello's occupation's gone.

IAGO Is't possible, my lord?

OTHELLO Villain, be sure thou prove my love a whore.
    Be sure of it, give me the ocular proof,   365
    Or by the worth of man's eternal soul,
    Thou hadst been better have been born a dog
    Than answer my waked wrath!

IAGO   Is't come to this?

OTHELLO Make me to see't, or at the least so prove it
    That the probation bear no hinge nor loop   370
    To hang a doubt on, or woe upon thy life!

IAGO My noble lord—

OTHELLO If thou dost slander her and torture me,
    Never pray more; abandon all remorse.
    On horror's head horrors accumulate;   375
    Do deeds to make heaven weep, all earth amazed;
    For nothing canst thou to damnation add
    Greater than that.

IAGO   O grace! O heaven defend me!
    Are you a man? Have you a soul or sense?
    God be wi' you, take mine office. O wretched fool,   380
    That livest to make thine honesty a vice!
    O monstrous world! Take note, take note, O world!
    To be direct and honest is not safe.
    I thank you for this profit, and from hence
    I'll love no friend, since love breeds such offence.   385

386   *shouldst.* Here the auxiliary has the force of reasonable supposition. In the next line 'should' means 'ought to' (as a consequence).

388   *And . . . for,* i.e. the honest man fails to achieve his proper, honest ends.

388–95   *By . . . satisfied!* It is curious that the Quarto does not include this important speech.

389   *honest.* Again in the sense of 'chaste', 'faithful'.

390   *just,* faithful, honourable.

392   *Dian's.* The point of this allusion is that Diana was the goddess of chastity.

392–3   *black . . . face.* This seems sufficient proof that Shakespeare intended his Othello to be a negro.

393–5   *If . . . it.* Othello is thinking of suicide.   *suffocating streams,* i.e. drowning.

400–1   *Would . . . topped?* Iago is now deliberately torturing Othello with a definite picture of Desdemona's alleged adulterous conduct.   *supervisor,* eye-witness.

404   *bolster,* share a pillow, i.e. sleep together.

408   *prime.* This and 'hot', 'salt in pride', are synonyms for 'lustful', 'on heat'.

409–10   *fools . . . drunk.* This—and especially 'ignorance'—is by no means clear. Perhaps Iago is saying that Othello cannot see the physical love-making of Cassio and Desdemona even if, in their 'intoxicated' state, they behave in the most foolishly reckless way. The Folio prints a comma after 'ignorance'.

411   *imputation . . . circumstance,* a charge (or accusation) based on circumstantial evidence.

412   *door.* Possibly Shakespeare employed this metaphor, subconsciously or not, for a suggestion of 'bedroom', etc.

414   *living.* Something that suggests the opposite of verbal report— 'real-life', 'actual', 'concrete', etc.

415   *office,* job, assignment.

416   *Pricked,* urged.

418–31   *I . . . Moor!* Again Iago's speech is cunningly filled with particulars and vivid physical pictures calculated to enflame Othello. The matador is playing the bull.

OTHELLO   Nay, stay. Thou shouldst be honest.

IAGO   I should be wise, for honesty's a fool
   And loses that it works for.

OTHELLO   By the world,
   I think my wife be honest, and think she is not.
   I think that thou art just, and think thou art not.   390
   I'll have some proof. Her name that was as fresh
   As Dian's visage is now begrimed and black
   As mine own face. If there be cords or knives,
   Poison or fire or suffocating streams,
   I'll not endure it. Would I were satisfied!   395

IAGO   I see, sir, you are eaten up with passion.
   I do repent me that I put it to you.
   You would be satisfied?

OTHELLO   Would! Nay, I will.

IAGO   And may. But how? How satisfied, my lord?
   Would you, the supervisor, grossly gape on—   400
   Behold her topped?

OTHELLO   Death and damnation! O!

IAGO   It were a tedious difficulty, I think,
   To bring them to that prospect. Damn them then
   If ever mortal eyes do see them bolster
   More than their own! What then? How then?   405
   What shall I say? Where's satisfaction?
   It is impossible you should see this
   Were they as prime as goats, as hot as monkeys,
   As salt as wolves in pride, and fools as gross
   As ignorance made drunk. But yet, I say,   410
   If imputation and strong circumstance,
   Which lead directly to the door of truth,
   Will give you satisfaction, you might have't.

OTHELLO   Give me a living reason she's disloyal.

IAGO   I do not like the office.   415
   But since I am entered into this cause so far,
   Pricked to't by foolish honesty and love,
   I will go on. I lay with Cassio lately,
   And being troubled with a raging tooth
   I could not sleep.   420

421   *loose*, unrestrained (with probably some suggestion of 'disso-
        lute').

425   *wary*. The Quarto reads 'merry'.

433   *forgone conclusion*, a previous physical consummation, i.e.
        Cassio's dreams were not merely lustful longings but re-
        collections of what had already occurred.

434   *'Tis . . . dream*. The Folio gives this line to Othello, and there are
        certainly some arguments in favour of such a reading. 'Doubt'
        probably means 'suspicion' here, but any gloss on 'shrewd'
        (which had several meanings) is uncertain, since the 'it' in
        ' 'Tis' might refer to the dream generally or to Othello's
        last remark.

435–6   *other . . . thinly*, i.e. other proofs that in themselves bear no
        very substantial evidence.

438   *Yet . . . done*. This is very ironical. For some while now Iago's
        whole concern has been that Othello's imagination should
        indeed 'see' things done, though of course this is not the
        'ocular proof' that Othello demanded. Now Iago is about to
        attempt some 'occular proof'.

440–5   *Have . . . with*. Bradley (*op. cit.*, p. 182) cites this as another
        example of the extraordinary luck that favours Iago, for if
        Othello had observed the handkerchief in ll.289–90, Iago's
        lying story would have been immediately exploded. This
        element of luck in the play leads Bradley to talk of a 'dark
        fatality' (p. 181) and of a feeling 'that fate has taken sides with
        villainy' (p. 182).

441   *spotted*, embroidered.

448–56 *O . . . tongues*. These lines may illustrate the typical Elizabethan
        hyperbole, not to say rant, that even Shakespeare was not
        immune from. But see the note on Act5Sc.2,ll.261–84. In
        any case it does not necessarily follow that this speech or
        ll.460–9 are evidence of a fondness for theatrical, rhetorical
        posing in Othello himself.

451   *fond*, foolish, infatuated.

453   *hollow cell!* A difficult allusion, possibly a quotation. But
        'hollow' may be a text corruption, and the Folio has 'hell' for
        'cell'.

454   *hearted throne*, throne in the heart.

455   *fraught*, freight.

456   *aspics'*, asps'.

There are a kind of men so loose of soul
That in their sleeps will mutter their affairs.
One of this kind is Cassio.
In sleep I heard him say 'Sweet Desdemona,
Let us be wary, let us hide our loves'. 425
And then, sir, would he gripe and wring my hand,
Cry 'O sweet creature!' and then kiss me hard,
As if he plucked up kisses by the roots,
That grew upon my lips; then laid his leg
Over my thigh, and sighed and kissed, and then 430
Cried 'Cursed fate that gave thee to the Moor!'

OTHELLO   O monstrous, monstrous!

IAGO   Nay, this was but his dream.

OTHELLO   But this denoted a foregone conclusion.

IAGO   'Tis a shrewd doubt, though it be but a dream:
And this may help to thicken other proofs 435
That dö demonstrate thinly.

OTHELLO   I'll tear her all to pieces!

IAGO   Nay, but be wise. Yet we see nothing done;
She may be honest yet. Tell me but this.
Have you not sometimes seen a handkerchief, 440
Spotted with strawberries, in your wife's hand?

OTHELLO   I gave her such a one; 'twas my first gift.

IAGO   I know not that, but such a handkerchief
(I am sure it was your wife's) did I today
See Cassio wipe his beard with.

OTHELLO   If it be that— 445

IAGO   If it be that, or any that was hers,
It speaks against her with the other proofs.

OTHELLO   O, that the slave had forty thousand lives!
One is too poor, too weak for my revenge.
Now do I see 'tis true. Look here, Iago— 450
All my fond love thus do I blow to heaven ...
'Tis gone.
Arise, black vengeance, from thy hollow cell!
Yield up, O love, thy crown and hearted throne
To tyrannous hate! Swell, bosom, with thy fraught, 455
For 'tis of aspics' tongues!

E

460–9   *Never . . . words.* Admitting the evil purpose, do we, like Swinburne, Bradley, Wilson Knight and others, take this speech (not in the Quarto) as reflection of Othello's intensely poetic imagination, or do we regard it, like Leavis, as a demonstration of 'self-dramatization', lack of 'self-knowledge', and a nobility 'no longer something real, but the disguise of an obtuse and brutal egotism'? ('Diabolic Intellect and the Noble Hero', *The Common Pursuit, Peregrine* ed. pp. 146–7). Or (the question we must always be asking) is it that the speech is not the revelation of Othello's 'character' but Shakespeare's poetic and rhetorical attempt to make us, the audience *feel* the enormity and terrible resolution of the decision?

460–3   *Like . . . Hellespont.* This description of the Pontic (Black) Sea is another echo of Pliny's *Natural History.*   *Propontic*, Sea of Marmora.   *Hellespont*, Dardanelles.

466   *capable.* Probably 'comprehensive', 'embracing'. Near perhaps to 'capacious'.

467   *by . . . heaven.* To appreciate Othello's 'chaos' and 'damnation' we must realize he is calling on heaven, not hell, to sanction his revenge. A 'sacrament of evil' Granville-Barker calls it, (*op. cit.*, p. 66).   *marble.* Probably suggesting a firm, enduring quality.   (Cf. *Antony and Cleopatra*, Act 5 Sc. 2, l. 240.)

468   *In . . . reverence*, in the reverential manner appropriate to.

471   *elements.* Possibly here the sky and its phenomena.   *clip*, enclose, surround.

473   *execution*, exercise, activity.   *wit*, intelligence.

475   *remorse.* See note on l. 374. Perhaps Iago is saying that his compassion ('remorse') will be for Othello (and therefore displayed in obeying him) and not for the victims of the 'bloody work'.

476   *soever.* Linked with the previous 'What'.

477   *Not . . . bounteous.* The thought seems to be that acceptance of Iago's offer is better than many words of thanks. The meaning of 'bounteous' (full?) must be something to stress 'acceptance' against 'vain thanks'.

478   *put thee to't*, put you to the test (of your love and offer).

481   *But . . . live.* 'Iago knows the surest way to secure that she shall not live is to suggest that she shall' (M. R. Ridley, *Arden* ed., p. 123 note).

485   *fair devil.* See note on l. 467 above. In Othello's 'damnation', his inversion of values, the 'divine' Desdemona has now become her opposite, a 'fair devil'.

486   *I . . . ever.* Sinister words, with much significant undertone and implication.

IAGO Pray be content.

OTHELLO O, blood, Iago, blood!

IAGO Patience, I say. Your mind perhaps may change.

OTHELLO Never, Iago. Like to the Pontic sea,   460
  Whose icy current and compulsive course
  Ne'er feels retiring ebb, but keeps due on
  To the Propontic and the Hellespont,
  Even so my bloody thoughts with violent pace
  Shall ne'er look back, ne'er ebb to humble love,   465
  Till that a capable and wide revenge
  Swallow them up. [*He kneels*] Now, by yond marble heaven,
  In the due reverence of a sacred vow
  I here engage my words.

IAGO   Do not rise yet. [*He kneels*]
  Witness you ever-burning lights above,   470
  You elements that clip us round about,
  Witness that here Iago doth give up
  The execution of his wit, hands, heart,
  To wronged Othello's service. Let him command,
  And to obey shall be in me remorse,   475
  What bloody work soever. [*They rise*]

OTHELLO   I greet thy love,
  Not with vain thanks, but with acceptance bounteous,
  And will upon the instant put thee to't.
  Within these three days let me hear thee say
  That Cassio's not alive.

IAGO   My friend is dead;   480
  'Tis done as you request. But let her live.

OTHELLO Damn her, lewd minx! O, damn her, damn her!
  Come go with me apart. I will withdraw
  To furnish me with some swift means of death
  For the fair devil. Now art thou my lieutenant.   485

IAGO I am your own for ever.   [*Exeunt*

Quite rightly this scene has not the continuous, acute tension of the last. It begins with a brief exchange between Desdemona and the Clown—a welcome moment of relief even if the humour is insipid; and there are periods of relative quietness, but charged, ominous quietness, as notably when Othello relates the magical history of the lost handkerchief. However, the scene contains passages of great dramatic intensity too, particularly when Desdemona's persistent, ill-timed plea for Cassio clashes with Othello's urgent demand for the handkerchief.

1–16   *Do . . . it.* This is feeble stuff, though it offers some relief in tension.

1   *lieutenant.* Ironic, with the penultimate line of the last scene still echoing in our ears.

6   *where I lie,* i.e. because I don't know.

9   *lie . . . throat.* To 'lie in the throat' was a common Elizabethan expression for infamous lying.

10   *edified,* instructed. Desdemona is probably guying the Clown's affected speech.

14   *moved,* appealed to.

15   *compass,* scope.

20   *crusadoes.* Portuguese coins marked with a cross.

24–5   *I . . . him.* Though Desdemona's knowledge of Othello may be limited, these words are to be noted. They support the belief that Othello is not 'jealous' in the chief modern sense, particularly as Desdemona speaks of 'humours', which to the Elizabethans meant basic qualities of temperament. At the very least Desdemona is asserting that Othello is not suspicious or mistrustful of her behaviour.

26–7   *I . . . him.* The Quarto reads, with a different sense:
    I will not leave him now. Let Cassio
    Be called to him.

Scene Four

Cyprus · The garden of the citadel

Enter DESDEMONA · EMILIA · *and* CLOWN

DESDEMONA Do you know, sirrah, where the lieutenant Cassio lies?

CLOWN I dare not say he lies anywhere.

DESDEMONA Why, man?

CLOWN He's a soldier, and for one to say a soldier lies is stabbing.

DESDEMONA Go to! Where lodges he?   5

CLOWN To tell you where he lodges is to tell you where I lie.

DESDEMONA Can anything be made of this?

CLOWN I know not where he lodges, and for me to devise a lodging
and say he lies here or he lies there were to lie in mine own throat.

DESDEMONA Can you inquire him out and be edified by report?   10

CLOWN I will catechize the world for him, that is, make questions,
and by them answer.

DESDEMONA Seek him; bid him come hither. Tell him I have
moved my lord on his behalf and hope all will be well.

CLOWN To do this is within the compass of man's wit, and therefore   15
I will attempt the doing of it.   [*Exit*

DESDEMONA Where should I lose that handkerchief, Emilia?

EMILIA I know not, madam.

DESDEMONA Believe me I had rather lose my purse
Full of crusadoes; and but my noble Moor   20
Is true of mind and made of no such baseness
As jealous creatures are, it were enough
To put him to ill thinking.

EMILIA   Is he not jealous?

DESDEMONA Who, he? I think the sun where he was born
Drew all such humours from him.

Enter OTHELLO

EMILIA   Look where he comes.   25

DESDEMONA I will not leave him now till Cassio
Be called to him. How is it with you, my lord?

28   *How . . . lord?* Desdemona is probably referring to the earlier
      mentioned headache.   *my good lady.* Note the formal
      address.

29   *Well . . . lord.* An innocently mocking repetition of Othello's
      first words.

30   *moist.* A hot, moist palm was thought to signify lustfulness.

31   *It . . . sorrow.* This line has a simple ringing pathos.

32   *fruitfulness, liberal.* Both these words mean 'generosity', 'liberal-
      ity', etc., but they can also denote sexual looseness.

34   *sequester,* sequestration, removal.

35   *castigation.* In this context of devotional exercises Othello may
      mean self-flagellation.

36   *devil.* Note the word.

37-8 *'Tis . . . one.* Ironical. Othello is of course not contradicting
      himself. 'frank' can have much the same meaning as 'liberal'
      in l.32, but it could also signify 'undisguised', 'revealing'.

41-2 *The . . . hearts.* A difficult passage. The general meaning might
      be that whereas in the old days 'heart' and 'hand' (outward
      appearances, manner, etc.) went together, today they do not.
      This in some sense would contradict Othello's belief that he
      has found truth in Desdemona's moist hand, but this shift of
      fancy would not be impossible. From 'heraldry' many com-
      mentators see a reference to the coat of arms, with a hand, de-
      signed for the new order of baronetage created by James in
      1612.

44   *chuck.* A common Elizabethan term of endearment.

46   *I . . . me.* The 'salt rheum' was a running cold; 'sullen' probably
      means 'obstinate'. (The Folio reads 'sorry' for 'sullen'.)

53-73 *That . . . hearts.* Whatever jokes may be made about the famous
      handkerchief of *Othello,* at least Shakespeare has given it a
      great imaginative significance.

55   *charmer,* enchantress.

57   *amiable,* loveable, desirable.

60   *spirits.* Probably 'feelings', 'sentiments'.

61   *fancies,* loves.

62   *when . . . wive,* when it was my fate to take a wife.

OTHELLO   Well, my good lady. [*aside*] O, hardness to dissemble!
  How do you, Desdemona?

DESDEMONA   Well, my good lord.

OTHELLO   Give me your hand. This hand is moist, my lady.   30

DESDEMONA   It yet has felt no age nor known no sorrow.

OTHELLO   This argues fruitfulness and liberal heart.
  Hot, hot and moist. This hand of yours requires
  A sequester from liberty, fasting and praying,
  Much castigation, exercise devout;   35
  For there's a young and sweating devil here
  That commonly rebels. 'Tis a good hand,
  A frank one.

DESDEMONA   You may, indeed, say so,
  For 'twas that hand that gave away my heart.   40

OTHELLO   A liberal hand! The hearts of old gave hands;
  But our new heraldry is hands, not hearts.

DESDEMONA   I cannot speak of this. Come now, your promise.

OTHELLO   What promise, chuck?

DESDEMONA   I have sent to bid Cassio come speak with you.   45

OTHELLO   I have a salt and sullen rheum offends me.
  Lend me thy handkerchief.

DESDEMONA   Here, my lord.

OTHELLO   That which I gave you.

DESDEMONA   I have it not about me.   50

OTHELLO   Not?

DESDEMONA   No, faith, my lord.

OTHELLO   This is a fault. That handkerchief
  Did an Egyptian to my mother give.
  She was a charmer and could almost read   55
  The thoughts of people. She told her, while she kept it,
  'Twould make her amiable and subdue my father
  Entirely to her love, but if she lost it
  Or made a gift of it, my father's eye
  Should hold her loathed and his spirits should hunt   60
  After new fancies. She, dying, gave it me,
  And bid me, when my fate would have me wive,
  To give it her. I did so. And take heed on't;

64   *darling*, Cf. Act1 Sc.2, l.68 and note.

65   *perdition*, damnation. See also Act3 Sc.3, l.90 for this charged, theological word.

67   *web*, woven fabric.

68   *sibyl*, prophetess.

68–9   *that . . . compasses*, i.e. the sibyl was two hundred years old.

70   *fury*, inspiration, especially of a frenzied kind. This 'fury' or 'furor' was a word often applied to poets.

71   *hallowed*, sacred, holy.

72   *mummy*. A substance from mummies used in medicine and magic.

72–3   *which . . . hearts*. There is some difficulty here, especially with the difference between the Quarto and the Folio text (printed opposite).   *Conserved of*, made a preservative from.

75   *Then . . . it!* The Desdemona who, during the courtship, had listened with such rapt attention to the wonders of Othello's life would still speak this line with simple, fearful intensity.

76   *Ha! Wherefore?* For the next few moments the scene is given great intensity by the short swift interchange between Othello and Desdemona, Othello's demand for the handkerchief being counterpointed against Desdemona's ill-timed insistence that he should see Cassio.

77   *startingly*. Probably 'in fits and starts'.   *rash*. Probably 'urgently' or 'intensely'.

81   *It . . . lost*. This is of course an untruth but to most of us excusable in the circumstances.   *an if*, if (the common, duplicated conditional conjunction).

89   *sufficient*, suitable for his office.

90   *talk*, talk to.

Make it a darling like your precious eye.
To lose or give't away were such perdition   65
As nothing else could match.

DESDEMONA   Is't possible?

OTHELLO 'Tis true; there's magic in the web of it.
A sibyl, that had numbered in the world
The sun to make two hundred compasses,
In her prophetic fury sewed the work.   70
The worms were hallowed that did breed the silk,
And it was dyed in mummy, which the skilful
Conserved of maidens' hearts.

DESDEMONA   I' faith, is't true?

OTHELLO Most veritable. Therefore look to't well.

DESDEMONA Then would to God that I had never seen it!   75

OTHELLO Ha! Wherefore?

DESDEMONA Why do you speak so startlingly and rash?

OTHELLO Is't lost? is't gone? Speak. Is't out o' the way?

DESDEMONA Heaven bless us!

OTHELLO Say you?   80

DESDEMONA It is not lost; but what an if it were?

OTHELLO Ha!

DESDEMONA I say it is not lost.

OTHELLO   Fetch it, let me see it.

DESDEMONA Why, so I can, sir, but I will not now.
This is a trick to put me from my suit.   85
Pray you let Cassio be received again.

OTHELLO Fetch me that handkerchief. My mind misgives.

DESDEMONA Come, come:
You'll never meet a more sufficient man.

OTHELLO The handkerchief!

DESDEMONA   I pray, talk me of Cassio—   90

OTHELLO The handkerchief!

DESDEMONA   a man that all his time
Hath founded his good fortunes on your love,
Shared dangers with you—

OTHELLO The handkerchief!

98   *Sure . . . handkerchief.* Spoken, no doubt, much in the tone of l.75—an artless, awed, rather numbed wonder. This line and the next completely give the lie to Iago's attempt to identify Desdemona with the sophisticated ladies of Venice.

100   *'Tis . . . two,* we don't require so much as a year or two, i.e. men show their natures rapidly.

101   *They . . . food.* The first 'all' goes with 'they', the second with 'we'.   *but,* only, merely.

102   *hungerly,* hungrily.

105   *happiness.* Probably in the sense of 'good fortune', i.e. 'here is Desdemona'.

109   *Exist.* Probably signifying 'really live'.

110   *duty.* The Folio prints 'office' (service).

112   *mortal,* deadly, fatal. Cf. Act3 Sc.3, l.360.

114   *Nor . . . futurity,* nor the estimation, or recompense ('merit'), that I intend to deserve in the future.

116   *But . . . benefit,* only to know this must (or would be) a gain, something to my good.

117–19   *So . . . alms.* A tricky, and possibly tautologous, passage 'Content' may mean 'contentment', or it may mean 'that which contains' and so, in the sense of 'dress', carry on the 'clothe' metaphor. In either case Cassio seems to be stressing here the compulsion ('forced') behind a new way of life. In the following line and a half he is emphasizing the comparative limitations of this new life. He would have to rely on Fortune for any blessings; and the implication is probably that these would be less than he would have received from Othello.

120   *advocation,* advocacy.

122   *favour,* appearance.   *humour,* mood, disposition.

123   *So . . . sanctified.* Notice the terms of Desdemona's supplication.

124   *As,* inasmuch as.

125   *blank,* target centre.

126   *free,* frank, outspoken.

DESDEMONA   I'faith you are to blame.

OTHELLO Zounds!   [*Exit* 95

EMILIA Is not this man jealous?

DESDEMONA I ne'er saw this before.
   Sure, there's some wonder in this handkerchief.
   I am most unhappy in the loss of it.

EMILIA 'Tis not a year or two shows us a man.   100
   They are all but stomachs, and we all but food;
   They eat us hungerly, and when they are full,
   They belch us.

Enter IAGO *and* CASSIO

               Look you, Cassio and my husband.

IAGO There is no other way; 'tis she must do it.
   And lo, the happiness! Go, and importune her.   105

DESDEMONA How now, good Cassio! What's the news with you?

CASSIO Madam, my former suit. I do beseech you
   That by your virtuous means I may again
   Exist and be a member of his love,
   Whom I with all the duty of my heart   110
   Entirely honour. I would not be delayed.
   If my offence be of such mortal kind
   That neither service past, nor present sorrows,
   Nor purposed merit in futurity,
   Can ransom me into his love again,   115
   But to know so must be my benefit.
   So shall I clothe me in a forced content,
   And shut myself up in some other course
   To fortune's alms.

DESDEMONA   Alas, thrice-gentle Cassio,
   My advocation is not now in tune.   120
   My lord is not my lord, nor should I know him,
   Were he in favour as in humour altered.
   So help me every spirit sanctified
   As I have spoken for you all my best
   And stood within the blank of his displeasure   125
   For my free speech! You must awhile be patient.
   What I can do, I will; and more I will

131–6   *Can ... angry.* Important evidence, even from Iago, of Othello's normal control over his emotions.

134   *brother . . . angry?* There may be some corruption here. As printed opposite, the unfinished construction ending with 'brother' includes the understood 'yet in these circumstances he was not angry'.

135   *moment,* consequence.

138   *unhatched practice,* undisclosed (or undeveloped) plot.

140   *puddled,* muddied.

140–5   *in . . . pain.* Not an easy passage. What Desdemona appears to be saying is that though in state affairs or plots Othello's real concern will be with 'great ones', in the usual human way his attitude (of grievance, anger, etc.) will spread to his treatment of inferiors. She draws the parallel of a finger-ache that spreads to the whole body.

141   *things.* This word, though usually employed contemptuously, can refer to human beings.

144   *indues.* Possibly in the sense of 'imbues with' or 'infects with'. But the following preposition 'to' creates difficulties, and there may be text corruption. 'Subdues' would be a tempting emendation.

147   *observances,* loving attentions.

148   *bridal,* wedding.   *Beshrew me.* A mild oath: 'devil take me'.

149   *unhandsome,* unfitting, inadequate.   *warrior.* Perhaps an echo of Act2Sc.1, l.176.

150   *Arraigning,* accusing, charging.   *unkindness,* lack of proper human feeling.   *with my soul.* This might mean that Desdemona's accusation of Othello was (at first) deeply felt.

151   *suborned,* caused to give false evidence.   *witness,* i.e. Desdemona herself.

154   *conception,* notion, fancy.   *jealous toy,* trifling suspicion.

157–60   *But . . . itself.* Emilia is arguing that 'jealousy' is self-generated: it has no rational cause. Compare Act3Sc.3, ll.169–71.

Than for myself I dare. Let that suffice you.

IAGO   Is my lord angry?

EMILIA   He went hence but now
  And certainly in strange unquietness.   130

IAGO   Can he be angry? I have seen the cannon
  When it hath blown his ranks into the air,
  And like the devil from his very arm
  Puffed his own brother—and can he be angry?
  Something of moment then. I will go meet him.   135
  There's matter in't indeed if he be angry.

DESDEMONA   I prithee do so.   [*Exit* IAGO
                Something, sure, of state,
  Either from Venice, or some unhatched practice
  Made demonstrable here in Cyprus to him,
  Hath puddled his clear spirit; and in such cases   140
  Men's natures wrangle with inferior things,
  Though great ones are their object.
  'Tis even so, for let our finger ache,
  And it indues our other healthful members
  Even to that sense of pain. Nay, we must think   145
  Men are not gods,
  Nor of them look for such observances
  As fits the bridal. Beshrew me much, Emilia,
  I was (unhandsome warrior as I am)
  Arraigning his unkindness with my soul;   150
  But now I find I had suborned the witness
  And he's indicted falsely.

EMILIA   Pray heaven it be state matters, as you think,
  And no conception nor no jealous toy
  Concerning you.   155

DESDEMONA   Alas the day, I never gave him cause.

EMILIA   But jealous souls will not be answered so;
  They are not ever jealous for the cause,
  But jealous for they are jealous. 'Tis a monster
  Begot upon itself, born on itself.   160

DESDEMONA   Heaven keep that monster from Othello's mind!

EMILIA   Lady, amen.

DESDEMONA   I will go seek him. Cassio, walk hereabout.

164   *move*, plead, press.

167   *Save*, God save.   *What . . . home?* What are you doing away
          from your house?

172   *Eight . . . hours?* 168 hours = 7 days and nights: an exact calcu-
          lation!

173   *dial*, clock, watch.

175   *I . . . pressed.* This might be coloured by a reference to the
          punishment in felony charges of being pressed to possible
          death (*la peine forte et dure*). Shakespeare has several allusions in
          his plays to this punishment, and such a reference here would
          be most apt for Cassio's state.

176   *convenient*, fitting, suitable. The Folio has 'continuate' (unin-
          terrupted, leisurely).

177   *score*, the reckoning of a bill to be paid. Cassio may be punning
          on Bianca's previous use of the word.

178   *Take . . . out*, make me a copy of this embroidery. That Cassio
          should decide to hand the handkerchief over to Bianca is
          another stroke of luck for Iago.   *O . . . this?* To some extent
          this jealous tiff between Cassio and Bianca over the hand-
          kerchief forms a comic and ironic parallel with what has
          happened in the main action of the play.

180   *To . . . cause.* I felt your absence; now I feel the cause of it.

181–4   *Go . . . remembrance.* Note the echo of the 'jealousy' theme.

186   *I . . . chamber.* Iago has carried out the plot announced in
          Act 3 Sc.3, l.325.

192   *addition.* Usually means 'title', but here possibly something
          like 'credit', 'testimonial'.

193   *womaned*, with a woman hanging on. Cassio's blunt term is
          appropriate to Bianca, but he tries to soften it with his next
          remark.

If I do find him fit, I'll move your suit
And seek to effect it to my uttermost.   165

CASSIO I humbly thank your ladyship.

[*Exeunt* DESDEMONA *and* EMILIA

Enter BIANCA

BIANCA Save you, friend Cassio.

CASSIO   What makes you from home?
How is it with you, my most fair Bianca?
I'faith, sweet love, I was coming to your house.

BIANCA And I was going to your lodging, Cassio.   170
What, keep a week away? seven days and nights?
Eight score eight hours? And lovers' absent hours
More tedious than the dial eight score times!
O weary reckoning!

CASSIO   Pardon me, Bianca.
I have this while with leaden thoughts been pressed,   175
But I shall in a more convenient time
Strike off this score of absence. Sweet Bianca,
Take me this work out. [*He gives her Desdemona's handkerchief*]

BIANCA   O Cassio, whence came this?
This is some token from a newer friend.
To the felt absence now I feel a cause.   180
Is't come to this? Well, well.

CASSIO   Go to, woman!
Throw your vile guesses in the devil's teeth
From whence you have them. You are jealous now
That this is from some mistress, some remembrance.
No, by my faith, Bianca.

BIANCA   Why, whose is it?   185

CASSIO I know not, sweet. I found it in my chamber.
i like the work well. Ere it be demanded
(As like enough it will) I'd have it copied.
Take it and do't, and leave me for this time.

BIANCA Leave you? Wherefore?   190

CASSIO I do attend here on the General,
And think it no addition, nor my wish,
To have him see me womaned.

199   *be circumstanced*, yield to circumstances, put up with it.

BIANCA   Why, I pray you?

CASSIO   Not that I love you not.

BIANCA   But that you do not love me.
   I pray you, bring me on the way a little,   195
   And say if I shall see you soon at night.

CASSIO   'Tis but a little way that I can bring you,
   For I attend here; but I'll see you soon.

BIANCA   'Tis very good. I must be circumstanced.   [*Exeunt*

This is another scene full of dramatic incident as Iago, determined for his own safety to get Desdemona out of the way, pours more of his 'medicine' into Othello. The effect is that Othello now decides to kill Desdemona. But more important than this advance of the plot is the horrifying spectacle of the heroic Othello's complete degradation: his foaming, physical collapse at the feet of the exultant Iago, his grotesquely undignified eavesdropping on Cassio, and his striking of Desdemona. 'The distinctive feature of the destructive process in *Othello* is its ugliness, for what the hero is subjected to is a deliberate and calculated degradation such as no other of Shakespeare's tragic heroes undergoes' (G. R. Hibbard, *Othello* and Shakespearian Tragedy, *Shakespeare Survey*, 21).

1   *Will . . . so?* Again, as in Act 1 Sc. 1, the illusion of a conversation in progress.   *Think so, Iago?* Bradley comments: 'when Othello reappears we see . . . that he is a changed man. He is physically exhausted, and his mind is dazed. He sees everything blurred through a mist of blood and tears' (*op. cit.*, p. 196).

3–4   *Or . . . harm.* Iago is enflaming Othello with vivid pictures of Desdemona's adultery.

6   *It . . . devil.* Probably Dr. Johnson's interpretation is correct. Such behaviour would be an hypocrisy in that the devil would be cheated by false hopes of a sin that was never in fact committed.

8   *they tempt heaven.* Either, such lovers run the risk of heaven's punishment; or, they will test heaven's mercy and forgiveness to the limits.

9   *So,* provided that.

16   *essence,* entity.

17   *They . . . not.* Possibly the meaning is that because honour is an invisible entity one can easily get away with a pretence to it. It cannot be tangibly tested or proved.

19–22 *By . . . handkerchief.* This suggests Othello had almost forgotten the story of the handkerchief.

21–2 *raven . . . all.* The raven was thought not only to bode death but to spread plague infection.

Act Four · Scene One

Cyprus · Before the citadel

Enter OTHELLO *and* IAGO

IAGO   Will you think so?

OTHELLO   Think so, Iago?

IAGO   What!
  To kiss in private?

OTHELLO   An unauthorized kiss.

IAGO   Or to be naked with her friend in bed
  An hour or more, not meaning any harm?

OTHELLO   Naked in bed, Iago, and not mean harm?   5
  It is hypocrisy against the devil.
  They that mean virtuously and yet do so,
  The devil their virtue tempts and they tempt heaven.

IAGO   So they do nothing, 'tis a venial slip.
  But if I give my wife a handkerchief—   10

OTHELLO   What then?

IAGO   Why, then, 'tis hers, my lord, and being hers,
  She may, I think, bestow't on any man.

OTHELLO   She is protectress of her honour too.
  May she give that?   15

IAGO   Her honour is an essence that's not seen;
  They have it very oft that have it not.
  But for the handkerchief—

OTHELLO   By heaven, I would most gladly have forgot it!
  Thou said'st (O, it comes o'er my memory   20
  As doth the raven o'er the infected house,
  Boding to all) he had my handkerchief.

IAGO   Ay, what of that?

OTHELLO   That's not so good now.

25-9   *as . . . blab.* The general sense is that knaves cannot help freely talking about the conquests they have achieved either through their own urgent persuasion or through the yielding nature of the woman concerned.   *abroad,* about, in the world. *dotage,* doting, foolish affection.   *Convinced or supplied,* conquered or satisfied their sexual desires.

36-7   *We . . . her.* In his distraction Othello is bitterly playing with a more acceptable meaning of 'lie on her', i.e. 'belie', tell lies about, calumniate. How ironically near to the truth he is at this instant!

37   *fulsome.* Either 'foul', 'filthy', 'sickening', or 'lustful', 'rank'.

38-43   *To . . . devil!* These lines are not in the Quarto.

39   *First . . . confess!* Probably intended to express Othello's utter disorder of mind.

40-1   *Nature . . . instruction.* If this sentence is intended to make sense, its difficulty centres on 'shadowing' and on the 'instruction' that produces the passion. If we take 'shadowing' to mean 'darkening' or 'overshadowing', we might gloss 'instruction' as 'reliable information', in antithesis to 'words' (mere reports?) in the next sentence. But the antithesis to 'words' might be 'shadowing' in the possible sense of 'calling forth images'. This second alternative would still leave 'instruction' unexplained.

41   *shakes.* 'words' (e.g. in the sense of 'report') is to be taken as a singular.

42   *Noses . . . lips!* Probably a reference to the love-making, but possibly the thought of mutilation punishment. See ll.142-4 later.

43   *devil!* Note this last word. Othello means it for the 'divine' Desdemona, but for the audience it ironically includes Iago. Here is a concentrated representation of Othello's mistake.

47   *reproach,* shame, degradation

48   (*stage direction*). That Cassio enters when Othello is unconscious is yet another stroke of luck for Iago.

51   *second fit.* Possibly an Iago lie.

53   *lethargy,* coma.

IAGO   What if I had said I had seen him do you wrong,
    Or heard him say—as knaves be such abroad,   25
    Who having by their own importunate suit
    Or voluntary dotage of some mistress
    Convinced or supplied them, cannot choose
    But they must blab—

OTHELLO   Hath he said anything?

IAGO   He hath, my lord, but be you well assured,   30
    No more than he'll unswear.

OTHELLO   What hath he said?

IAGO   Faith, that he did—I know not what he did.

OTHELLO   What? what?

IAGO   Lie—

OTHELLO   With her?

IAGO   With her, on her, what you will.   35

OTHELLO   Lie with her? Lie on her? We say lie on her when they
belie her. Lie with her! Zounds, that's fulsome! Handkerchief...
confessions . . . handkerchief! To confess and be hanged for his
labour. First to be hanged and then to confess! I tremble at it.
Nature would not invest herself in such shadowing passion   40
without some instruction. It is not words that shakes me thus!
Pish! Noses, ears, and lips! Is't possible? . . . Confess? . . . Handkerchief! . . . O devil! [He falls in a fit]

IAGO   Work on,
    My medicine, work! Thus credulous fools are caught,   45
    And many worthy and chaste dames even thus,
    All guiltless, meet reproach. What ho, my lord!
    My lord, I say! Othello!

Enter CASSIO

                How now, Cassio!

CASSIO   What's the matter?

IAGO   My lord is fallen into an epilepsy.   50
    This is his second fit; he had one yesterday.

CASSIO   Rub him about the temples.

IAGO   No, forbear.
    The lethargy must have his quiet course.

58   *on great occasion*, on a matter of importance. For the moment
       Iago wants Cassio out of the way, but he requires him back
       soon, as he has presumably—on the instant—thought of the
       next scheme that he is to unfold in ll.78–81. Shakespeare's
       joinery is distinctly crude here.

60   *mock.* Othello takes Iago's last words as a reference to the
       cuckhold's horns joke.

64   *civil*, citizen.

65   *Did . . . it?* Othello is of course returning to their earlier con-
       versation: he has had no awareness of Cassio's visit.

66   *yoked*, married, or 'hitched', as we say. Presumably a picture
       of oxen pulling the plough, etc.

67   *May . . . you*, i.e. are likely to be in your state, cuckholds,
       horned beasts under a yoke.

68   *unproper*, not their own exclusively, shared with other lovers of
       their wives.

69   *peculiar*, entirely their own.   *Your . . . better*, i.e. because you
       know you have been cuckolded.

71   *lip*, kiss.   *secure*, free from concern (possibly, suspicion).

73   *And . . . be.* This probably means: 'knowing I'm a cuckold, I
       know what she is, a whore; and I know what to do with her'.
       He is attempting to project from himself, as it were, a desired
       attitude into Othello. Othello has become his puppet.

75   *patient list*, bounds of patience.

79   *'scuse*, excuse.   *ecstasy.* Probably synonymous with 'mad' in
       l.76.

81   *encave*, conceal. An unusual word, unless in reference to the
       curtained back-stage.

82   *fleers*, sneers or contemptuous grins.   *notable*, discernible,
       obvious.

86   *cope*, copulate with.

87   *Marry, patience!* A merciless stroke this: to urge patience after
       what he has just been saying.   *Marry*, by the Virgin Mary.

88   *all in all*, utterly, in all respects.   *spleen.* The Elizabethans
       regarded the physical spleen as the source of various psycho-
       logical conditions. They believed, among other things, that
       it produced excited or violent outbursts of different kinds. A
       possible paraphrase of Iago's words might be: 'utterly carried
       away by your raging passion'.

If not, he foams at mouth, and by and by
Breaks out to savage madness. Look, he stirs.   55
Do you withdraw yourself a little while.
He will recover straight. When he is gone,
I would on great occasion speak with you.   [*Exit* CASSIO
How is it, General? Have you not hurt your head?

OTHELLO   Dost thou mock me?

IAGO   I mock you? No, by heaven!   60
Would you would bear your fortune like a man!

OTHELLO   A horned man's a monster and a beast.

IAGO   There's many a beast then in a populous city,
And many a civil monster.

OTHELLO   Did he confess it?

IAGO   Good sir, be a man.   65
Think every bearded fellow that's but yoked
May draw with you. There's millions now alive
That nightly lie in those unproper beds
Which they dare swear peculiar. Your case is better.
O, 'tis the spite of hell, the fiend's arch-mock,   70
To lip a wanton in a secure couch,
And to suppose her chaste! No, let me know;
And knowing what I am, I know what she shall be.

OTHELLO   O, thou art wise, 'tis certain.

IAGO   Stand you awhile apart;
Confine yourself but in a patient list.   75
Whilst you were here erewhile, mad with your grief
(A passion most unsuiting such a man)
Cassio came hither. I shifted him away
And laid good 'scuse upon your ecstasy,
Bade him anon return and here speak with me,   80
The which he promised. Do but encave yourself,
And mark the fleers, the gibes and notable scorns
That dwell in every region of his face,
For I will make him tell the tale anew,
Where, how, how oft, how long ago and when   85
He hath and is again to cope your wife.
I say, but mark his gesture. Marry, patience!
Or I shall say you're all in all in spleen

90–1   *I . . . bloody.* Othello is speaking of an impossible tension—
         between patience and his bloody thoughts.

92   *keep time,* be controlled. The expression is probably from music.
         will you withdraw? In the somewhat grotesque eavesdropping
         episode that follows Othello sinks to his lowest degradation.
         He comes dangerously close to a comic figure.

94   *housewife,* hussy.   *selling her desires.* Probably something like:
         'turning her sexual appetite to profitable account'.

101   *unbookish,* ignorant, inexperienced.   *conster,* construe. The
         background image is of a poor scholar grossly mistranslating.

104   *addition,* title, rank (i.e. of lieutenant).

107–8   *Now . . . speed!* Is this shift to Bianca a little clumsily managed
         by Shakespeare?

108   *caitiff,* wretch.

112   *faintly,* lightly, hardly at all.

115   *said.* Probably 'done', as in Act2Sc.1, l.165.

119   *Roman.* This would appear to make no sense except in asso-
         ciation with 'triumph'. No one has yet suggested a satisfac-
         tory explanation of 'Roman' by itself.

And nothing of a man.

OTHELLO   Dost thou hear, Iago?
  I will be found most cunning in my patience,   90
  But (dost thou hear?) most bloody.

IAGO   That's not amiss,
  But yet keep time in all. Will you withdraw? [OTHELLO *conceals himself*]
  Now will I question Cassio of Bianca,
  A housewife that by selling her desires
  Buys herself bread and clothes. It is a creature   95
  That dotes on Cassio—as 'tis the strumpet's plague
  To beguile many and be beguiled by one.
  He, when he hears of her, cannot refrain
  From the excess of laughter. Here he comes.

Re-enter CASSIO

  As he shall smile, Othello shall go mad,   100
  And his unbookish jealousy must conster
  Poor Cassio's smiles, gestures and light behaviour
  Quite in the wrong. How do you now, lieutenant?

CASSIO   The worser that you give me the addition
  Whose want even kills me.   105

IAGO   Ply Desdemona well and you are sure on't.
  [*speaking lower*] Now if this suit lay in Bianca's power,
  How quickly should you speed!

CASSIO   Alas, poor caitiff!

OTHELLO   [*aside*] Look, how he laughs already!

IAGO   I never knew a woman love man so.   110

CASSIO   Alas, poor rogue! I think i'faith she loves me.

OTHELLO [*aside*] Now he denies it faintly and laughs it out.

IAGO   Do you hear, Cassio?

OTHELLO [*aside*] Now he importunes him
  To tell it o'er . . . Go to, well said, well said!   115

IAGO   She gives it out that you shall marry her.
  Do you intend it?

CASSIO   Ha, ha, ha!

OTHELLO [*aside*] Do you triumph, Roman? Do you triumph?

120 *customer*, prostitute.

120–1 *Prithee . . . wit*, pray, have some respect for my intelligence (or judgment)—'I'm not all that stupid'.

121 *it*, i.e. my wit.

122 *They . . . win*, i.e. Cassio's triumphant laugh proves that he has had a conquest over Desdemona.

123 *cry*, rumour.

126 *scored*. Possibly 'branded'; otherwise 'wounded'.

128 *flattery*, self-flattery.

129 *beckons*, signals to (not summons).

131 *sea-bank*, sea-shore; possibly here, promenade.

132 *bauble*, plaything—a bit of stuff, as we might say.

134 *imports*, indicates, implies.

139 *but . . . to!* i.e. the revenge of cutting off Cassio's nose has still to come.

140 (*stage direction*). More good luck for Iago with the arrival of Bianca and the handkerchief.

141 *Before me!* An exclamatory oath: 'Upon my soul!'

142 *'Tis . . . one!* The 'fitchew' (pole-cat) was associated with lust-fulness and smell. Possibly 'such another' means that Bianca is really a pole-cat, though her perfume disguises the fact a little.

146 *piece of work*. Possibly means 'thing', with a punning shift of meaning from the previous 'work'. Compare 'What a piece of work is a man!' (*Hamlet*, Act 2 Sc. 2, ll. 290–1).

149 *hobby-horse*, whore.

153–4 *If . . . for*. Is this a provocative way of saying 'when *I* am ready'?

CASSIO I marry her! What, a customer! Prithee bear some charity to 120
my wit. Do not think it so unwholesome. Ha, ha, ha!

OTHELLO [*aside*] So, so, so, so. They laugh that win.

IAGO Faith, the cry goes that you shall marry her.

CASSIO Prithee, say true.

IAGO I am a very villain else.   125

OTHELLO [*aside*] Have you scored me? Well.

CASSIO This is the monkey's own giving out. She is persuaded I will
marry her out of her own love and flattery, not out of my promise.

OTHELLO [*aside*] Iago beckons me. Now he begins the story.

CASSIO She was here even now. She haunts me in every place. I 130
was the other day talking on the sea-bank with certain Venetians,
and thither comes this bauble. By this hand, she falls thus about
my neck—

OTHELLO [*aside*] Crying 'O dear Cassio!' as it were. His gesture imports
it.   135

CASSIO So hangs and lolls and weeps upon me, so hales and pulls
me. Ha, ha, ha!

OTHELLO [*aside*] Now he tells how she plucked him to my chamber.
O, I see that nose of yours, but not that dog I shall throw it to!

CASSIO Well, I must leave her company.   140

Enter BIANCA

IAGO Before me! Look where she comes.

CASSIO 'Tis such another fitchew! Marry, a perfumed one! What
do you mean by this haunting of me?

BIANCA Let the devil and his dam haunt you! What did you mean
by that same handkerchief you gave me even now? I was a fine 145
fool to take it. I must take out the work! A likely piece of work,
that you should find it in your chamber and not know who left it
there! This is some minx's token—and I must take out the work!
There, give it your hobby-horse, wheresoever you had it. I'll
take out no work on't.   150

CASSIO How now, my sweet Bianca! How now, how now!

OTHELLO [*aside*] By heaven, that should be my handkerchief!

BIANCA If you'll come to supper tonight, you may. If you will not,
come when you are next prepared for.   [*Exit*

159   *would . . . speak,* would be very glad (or pleased) to speak.

164   *vice,* sinful act.

170–1   *A fine . . . woman!* From here till the entry of Ludovico the
           struggle between Othello's sense of revenge and outrage and
           his surviving love for Desdemona is very marked. He is not
           speaking ironically, as is proved by Iago's next words.

173   *damned.* Note this word and its strong theological meaning in
           Shakespeare's time.

178–80   *so . . . invention.* An epitome of all the admired womanly graces
           at the time.

179   *O . . . sing.* A prelude to the 'Willow' song of the next scene.
           savageness . . . bear. Shakespeare has several references to the
           belief in the power of music to charm and tame wild animals,
           e.g. *The Merchant of Venice,* Act5Sc.1,ll.70–8. There is no very
           evident reason, however, why 'bear' is particularly chosen
           here.   *high,* excellent; or possibly, highly developed.

180   *wit,* general mental liveliness; or perhaps, the ability to say
           clever, amusing things.   *invention,* fancy.

182   *so . . . condition,* so much the gentlewoman.

184   *gentle.* Iago twists the word to its other meanings of 'pleasant',
           'pliant', etc.

185–6   *But . . . Iago!* Some especially poignant lines.

187   *fond,* foolishly infatuated.   *patent,* licensed permission.

188   *touches.* Probably in the sense of 'wounds', 'injures', rather than
           of the neutral 'concerns'.

189   *messes,* portions of meat.

IAGO After her, after her!   155

CASSIO Faith, I must. She'll rail in the street else.

IAGO Will you sup there?

CASSIO Faith, I intend so.

IAGO Well, I may chance to see you, for I would very fain speak
    with you.   160

CASSIO Prithee come, will you?

IAGO Go to. Say no more.   [*Exit* CASSIO

OTHELLO [*coming forward*] How shall I murder him, Iago?

IAGO Did you perceive how he laughed at his vice?

OTHELLO O, Iago!   165

IAGO And did you see the handkerchief?

OTHELLO Was that mine?

IAGO Yours, by this hand. And to see how he prizes the foolish
    woman your wife! She gave it him, and he hath given it his whore.

OTHELLO I would have him nine years a-killing! A fine woman, a   170
    fair woman, a sweet woman!

IAGO Nay, you must forget that.

OTHELLO Ay, let her rot and perish, and be damned tonight, for she
    shall not live! No, my heart is turned to stone—I strike it, and it
    hurts my hand. O, the world hath not a sweeter creature! She   175
    might lie by an emperor's side and command him tasks.

IAGO Nay, that's not your way.

OTHELLO Hang her! I do but say what she is—so delicate with her
    needle, an admirable musician! O, she will sing the savageness out
    of a bear! Of so high and plenteous wit and invention!   180

IAGO She's the worse for all this.

OTHELLO O, a thousand thousand times! And then of so gentle a
    condition.

IAGO Ay, too gentle.

OTHELLO Nay, that's certain . . . But yet the pity of it, Iago! O, Iago,   185
    the pity of it, Iago!

IAGO If you be so fond over her iniquity, give her patent to offend,
    for if it touches not you, it comes near nobody.

OTHELLO I will chop her into messes! Cuckold me!

193   *expostulate*, talk (argue) at length.
194   *unprovide*, weaken the resolution of.
199   *let … undertaker*, let me manage him. Just possibly a pun, though it is not certain that 'undertaker' has assumed its modern meaning by Shakespeare's time.
206   *instrument*, official document.
211   *Lives, sir.* A typical little Iago evasion.
213   *unkind*, unnatural; not showing generous (and proper) fellow-feeling.

IAGO   O, 'tis foul in her.   190

OTHELLO   With mine officer!

IAGO   That's fouler.

OTHELLO   Get me some poison, Iago, this night. I'll not expostulate
   with her, lest her body and beauty unprovide my mind again.
   This night, Iago.   195

IAGO   Do it not with poison. Strangle her in her bed, even the bed
   she hath contaminated.

OTHELLO   Good, good! The justice of it pleases. Very good!

IAGO   And for Cassio, let me be his undertaker. You shall hear more
   by midnight.   200

OTHELLO   Excellent good. [trumpet within] What trumpet is that same?

IAGO   Something from Venice, sure.

Enter LODOVICO · DESDEMONA · *and Attendants*

                              'Tis Lodovico,
   Come from the Duke; and see, your wife is with him.

LODOVICO   God save you, worthy General!

OTHELLO   With all my heart, sir.

LODOVICO   The Duke and senators of Venice greet you. [*gives him a*   205
   letter]

OTHELLO   I kiss the instrument of their pleasures. [*opens the letter and*
   reads]

DESDEMONA   And what's the news, good cousin Lodovico?

IAGO   I am very glad to see you, signior.
   Welcome to Cyprus.

LODOVICO   I thank you. How does lieutenant Cassio?   210

IAGO   Lives, sir.

DESDEMONA   Cousin, there's fallen between him and my lord
   An unkind breach; but you shall make all well.

OTHELLO   Are you sure of that?

DESDEMONA   My lord?   215

OTHELLO [*reads*] 'This fail you not to do, as you will'—

LODOVICO   He did not call; he's busy in the paper.
   Is there division between thy lord and Cassio?

DESDEMONA   A most unhappy one. I would do much

220   *atone*, make one, reconcile.

221   *Fire and brimstone!* Othello presumably hears Desdemona's last words: hence this exclamation. From his incredulity that Desdemona could speak so openly of her love for Cassio follows his next question, 'Are you wise?'

224   *Deputing . . . government*, appointing Cassio to take over control in his place. Now that there was no danger of a Turkish attack Othello's mission was over.

225   *on't*, of it.   *Indeed!* Othello of course entirely mistakes the reason for Desdemona's gladness.

226   *mad*, i.e. in so openly confessing your feelings for Cassio.

227   *Devil!* Again notice this word at a key point in the action. Bradley's unease about this episode of the striking of Desdemona—'I confess that, do what I will, I cannot reconcile myself to it' (*op. cit.*, p. 184)—makes curious reading today for its attitude towards violence in drama and is a reminder how radically our general outlook can change.

230   *'Tis very much.* Something like ' 'tis incredible'.

232–3   *If . . . crocodile.* The general sense is clear enough: Othello dismisses Desdemona's weeping as crocodile tears, that is to say, falsely insincere (and perhaps, positively deceptive). But it is not quite clear whether 'she' in l.233 refers to the earth or to Desdemona: 'teem' might mean either 'bring forth' or 'conceive by', and 'falls' either 'lets fall' or 'delivers in birth'. Behind the lines there may be some trace of curious Elizabethan notions about the generation of creatures. (See *Antony and Cleopatra*, Act 2 Sc.7, ll.26–7.)   *prove*, turn out to be.

238   *Mistress!* Perhaps an intended double meaning in this word.

240   *What . . . sir?* In this and his following remarks Othello pretends to be a bawd soliciting custom for a prostitute.

246–50   *Proceed . . . avaunt.* In these lines Othello counterpoints his remarks to Lodovico on the order of his recall with asides to Desdemona.

247   *passion*, grief.

To atone them, for the love I bear to Cassio.   220
OTHELLO   Fire and brimstone!
DESDEMONA   My lord?
OTHELLO   Are you wise?
DESDEMONA   What, is he angry?
LODOVICO   Maybe the letter moved him,
   For, as I think, they do command him home,
   Deputing Cassio in his government.
DESDEMONA   By my troth, I am glad on't.
OTHELLO   Indeed!
DESDEMONA   My lord?   225
OTHELLO   I am glad to see you mad.
DESDEMONA   How, sweet Othello?
OTHELLO   Devil! [*He strikes her*]
DESDEMONA   I have not deserved this.
LODOVICO   My lord, this would not be believed in Venice,
   Though I should swear I saw't. 'Tis very much.   230
   Make her amends—she weeps.
OTHELLO   O devil, devil!
   If that the earth could teem with women's tears,
   Each drop she falls would prove a crocodile.
   Out of my sight!
DESDEMONA   I will not stay to offend you. [*starts to go*]   235
LODOVICO   Truly an obedient lady.
   I do beseech your lordship, call her back.
OTHELLO   Mistress!
DESDEMONA   My lord?
OTHELLO   What would you with her, sir?   240
LODOVICO   Who, I, my lord?
OTHELLO   Ay, you did wish that I would make her turn.
   Sir, she can turn, and turn, and yet go on,
   And turn again. And she can weep, sir, weep.
   And she's obedient, as you say, obedient,   245
   Very obedient. Proceed you in your tears.
   Concerning this, sir—O, well-painted passion!—
   I am commanded home. Get you away;

F

253 *Goats and monkeys!* Animal imagery taken over from Iago (see (Act3 Sc.3, l.408).

254–8 *Is . . . pierce?* This comment of the detached Lodovico on the 'normal' Othello must always be considered in any interpretation. Note particularly 'noble' and the tribute to Othello's control over his emotions. No critic has more strongly stressed the nobility of Othello than Swinburne, who wrote: 'Othello is the noblest man of man's making' (*A Study of Shakespeare*).

255 *all-in-all sufficient*, utterly suitable to his office.

257 *accident.* Could mean either 'disaster', 'unforeseen contingency', or 'fate'. If the word is synonymous with the following 'chance', such tautologies are not rare in Shakespeare.

258–62 *He's . . . were.* Some of Iago's most cryptic and perhaps deliberately meaningless lines. Any attempted paraphrase runs the risk of absurdity, but perhaps the meaning might be something like the following. 'Let's just say he is what he is. I dare not give my considered opinion ("censure") of what he might be (i.e. out of his mind). If he is not out of his mind, I wish he were'—with understood, 'because of the way his wife has behaved'.

264 *use*, habit, custom.

265 *blood*, passions. It is a little odd that Lodovico should think that the recall order might be the cause of Othello's anger, for on the surface at least there was nothing abnormal or degrading about the recall. But perhaps the governorship of Cyprus is intended to be an office of importance.

269 *denote*, reveal. *so*, i.e. through your observing.

Scene Two

In this so-called 'brothel' scene Othello, for the first time, accuses Desdemona to her face. But, like the next, the scene really contributes little to the plot. Its essential importance lies in the further dramatic demonstration of the corruption and degradation of Othello and of the pitiful, hopeless plight of Desdemona. It also presents a further triumph for Iago, since in some sense Desdemona's pathetic (and ironic) request for his assistance parallels the moment in the previous scene when he had stood conqueror over the helpless, unconscious Othello. On the other hand, Roderigo, the worm turning, now offers some threat.

2 *Nor . . . suspect.* 'Anything' to be understood as the object of 'heard' and 'suspect'.

I'll send for you anon. Sir, I obey the mandate,
And will return to Venice. Hence, avaunt!   [*Exit* DESDEMONA 250
Cassio shall have my place. And sir, tonight
I do entreat that we may sup together.
You are welcome, sir, to Cyprus . . . Goats and monkeys!   [*Exit*

LODOVICO Is this the noble Moor, whom our full senate
Call all in all sufficient? Is this the nature   255
Whom passion could not shake? whose solid virtue
The shot of accident nor dart of chance
Could neither graze nor pierce?

IAGO   He is much changed.

LODOVICO Are his wits safe? Is he not light of brain?

IAGO He's that he is: I may not breathe my censure   260
What he might be. If what he might he is not,
I would to heaven he were.

LODOVICO   What! strike his wife!

IAGO Faith, that was not so well; yet would I knew
That stroke would prove the worst!

LODOVICO   Is it his use,
Or did the letters work upon his blood   265
And new-create this fault?

IAGO   Alas, alas!
It is not honesty in me to speak
What I have seen and known. You shall observe him,
And his own courses will denote him so,
That I may save my speech. Do but go after   270
And mark how he continues.

LODOVICO I am sorry that I am deceived in him.   [*Exeunt*

Scene Two

Cyprus · A room in the citadel

Enter OTHELLO *and* EMILIA

OTHELLO You have seen nothing then?

EMILIA Nor ever heard, nor ever did suspect.

3   *she.* In modern grammar this would of course be 'her'.

9   *mask.* Probably to be worn at a masquerade or some similar entertainment. Shakespeare several times makes use of these masquerades in his plays. See, for example, *The Merchant of Venice.*

12   *honest,* chaste, faithful.

13   *Lay . . . stake,* I'd stake my soul on it.

14   *abuse.* Could carry the meaning of both 'wrong' and 'deceive'.

15–16   *If . . . curse!* This unconscious reference to her husband is highly ironical.

16   *serpent's curse!* Probably a reference to the curse God put on the Garden of Eden serpent after it had deceived Eve: to crawl on its belly, to eat dust, and to be crushed beneath the heels of men (*Genesis,* Ch. 3, vv.14–15).

19   *as slander.* What may have prompted Emilia to this particular comparison, is her belief that Desdemona has been slandered.

20   *yet . . . bawd.* Here Othello's grim game of pretending Emilia is a bawd and Desdemona a prostitute begins. This is another scene that troubled the susceptibilities of Bradley, though he is probably right in saying that 'it is far more painful than the murder scene' (*op. cit.,* p. 178).   *simple,* inexperienced, a beginner.

21   *This,* i.e. Desdemona.

22   *closet.* Probably has the modern American meaning of 'cup-board'.

27   *Some . . . function,* do your job.

28   *procreants,* copulators.

30   *mystery.* The old meaning of 'trade' or 'craft'.

OTHELLO   Yes, you have seen Cassio and she together.

EMILIA   But then I saw no harm, and then I heard
Each syllable that breath made up between them.   5

OTHELLO   What, did they never whisper?

EMILIA   Never, my lord.

OTHELLO   Nor send you out o' the way?

EMILIA   Never.

OTHELLO   To fetch her fan, her gloves, her mask, nor nothing?

EMILIA   Never, my lord.   10

OTHELLO   That's strange.

EMILIA   I durst, my lord, to wager she is honest,
Lay down my soul at stake. If you think other,
Remove your thought—it doth abuse your bosom.
If any wretch have put this in your head,   15
Let heaven requite it with the serpent's curse!
For if she be not honest, chaste, and true,
There's no man happy—the purest of their wives
Is foul as slander.

OTHELLO   Bid her come hither. Go.

                                          [Exit EMILIA
She says enough; yet she's a simple bawd   20
That cannot say as much. This is a subtle whore,
A closet lock and key of villainous secrets;
And yet she'll kneel and pray. I have seen her do't.

Enter DESDEMONA *and* EMILIA

DESDEMONA   My lord, what is your will?

OTHELLO   Pray, chuck, come hither.

DESDEMONA   What is your pleasure?

OTHELLO   Let me see your eyes.   25
Look in my face.

DESDEMONA   What horrible fancy's this?

OTHELLO [*to* EMILIA]   Some of your function, mistress.
Leave procreants alone and shut the door.
Cough or cry 'hem' if anybody come.
Your mystery, your mystery! Nay, dispatch!   [*Exit* EMILIA 30

DESDEMONA   Upon my knees, what doth your speech import?

36–9   *Come . . . honest.* Notice the insistence on damnation and the belief now that the 'divine' Desdemona merely resembles a heavenly creature. Full of unconscious irony, these lines epitomize the 'chaos' that has come on Othello.

44   *motive,* instigator or cause.

47   *If . . . him.* Desdemona must mean that if her father had a hand in the recall that is a *further* example of an alienation that had already taken place.

49   *they.* This reads 'he' in the Quarto, and there has probably been a bowdlerization for 'God'.

51   *Steeped . . . lips.* Presumably the image is of poverty as a lake, sea, etc. that nearly drowns Othello.

52   *captivity.* Perhaps Othello is recalling the captivity mentioned in Act1 Sc.3, l.138.   *hopes.* Almost in the sense of 'dearest concerns' (e.g. a happy married life with Desdemona).

54–6   *But . . . at!* The only certainties about these lines are (1) that Othello is seeing himself as an object of scorn and mockery, and (2) that this scorn will be inescapable (and possibly slow to pass). The commonly assumed clock image would make sense of 'slow unmoving finger' as the dial-hand that never appears to move; but there is no certainty about the existence of such an image. The Folio reads: 'slow and moving'.

58–61   *But . . . thence!* This seems to be the heart of Othello's distress: that, with the loss of Desdemona's love, his whole existence is shattered. Jealousy is barely relevant to this predicament.

58   *there,* i.e. in Desdemona's heart or love.   *garnered up,* stored.

60   *fountain.* In the sense of 'source'.

62   *cistern.* In this parallel with 'fountain' the image of Desdemona's heart changes from that of a dried-up spring to that of a reservoir tank where vice and foulness engender.

63–5   *Turn . . . hell.* In this Folio text the patience (personified) that Othello is trying to maintain is told to change colour or appearance or even nature ('complexion') at the sight of Desdemona's cistern-soul and to look grim as hell. This is another interesting religious allusion, and again there is another potential inversion—of the 'cherubin' into a thing of 'hell'. But the passage is uncertain, and the Quarto reads differently.

67–8   *O . . . blowing.* Very Iago-like imagery (compare Act1 Sc.1, ll.70-1). *shambles,* slaughter-house.   *quicken . . . blowing,* come to life as soon as the eggs are laid. The point presumably is the rapidity with which foulness has developed in Desdemona.

        I understand a fury in your words,
        But not the words.

OTHELLO   Why, what art thou?

DESDEMONA   Your wife, my lord; your true and loyal wife.   35

OTHELLO   Come, swear it, damn thyself,
        Lest, being like one of heaven, the devils themselves
        Should fear to seize thee. Therefore be double-damned;
        Swear thou art honest.

DESDEMONA   Heaven doth truly know it.

OTHELLO   Heaven truly knows that thou art false as hell.   40

DESDEMONA   To whom, my lord? With whom? How am I false?

OTHELLO   O Desdemona! Away, away, away!

DESDEMONA   Alas, the heavy day! Why do you weep?
        Am I the motive of these tears, my lord?
        If haply you my father do suspect   45
        An instrument of this your calling back,
        Lay not your blame on me. If you have lost him,
        Why, I have lost him too.

OTHELLO   Had it pleased heaven
        To try me with affliction, had they rained
        All kinds of sores and shames on my bare head,   50
        Steeped me in poverty to the very lips,
        Given to captivity me and my utmost hopes,
        I should have found in some part of my soul
        A drop of patience. But alas, to make me
        A fixed figure for the time of scorn   55
        To point his slow unmoving finger at!
        Yet could I bear that too, well, very well.
        But there where I have garnered up my heart,
        Where either I must live or bear no life,
        The fountain from the which my current runs   60
        Or else dries up—to be discarded thence!
        Or keep it as a cistern for foul toads
        To knot and gender in! Turn thy complexion there,
        Patience, thou young and rose-lipped cherubin,
        Ay, there look grim as hell!   65

DESDEMONA   I hope my noble lord esteems me honest.

OTHELLO   O, ay! as summer flies are in the shambles,

71   *committed.* For the play that Othello goes on to make with this innocently intended word its almost inevitable association with adultery must be appreciated.

74   *commoner,* whore.

75-7   *I . . . deeds.* This is perhaps near to rhetorical bombast, but it is an Elizabethan style of writing by no means uncommon in Shakespeare. It does not necessarily discredit Othello himself.

78   *the moon winks,* the moon, the symbol of chastity, closes up her eyes.

80   *hollow . . . earth.* Some cavity where the winds are shut up; perhaps vaguely echoing a classical idea about the winds.

84   *vessel.* Biblical for 'body'.

85   *other,* i.e. of another man. The Quarto reads 'hated'.

87   *as . . . saved.* Note another 'salvation' reference.

89   *I . . . then,* pardon me then.

93   *keeps . . . hell!* i.e. as bawd in a brothel.

94   *done our course,* concluded our business (or, goings-on).

95   *keep our counsel,* say nothing about our private, secret business.

96   *conceive,* imagine, i.e. 'what worm is in his brain?'

That quicken even with blowing. O, thou weed,
Who art so lovely fair and smell'st so sweet
That the sense aches at thee, would thou hadst ne'er been born! 70

DESDEMONA   Alas, what ignorant sin have I committed?

OTHELLO   Was this fair paper, this most goodly book,
Made to write 'whore' on? What committed!
Committed! O, thou public commoner!
I should make very forges of my cheeks,   75
That would to cinders burn up modesty,
Did I but speak thy deeds. What committed!
Heaven stops the nose at it, and the moon winks;
The bawdy wind, that kisses all it meets,
Is hushed within the hollow mine of earth   80
And will not hear it. What committed!
Impudent strumpet!

DESDEMONA   By heaven, you do me wrong.

OTHELLO   Are you not a strumpet?

DESDEMONA   No, as I am a Christian.
If to preserve this vessel for my lord
From any other foul unlawful touch   85
Be not to be a strumpet, I am none.

OTHELLO   What, not a whore?

DESDEMONA   No, as I shall be saved.

OTHELLO   Is't possible?

DESDEMONA   O, heaven forgive us!

OTHELLO   I cry you mercy then.
I took you for that cunning whore of Venice   90
That married with Othello. [*shouting to* EMILIA] You, mistress,
That have the office opposite to Saint Peter
And keeps the gate of hell!—

Re-enter EMILIA

                  You, you, ay, you!
We have done our course; there's money for your pains.
I pray you turn the key and keep our counsel.   [*Exit* 95

EMILIA   Alas, what does this gentleman conceive?
How do you, madam? How do you, my good lady?

100   *who?* 'whom' in modern grammar.

105   *water,* i.e. tears. But since Desdemona is too stunned to weep
          this is tantamount to saying that she cannot give Emilia any
          answer at all.

106   *Lay . . . sheets.* A touchingly simple, but hopeless, move by
          Desdemona. She thinks this reminder of their wedding may
          perhaps restore Othello's love.

108   *'Tis . . . meet.* This must be a most rare outburst of indignant
          irony from Desdemona since a literal reading of the line
          would make her much too submissive.   *meet,* proper,
          fitting.

109–10   *How . . . abuse?* A difficult passage. Apart from possible text
          corruption, 'opinion' can have several different meanings,
          and we have to choose between the Quarto 'greatest abuse'
          and the Folio 'least misuse'. Following Onions' unsupported
          assertion in his *Shakespeare Glossary* that 'opinion' here means
          'censure', a conservative paraphrase might be: 'What have I
          done that he might level the slightest censure against my very
          worst offence?' But this paraphrase is open to several ob-
          jections.

115   *I . . . chiding,* I am unused to reproof.

116–18   *Alas . . . bear.* Evidently Emilia has been listening at the door.

117   *despite.* Probably near to 'abuse'.   *heavy.* Possibly 'grievous',
          'distressing'.

122   *callet,* drab, slut.

DESDEMONA Faith, half asleep.

EMILIA Good madam, what's the matter with my lord?

DESDEMONA With who?   100

EMILIA Why, with my lord, madam.

DESDEMONA Who is thy lord?

EMILIA   He that is yours, sweet lady.

DESDEMONA I have none. Do not talk to me, Emilia.
  I cannot weep, nor answer have I none
  But what should go by water. Prithee, tonight   105
  Lay on my bed my wedding sheets—remember;
  And call thy husband hither.

EMILIA   Here's a change indeed!   [*Exit*

DESDEMONA 'Tis meet I should be used so, very meet.
  How have I been behaved, that he might stick
  The smallest opinion on my greatest abuse?   110

Re-enter EMILIA *with* IAGO

IAGO What is your pleasure, madam? How is't with you?

DESDEMONA I cannot tell. Those that do teach young babes
  Do it with gentle means and easy tasks.
  He might have chid me so, for, in good faith,
  I am a child to chiding.

IAGO   What is the matter, lady?   115

EMILIA Alas, Iago, my lord hath so bewhored her,
  Thrown such despite and heavy terms upon her
  As true heart cannot bear.

DESDEMONA Am I that name, Iago?

IAGO   What name, fair lady?

DESDEMONA Such as she says my lord did say I was.   120

EMILIA He called her whore. A beggar in his drink
  Could not have laid such terms upon his callet.

IAGO Why did he so?

DESDEMONA I do not know; I am sure I am none such.

IAGO Do not weep, do not weep. Alas the day!   125

EMILIA Hath she forsook so many noble matches,
  Her father and her country, all her friends,

129   *Beshrew*, curse.

130   *trick*, freakish behaviour.   *heaven doth know*. Notice Desdemona's frequent references to 'heaven', which contrast so sharply, and significantly, with those of Othello to 'hell', 'devils', etc.

131   *eternal*, everlasting, utter. (But mainly for vague colloquial emphasis, like our 'infernal'.)

132   *busy*, meddling, interfering.   *insinuating*, worming into things. (Not the modern meaning.)

133   *cogging, cozening*. Synonymous for 'deceiving', 'cheating', etc. *get some office*. It may seem odd that Emilia should come so near the truth, since she has not the slightest suspicion of Iago, as we may see from her reaction in the last scene of the play. But at least her words produce strong dramatic irony, and this presumably was Shakespeare's chief intention. This is a small but interesting example of something that is fundamental to our appreciation of Shakespeare: that he was often much more concerned with emotional impact on his audience than with 'realistic' facts of story or character.

137   *A halter . . . him*, i.e. may he be hanged!

139   *form*. Emilia is saying something like 'Where has any adultery shown itself in definite shape (or appearance)?'

140   *outrageous*. Mainly an intensive word. So probably is the following 'notorious'.

142   *companions*, fellows (contemptuously used).   *unfold*, reveal, disclose.

145   *Speak within door*, don't speak so loud. Compare our modern expression 'let the whole street hear'.

146–8   *Some . . . Moor*. This fits with what Iago says in Act1 Sc.3, ll.368–70 and Act2 Sc.1, ll.278–80 and seems to confirm that at least one of his self-stated motives is important and genuine.

146   *squire*, fellow (contemptuously used).

147   *seamy*, wrong. See a similar expression in Act2 Sc.3, l.44.

149   *Go to*. An idiomatic expression variously used. Here possibly 'Shut up'.

152   *Here I kneel*. This proper address to heaven parallels, but in significant contrast, Othello's kneeling to heaven to sanctify his revenge in Act3 Sc.3, ll.467–9.

153   *will*. This probably has some shade of the meaning 'sexual desire'.   *trespass*, sin.

154   *discourse*, process or course.

156   *other*, i.e. than Othello.

157   *yet*, still.

157–9   *Or . . . dearly*. A somewhat clumsy turn of expression for Desdemona's protest of everlasting love.

160   *Comfort*, well-being, happiness. (See note to Act2 Sc.1, l.186). *forswear*, forsake, or repudiate.   *unkindness*. As usual in Shakespeare, 'kind' and its cognates have a much wider significance than in modern use. Here the meaning is something like 'inhuman treatment'.

161   *defeat*, end, destroy.

To be called whore? Would it not make one weep?

DESDEMONA   It is my wretched fortune.

IAGO   Beshrew him for't!
How comes this trick upon him?

DESDEMONA   Nay, heaven doth know.   130

EMILIA   I will be hanged if some eternal villain,
Some busy and insinuating rogue,
Some cogging, cozening slave, to get some office,
Have not devised this slander—I'll be hanged else.

IAGO   Fie, there is no such man! It is impossible.   135

DESDEMONA   If any such there be, heaven pardon him!

EMILIA   A halter pardon him and hell gnaw his bones!
Why should he call her whore? Who keeps her company?
What place, what time, what form, what likelihood?
The Moor's abused by some outrageous knave,   140
Some base notorious knave, some scurvy fellow.
O heaven, that such companions thou'ldst unfold,
And put in every honest hand a whip
To lash the rascals naked through the world,
Even from the east to the west!

IAGO   Speak within door.   145

EMILIA   O, fie upon him. Some such squire he was
That turned your wit the seamy side without
And made you to suspect me with the Moor.

IAGO   You are a fool. Go to.

DESDEMONA   O good Iago,
What shall I do to win my lord again?   150
Good friend, go to him, for by this light of heaven
I know not how I lost him. Here I kneel.
If e'er my will did trespass 'gainst his love
Either in discourse of thought or actual deed,
Or that mine eyes, mine ears, or any sense   155
Delighted them in any other form,
Or that I do not yet, and ever did,
And ever will (though he do shake me off
To beggarly divorcement) love him dearly,
Comfort forswear me! Unkindness may do much,   160
And his unkindness may defeat my life,

163   *abhor*, fill with abhorrence. A good example of the way the
       Elizabethans used the pun in quite serious contexts.

164   *addition*, title (i.e. of whore).

165   *vanity*. Presumably 'vain' (i.e. empty, futile) temptations and
       inducements, however glittering.   *make*. Here used in the
       modern sense of 'constrain', 'compel'.

166   *humour*, mood.

167   *The . . . offence*. Perhaps Iago has taken the hint from Lodovico's
       remark in Act4 Ss.1, ll265–6. Also he was just making his exit
       when Desdemona offered this excuse (Act3 Sc.4, ll.137–40).
       does him offence, annoys (or exasperates) him.

171   *stay the meat*, wait for the meal. For this line the Quarto reads:
       'And the great messengers of Venice stay'.

172   *all . . . well*. Had this expression an ironical touch arising from
       its use in religious contexts?

176   *daff'st*, dost put off.   *device*, scheme, contrivance.

177   *conveniency*. Possibly 'advantage' or 'opportunity'. But un-
       certain in meaning.

179   *put up*, put up with.

183   *are . . . together*, are not akin, don't go together.

187   *votarist*, nun (and therefore vowed to chastity).

188–90 *returned . . . none*. A difficult passage here printed in the
       Quarto version. It can perhaps be clarified if we understand
       'comforts' and 'acquittance' as examples of the 'expectation'.
       comforts . . . respect, joys, delights, of an immediate aspect or
       kind, i.e. soon to be realized.   *acquittance*, payment of debt,
       i.e. Desdemona's love in return for Roderigo's jewels.

190   *go to*. More mildly used than in l.149. In picking up the
       phrase Roderigo appears to be using it more literally and
       perhaps obscenely: he cannot 'go to' Desdemona.

192   *fopped*, tricked, fooled.

But never taint my love. I cannot say 'whore';
It does abhor me now I speak the word.
To do the act that might the addition earn
Not the world's mass of vanity could make me.   165

IAGO   I pray you, be content; 'tis but his humour.
The business of the state does him offence,
And he does chide with you.

DESDEMONA   If 'twere no other—
IAGO   'Tis but so, I warrant you.
    [*trumpets within*]
Hark how these instruments summon you to supper!   170
The messengers of Venice stay the meat.
Go in, and weep not; all things shall be well.
                                    [*Exeunt* DESDEMONA *and* EMILIA

Enter RODERIGO

How now, Roderigo?
RODERIGO   I do not find that thou deal'st justly with me.

IAGO   What in the contrary?   175

RODERIGO   Every day thou daff'st me with some device, Iago, and
    rather, as it seems to me, thou keepest from me all conveniency
    than suppliest me with the least advantage of hope. I will indeed
    no longer endure it, nor am I yet persuaded to put up in peace
    what already I have foolishly suffered.   180

IAGO   Will you hear me, Roderigo?

RODERIGO   Faith, I have heard too much, for your words and
    performances are no kin together.

IAGO   You charge me most unjustly.

RODERIGO   With naught but truth. I have wasted myself out of my 185
    means. The jewels you have had from me to deliver to Desde-
    mona would half have corrupted a votarist. You have told me
    she hath received them, and returned me expectation and
    comforts of sudden respect and acquittance, but I find none.

IAGO   Well, go to; very well.   190

RODERIGO   Very well, go to! I cannot go to, man, nor 'tis not very
    well. Nay, I think it is scurvy and begin to find myself fopped in it.

IAGO   Very well.

198   *You . . . now.* This is some expression of pretended affirmation like 'that's right'. As his next words make clear, Iago attempts to give the impression that he is admiring Roderigo's spirited resolution. But of course this threatened action of Roderigo puts him on the spot.

199   *intendment,* intention.

204   *directly,* straightforwardly, honestly.

207   *wit,* good sense, intelligence.

211   *engines for,* plots or schemes against.

212   *compass,* scope (as in Act3Sc.4,l.15).

213   *depute,* appoint.

217   *He . . . Mauritania.* Iago risks this lie because he wishes to rush Roderigo into the plan of murdering Cassio. If Desdemona were returning to Venice, the home of herself and Roderigo, there would be less need for this killing of Cassio that will force Othello to stay on in Cyprus.

219   *determinate,* decisive, conclusive.

225   *right,* satisfaction, or, act of justice.

RODERIGO I tell you, 'tis not very well. I will make myself known to
Desdemona. If she will return me my jewels, I will give over my 195
suit and repent my unlawful solicitation. If not, assure yourself
I will seek satisfaction of you.

IAGO You have said now.

RODERIGO Ay, and said nothing but what I protest intendment of
doing.   200

IAGO Why, now I see there's mettle in thee, and even from this
instant do build on thee a better opinion than ever before. Give
me thy hand, Roderigo. Thou hast taken against me a most just
exception; but yet I protest I have dealt most directly in thy affair.

RODERIGO It hath not appeared.   205

IAGO I grant indeed it hath not appeared, and your suspicion is not
without wit and judgment. But, Roderigo, if thou hast that in
thee indeed, which I have greater reason to believe now than
ever—I mean purpose, courage, and valour—this night show it.
If thou the next night following enjoy not Desdemona, take me 210
from the world with treachery and devise engines for my life.

RODERIGO Well, what is it? Is it within reason and compass?

IAGO Sir, there is especial commission come from Venice to depute
Cassio in Othello's place.

RODERIGO Is that true? Why, then Othello and Desdemona return 215
again to Venice.

IAGO O, no. He goes into Mauritania and takes away with him the
fair Desdemona, unless his abode be lingered here by some
accident, wherein none can be so determinate as the removing
of Cassio.   220

RODERIGO How do you mean 'removing' of him?

IAGO Why, by making him uncapable of Othello's place, knocking
out his brains.

RODERIGO And that you would have me to do?

IAGO Ay, if you dare do yourself a profit and a right. He sups 225
tonight with a harlot, and thither will I go to him. He knows not
yet of his honourable fortune. If you will watch his going thence,
which I will fashion to fall out between twelve and one, you may
take him at your pleasure. I will be near to second your attempt,
and he shall fall between us. Come, stand not amazed at it, but 230

232   *it*, i.e. death.
233   *high*, fully.   *grows to waste*, is wasting apace, swiftly passing.

Scene Three   This scene of Desdemona preparing for bed, one of the most poignant in all Shakespeare's tragedies, without a single false stroke of sentimentality, presents a brief moment of ordered calm (but once more, as always in the play, of ominous quietness); and it provides a sharp contrast with both the grim bitterness of the preceding scene and the confusion and violence of the final Act. Wilson Knight makes a pertinent comment when he writes: 'The extreme beauty and pathos of this scene are largely dependent on the domesticity of it' (*op. cit.*, p. 108).

1   *I ... further.* Presumably Othello has offered to escort Lodovico to his lodging.
10   *He ... did.* By now Othello has regained more self-control.
11   *uncontinent*, immediately.
18–20 *So ... them.* A most heartfelt utterance.
19   *stubbornness*, roughness, harshness (see Act1Sc.3,l.226 for a similar use of 'stubborn').   *checks*, reproofs.
20   *Prithee, unpin me.* These intimate touches contribute greatly to the poignancy of the scene. To tastes at certain times they have seemed out of keeping with high tragedy.   *grace.* Probably with the suggestion of 'divine favour'.   *favour.* This may be synonymous with 'grace', or it may mean 'charm'. Both words have shades of meaning that may overlap.

go along with me. I will show you such a necessity in his death
that you shall think yourself bound to put it on him. It is now
high supper-time and the night grows to waste. About it!

RODERIGO   I will hear further reason for this.

IAGO   And you shall be satisfied.   [*Exeunt* 235

Scene Three

Cyprus · Another room in the citadel

Enter OTHELLO · LODOVICO · DESDEMONA · EMILIA · *and Attendants*

LODOVICO   I do beseech you, sir, trouble yourself no further.

OTHELLO   O, pardon me, 'twill do me good to walk.

LODOVICO   Madam, good night. I humbly thank your ladyship.

DESDEMONA   Your honour is most welcome.

OTHELLO   Will you walk, sir?...
  O, Desdemona!   5

DESDEMONA   My lord?

OTHELLO   Get you to bed on the instant. I will be returned forthwith.
  Dismiss your attendant there. Look it be done.

DESDEMONA   I will, my lord.
                    [*Exeunt* OTHELLO · LODOVICO · *and Attendants*

EMILIA   How goes it now? He looks gentler than he did.   10

DESDEMONA   He says he will return incontinent.
  He hath commanded me to go to bed,
  And bade me to dismiss you.

EMILIA   Dismiss me?

DESDEMONA   It was his bidding. Therefore, good Emilia,
  Give me my nightly wearing, and adieu.   15
  We must not now displease him.

EMILIA   I would you had never seen him!

DESDEMONA   So would not I. My love doth so approve him
  That even his stubbornness, his checks, his frowns—
  Prithee, unpin me—have grace and favour in them.   20

Notes &
Commentary

22	*All's one,* all right, no matter.　　*faith.* The Folio reads 'father'.
24	*talk,* i.e. idly.
25	*My mother.* Possibly in Desdemona's sleepy wanderings of mind it is the previous reference to 'shrouds' that has brought back the memory of her mother, and this in turn the maid Barbary (our modern Barbara) and her song.
26	*mad.* Perhaps, to fit the ballad, in the sense of 'faithless'.
27	*'willow'.* The willow was the emblem of deserted love.
30–50	*I . . . next.* This passage is not in the Quarto. It may therefore be a later addition.
30–1	*I . . . But,* it is all I can do not to, etc.
33	*night-gown,* dressing gown.
34	*proper,* handsome. Some critics have been puzzled that Desdemona should speak here of Lodovico, and in this manner. But surely this female chatter about the guest is quite natural.
36–7	*walked . . . Palestine,* i.e. gone on a pilgrimage.
38	*sycamore.* This could be a type of fig-tree rather than a maple.
45	*Lay by these.* These interruptions of everyday remarks intensify rather than spoil the poignancy of this artless song, and in some sense they are in keeping with it.　　*these,* Desdemona's jewels, etc.
47	*hie,* hasten.
50	*Nay . . . knocks.* A beautifully effective line. Not only does the interruption 'Nay, that's not next' give a general touch of realism but it may be that Desdemona has unconsciously got the last song-words out of order because they are so relevant to Othello and herself. Also her question has an appropriately chilling—or sinister—suggestion.

EMILIA   I have laid those sheets you bade me on the bed.

DESDEMONA   All's one. Good faith, how foolish are our minds!
　　If I do die before thee, prithee shroud me
　　In one of those same sheets.

EMILIA　　　　　　　　　　Come, come, you talk.

DESDEMONA   My mother had a maid called Barbary—　　25
　　She was in love, and he she loved proved mad
　　And did forsake her. She had a song of 'willow'—
　　An old thing 'twas, but it expressed her fortune,
　　And she died singing it. That song tonight
　　Will not go from my mind. I have much to do　　30
　　But to go hang my head all at one side
　　And sing it like poor Barbary. Prithee, dispatch.

EMILIA   Shall I go fetch your night-gown?

DESDEMONA　　　　　　　　　　No, unpin me here . . .
　　This Lodovico is a proper man.

EMILIA   A very handsome man.

DESDEMONA　　　　　　　He speaks well.　　35

EMILIA   I know a lady in Venice would have walked barefoot to
　　Palestine for a touch of his nether lip.

DESDEMONA [*sings*]
　　　　　The poor soul sat sighing by a sycamore tree,
　　　　　　Sing all a green willow;
　　　　　Her hand on her bosom, her head on her knee,　　40
　　　　　　Sing willow, willow, willow.
　　　　　The fresh streams ran by her and murmured her moans;
　　　　　　Sing willow, willow, willow;
　　　　　Her salt tears fell from her and softened the stones—
　　Lay by these.　　45
　　[*sings*]　　　　Sing willow, willow, willow—
　　Prithee hie thee. He'll come anon.
　　[*sings*]　　Sing all a green willow must be my garland.
　　　　　Let nobody blame him; his scorn I approve—
　　Nay, that's not next. Hark, who's that knocks?　　50

EMILIA   It is the wind.

DESDEMONA [*sings*]
　　　　　I called my love false love, but what said he then?
　　　　　　Sing willow, willow, willow:

54   *moe*, more.   *you'll . . . men*. For those who know the play
          these words have some irony—and pathos, since this is one of
          the reasons that Othello is to give in his great soliloquy at
          the beginning of Act5Sc.2 to justify his killing of Desdemona.

56   *'Tis . . . there*. Perhaps 'it might or might not'.

58   *in conscience*, very truly, honestly.

62   *this heavenly light*, the moon.

66   *price*. The spelling of 'price' and 'prize' was still confused in
          Shakespeare's time. 'Prize' would make better sense here.

68   *undo't*. The word undo could mean 'cancel', 'annul'. Probably
          Emilia means she would deny any adultery.

69   *joint-ring*. A ring made in two separable parts.

70   *lawn*, fine linen.

71   *exhibition*, allowance, gift, present. Cf. Act1Sc.3,l.236. *Ud's*,
          God's.

80   *to the vantage*, in addition.   *store*, stock with people, populate.

82–99   *But . . . so*. The purpose of the exchange between Desdemona
          and Emilia up to this point has been mainly to bring out the
          innocence and purity of Desdemona by contrast with the
          worldliness of Emilia. But in what now follows Shakespeare
          appears to be giving Emilia the chance to express a valid
          woman's point of view. Emilia has spoken in something of
          this vein before (Act3Sc.4,ll.100–4). There are some striking
          similarities between this speech (which is not in the Quarto)
          and Shylock's argument for the Jews in *The Merchant of Venice*,
          Act3Sc.1,ll.42–57.

83–4   *Say . . . laps*. All of this may have a crude meaning.   *duties*.
          Probably sexual duties.   *foreign*, of strangers.

87   *scant . . . despite*. Probably 'cut down our former allowance out
          of spite'.

    If I court moe women, you'll couch with moe men.
So get thee gone; good night. Mine eyes do itch—   55
Does that bode weeping?

EMILIA   'Tis neither here nor there.

DESDEMONA   I have heard it said so. O, these men, these men!
    Dost thou in conscience think—tell me, Emilia—
    That there be women do abuse their husbands
    In such gross kind?

EMILIA   There be some such, no question.   60

DESDEMONA   Wouldst thou do such a deed for all the world?

EMILIA   Why, would not you?

DESDEMONA   No, by this heavenly light!

EMILIA   Nor I neither by this heavenly light. I might do it as well in
    the dark.

DESDEMONA   Wouldst thou do such a deed for all the world?   65

EMILIA   The world is a huge thing. It is a great price for a small vice.

DESDEMONA   In troth, I think thou wouldst not.

EMILIA   In troth I think I should; and undo't when I had done it.
    Marry, I would not do such a thing for a joint-ring, nor for
    measures of lawn, nor for gowns or petticoats, nor caps, nor any 70
    such exhibition. But for the whole world! Ud's pity, who would
    not make her husband a cuckold, to make him a monarch? I
    should venture purgatory for it.

DESDEMONA   Beshrew me, if I would do such a wrong for the whole
    world!   75

EMILIA   Why, the wrong is but a wrong i' the world, and having the
    world for your labour, 'tis a wrong in your own world, and you
    might quickly make it right.

DESDEMONA   I do not think there is any such woman.

EMILIA   Yes, a dozen—and as many to the vantage as would store 80
    the world they played for.
    But I do think it is their husbands' faults
    If wives do fall. Say that they slack their duties
    And pour our treasures into foreign laps,
    Or else break out in peevish jealousies,   85
    Throwing restraint upon us; or say they strike us,
    Or scant our former having in despite—

88   *galls*, tempers, spirits (to retaliate). Not necessarily bad
          temper.   *grace*. Probably here in the sense of 'kindness',
          'beneficence'.
89   *revenge*. We probably have to understand 'instincts for revenge'.
90   *sense*, sensation.
93   *sport*. Probably 'sexual intercourse'.
94   *affection*, feeling, emotion, passion.
100–1   *God . . . mend*. A difficult line and a half, but if 'such uses' refers
          back to Emilia's 'use us well' in l.100, Desdemona is praying
          that she will be well used and therefore, following Emilia's
          argument, under no need to repay bad treatment by bad
          conduct. So far as badness is concerned she hopes that for her
          it will be rather an example or stimulus to 'mend' (amend,
          improve) her conduct.

Why, we have galls, and though we have some grace,
Yet have we some revenge. Let husbands know
Their wives have sense like them. They see and smell   90
And have their palates both for sweet and sour
As husbands have. What is it that they do
When they change us for others? Is it sport?
I think it is. And doth affection breed it?
I think it doth. Is't frailty that thus errs?   95
It is so too. And have not we affections,
Desires for sport, and frailty, as men have?
Then let them use us well; else let them know
The ills we do, their ills instruct us so.
DESDEMONA   Good night, good night. God me such uses send,   100
Not to pick bad from bad, but by bad mend!   [*Exeunt*

With swords out, the clash in the midnight street, and the presence of Iago and Roderigo, this short scene reminds us a little of the opening of the play. It forms a kind of prologue to Iago's final defeat, since, for the first time, his plans misfire.

1   *bulk*. Usually understood as something (e.g. a stall) projecting from a shop front.

2   *bare*, unsheathed.

4   *It . . . us*. The 'make'—'mar' antithesis was a common Elizabethan idiom.

8   *I . . . deed*, I'm not much inclined to this action.

10   *Forth . . . dies!* As he draws his sword Roderigo is, as it were, rehearsing the assassination, perhaps to give himself courage.

11   *quat*, pimple or boil.   *to the sense*, to the quick, to acute irritation.

14   *gain*. The Quarto has 'game', which would suggest winning a gamble.   *Live Roderigo*, if Roderigo lives.

16   *bobbed*, swindled.

19–20   *He . . . ugly*. Wilson Knight finds his key to Iago's motive in these lines—'He is cynicism loathing beauty, refusing to allow its existence' (*op. cit.*, p. 114). Later he says: 'Iago, himself a kind of devil, insidiously eats his way into this world of romance, chivalry, nobility' (p. 115).

21   *May . . . him*, may reveal to him how I have been accusing him.

25   *coat*. Either of mail or strong leather. Probably an under-coat.

Act Five · Scene One

Cyprus · A street

Enter IAGO *and* RODERIGO

IAGO Here, stand behind this bulk; straight will he come.
  Wear thy good rapier bare, and put it home.
  Quick, quick! Fear nothing—I'll be at thy elbow.
  It makes us or it mars us. Think on that
  And fix most firm thy resolution.   5

RODERIGO Be near at hand; I may miscarry in't.

IAGO Here, at thy hand. Be bold, and take thy stand. [*He retires*]

RODERIGO I have no great devotion to the deed,
  And yet he hath given me satisfying reasons—
  'Tis but a man gone. Forth my sword; he dies!   10

IAGO I have rubbed this young quat almost to the sense,
  And he grows angry. Now, whether he kill Cassio,
  Or Cassio him, or each do kill the other,
  Every way makes my gain. Live Roderigo,
  He calls me to a restitution large   15
  Of gold and jewels, that I bobbed from him
  As gifts to Desdemona.
  It must not be. If Cassio do remain
  He hath a daily beauty in his life
  That makes me ugly. And besides, the Moor   20
  May unfold me to him—there stand I in peril.
  No, he must die. Be't so. I hear him coming.

Enter CASSIO

RODERIGO I know his gait; 'tis he. Villain, thou diest! [*He makes a pass at* CASSIO]

CASSIO That thrust had been mine enemy indeed,
  But that my coat is better than thou think'st.   25
  I will make proof of thine. [*He draws and wounds* RODERIGO]

27   (*stage direction*). In Shakespeare's theatre Othello probably appeared on the balcony above the back stage.

29   *It . . . so.* The reference of Othello's words is by no means clear. He may be confirming Roderigo's 'villain' remark but imagining that it comes from Cassio. The incident is of course played in dark confusion.

31   *brave*, admirable, excellent.   *just*, faithful, honourable.

32   *noble*, Even more ironically striking than 'honest' is this transfer of what one might call an Othello word to Iago.

33   *Minion*. Probably something like 'hussy'. The reference is to Desdemona.

35   *Forth of*. This reads awkwardly with 'blotted' and would have to be understood as 'from'. The Folio reads 'For of'.

36   *lust's blood*. Since Othello has decided to strangle Desdemona these words are odd.

37   *watch*. The Elizabethan body of watchmen who patrolled the streets at night—a primitive form of policing. See *Much Ado* for Shakespeare's fullest, amusing picture of the watch. *passage*, people passing by.

42   *heavy*. Possibly in the sense of 'dark', 'thick'.

43   *counterfeits*, decoys. Lodovico fears that the obscure cries in the dark may be some robbers' trick.

44   *come in to*, approach.

47   *in his shirt*, i.e. a sign of a hurried, alarmed rising from sleep.

48   *on*, out.

RODERIGO   O, I am slain!

[IAGO *from behinds wounds* CASSIO *in the leg and exit*

CASSIO   I am maimed for ever. Help, ho! Murder, murder! [*He falls*]

Enter OTHELLO

OTHELLO   The voice of Cassio. Iago keeps his word.

RODERIGO   O, villain that I am!

OTHELLO   It is even so.

CASSIO   O, help, ho! Light! A surgeon!   30

OTHELLO   'Tis he! O brave Iago, honest and just,
That hast such noble sense of thy friend's wrong,
Thou teachest me. Minion, your dear lies dead,
And your fate hies apace. Strumpet, I come!
Forth of my heart those charms, thine eyes, are blotted;   35
Thy bed, lust-stained, shall with lust's blood be spotted.   [*Exit*

Enter LODOVICO *and* GRATIANO *at a distance*

CASSIO   What ho! No watch? No passage? Murder, murder!

GRATIANO   'Tis some mischance; the cry is very direful.

CASSIO   O, help!

LODOVICO   Hark!   40

RODERIGO   O wretched villain!

LODOVICO   Two or three groan. It is a heavy night.
These may be counterfeits. Let's think't unsafe
To come in to the cry without more help.

RODERIGO   Nobody come?—then shall I bleed to death.   45

LODOVICO   Hark!

Re-enter IAGO, *with a light*

GRATIANO   Here's one comes in his shirt, with light and weapons.

IAGO   Who's there? Whose noise is this that cries on murder?

LODOVICO   We do not know.

IAGO   Did you not hear a cry?

CASSIO   Here, here. For heaven's sake help me!

IAGO   What's the matter?   50

GRATIANO   This is Othello's ancient, as I take it.

53   *What*, who.
54   *spoiled*, wounded to death.
58   *make away*, get away, escape.
59   *come in.* As in l.43 'approach'.
66   *praise*, appraise, judge. See the note to Act2Sc.3,l.117.
69   *I . . . mercy*, pardon me.
75   *Who . . . cried?* There seems no clear point in Iago's repetition of Bianca's question. Possibly there is some corruption of the text hereabouts.
76   *O . . . Cassio!* Shakespeare's treatment of Bianca deserves some second thought. Prostitute as she is, and in spite of the strictures of most commentators, she seems to love Cassio genuinely, and perhaps she contributes something to the theme of true faithful love embodied in Desdemona. Possibly Shakespeare, with his extraordinary range of human sympathy and generosity, is implying that truly felt love can be found in a common whore as well as in a high-born lady. His treatment of Doll Tearsheet in *Henry the Fourth*, Part II prompts the same reflection.
78   *may*, can.
79   *mangled*, wounded (possibly, but not necessarily, with the sense of 'mutilation').

LODOVICO   The same indeed, a very valiant fellow.

IAGO   What are you here that cry so grievously?

CASSIO   Iago? O, I am spoiled, undone by villains!
  Give me some help.   55

IAGO   O, my lieutenant! What villains have done this?

CASSIO   I think that one of them is hereabout
  And cannot make away.

IAGO   O treacherous villains!
  [*to* LODOVICO *and* GRATIANO]
  What are you there? Come in, and give some help.

RODERIGO   O, help me here!   60

CASSIO   That's one of them.

IAGO   O murderous slave! O villain! [*He stabs*
  RODERIGO]

RODERIGO   O damned Iago! O inhuman dog!

IAGO   Kill men i' the dark? Where be these bloody thieves?
  How silent is the town! Ho, murder, murder! [LODOVICO *and*
  GRATIANO *come forward*]
  What may you be? Are you of good or evil?   65

LODOVICO   As you shall prove us, praise us.

IAGO   Signor Lodovico?

LODOVICO   He, sir.

IAGO   I cry you mercy. Here's Cassio hurt by villains.

GRATIANO   Cassio?   70

IAGO   How is it, brother?

CASSIO   My leg is cut in two.

IAGO   Marry, heaven forbid!
  Light, gentlemen. I'll bind it with my shirt.

Enter BIANCA

BIANCA   What is the matter, ho? Who is't that cried?

IAGO   Who is't that cried?   75

BIANCA   O, my dear Cassio, O, my sweet Cassio,
  O Cassio, Cassio, Cassio!

IAGO   O notable strumpet! Cassio, may you suspect
  Who they should be that have thus mangled you?

82   *Lend . . . garter.* Presumably for tourniquet purposes.

85   *trash,* worthless hussy. To cover himself Iago is hurriedly incriminating Bianca, suggesting there has been some brothel squabble etc. and that Cassio's assailants are in league with her.

98   *well said,* well done.

101   *Save . . . labour.* Bianca is giving attention to Cassio.

102   *malice,* enmity, bad feeling.

105   *gentlemen.* The Quarto has 'gentlewoman', and this would mean that Iago is stopping Bianca from accompanying Cassio.

106–7   *Do . . . anon.* Some sense can be given to the Folio text printed opposite. 'gastness' could mean a fearful (or wild) look; and though the connection between the way Bianca is looking and 'hear more' may seem strained, in the light of the last lines of this speech Iago's meaning may be that Bianca's guilty looks and manner will give her further away. The Quarto reads 'gestures' for 'gastness', 'stir' for 'stare', and 'have' for 'hear'.

CASSIO No.   80

GRATIANO I am sorry to find you thus. I have been to seek you.

IAGO Lend me a garter—so. O, for a chair
    To bear him easily hence!

BIANCA   Alas, he faints!
    O Cassio, Cassio, Cassio!

IAGO Gentlemen all, I do suspect this trash   85
    To be a party in this injury.
    Patience awhile, good Cassio. Come, come;
    Lend me a light. Know we this face or no?
    Alas, my friend and my dear countryman
    Roderigo? No—yes, sure—O heaven, Roderigo!   90

GRATIANO What, of Venice?

IAGO Even he, sir. Did you know him?

GRATIANO   Know him? Ay.

IAGO Signor Gratiano? I cry you gentle pardon.
    These bloody accidents must excuse my manners
    That so neglected you.

GRATIANO   I am glad to see you.   95

IAGO How do you, Cassio? O, a chair, a chair!

GRATIANO Roderigo!

IAGO He, he, 'tis he. [*A chair is brought in*]
              O, that's well said, the chair!
    Some good man bear him carefully from hence;
    I'll fetch the General's surgeon. [*to* BIANCA] For you, mistress,   100
    Save you your labour. He that lies slain here, Cassio,
    Was my dear friend. What malice was between you?

CASSIO None in the world, nor do I know the man.

IAGO [*to* BIANCA] What, look you pale? O, bear him out o'the air.
    [CASSIO *and* RODERIGO *are borne off*]
    Stay you, good gentlemen. Look you pale, mistress?   105
    Do you perceive the gastness of her eye?
    Nay, if you stare, we shall hear more anon.
    Behold her well—I pray you look upon her.
    Do you see, gentlemen? Nay, guiltiness will speak
    Though tongues were out of use.   110

G

122–3   *life . . . me.* In view of Emilia's theft of the handkerchief, and lies, there is some ironic truth in Bianca's retort.

124   *Kind.* Here in a most general sense: 'good'.   *dressed,* have his wound attended to.

128–9   *This . . . quite.* Iago's schemes have not gone to plan. Notice, for the first time, some confession of uncertainty.   *makes me,* sets me up.   *fordoes,* ruins, destroys.

Scene Two

This is perhaps the finest last scene in all Shakespeare's tragedies, and much could be written in praise of its great variety of tone and tension, its management of the two main climaxes, its economy and avoidance of tedious concluding matter, and its splendidly sustained poetry. But one can also have some sympathy for Dr. Johnson's reaction when he confessed: 'I am glad that I have ended my revisal of this dreadful scene. It is not to be endured'. As Granville-Barker wrote: 'It is a terrible, shameful spectacle, of which Shakespeare spares us nothing, which, indeed, he elaborates and prolongs until the man's death comes as a veritable relief, a happy restoring of him to dignity'.

1–22   *It . . . wakes.* There can be little question that this is one of the most memorable speeches in Shakespeare.

1   *It . . . cause.* As the next line shows, 'cause' certainly refers to Desdemona's inchastity. (It might also carry a suggestion of 'disease', which was one meaning of the word.) But, in the light of the speech as a whole, the complete sentence may imply: 'All that concerns me now is the just punishment of Desdemona's adultery'. Behind this problem of expression there is a wider interpretative one. If Othello is now regarding the killing of Desdemona not in terms of bloody revenge but as an inevitable, though difficult, act of justice, is this change valid and justifiable, or is it, as some recent critics have maintained, a final act of self-delusion?

       Othello's calm and control are precarious: this speech reveals a tremendous tension of conflicting attitudes.

4   *whiter.* More clearly understood in front of 'than'.

5   *monumental alabaster.* Tomb figures were often in alabaster. See *The Merchant Of Venice,* Act1 Sc.1, l.84.

7   *Put . . . light.* A common interpretation of this difficult line is that the first 'light' refers to the torch, the second to Desdemona's life (or life in general).

Enter EMILIA

EMILIA 'Las what's the matter? What's the matter, husband?

IAGO Cassio has here been set on in the dark
    By Roderigo and fellows that are 'scaped.
    He's almost slain and Roderigo dead.

EMILIA Alas, good gentleman! Alas, good Cassio!　　　　　115

IAGO This is the fruit of whoring. Prithee, Emilia,
    Go know of Cassio where he supped tonight.
    [*to* BIANCA] What, do you shake at that?

BIANCA He supped at my house, but I therefore shake not.

IAGO O, did he so? I charge you go with me.　　　　　120

EMILIA O, fie upon thee, strumpet!

BIANCA I am no strumpet, but of life as honest
    As you that thus abuse me.

EMILIA　　　　　　　　　　As I? Foh! Fie upon thee!

IAGO Kind gentlemen, let's go see poor Cassio dressed.
    Come mistress, you must tell's another tale.　　　　　125
    Emilia, run you to the citadel,
    And tell my lord and lady what has happed.
    Will you go on, I pray? [*aside*] This is the night
    That either makes me or fordoes me quite.　　　　　[*Exeunt*

Scene Two

Cyprus · A bedchamber in the citadel

DESDEMONA *in bed asleep · Enter* OTHELLO *with a light*

OTHELLO It is the cause, it is the cause, my soul—
    Let me not name it to you, you chaste stars!—
    It is the cause. Yet I'll not shed her blood,
    Nor scar that whiter skin of hers than snow
    And smooth as monumental alabaster.　　　　　5
    Yet she must die, else she'll betray more men.
    Put out the light, and then put out the light.
    If I quench thee, thou flaming minister,

11 *cunning'st*, skilfully wrought. *pattern.* Perhaps simply 'form' or 'product'. *excelling nature.* This could have the sense of nature surpassing herself.

12 *Promethean.* In classical legend Prometheus was the fire-giver to men.

13 *relume*, relight.

16–17 *O . . . sword!* Othello is seeing himself as the agent, almost the personification, of Justice. The sword (and scales) were traditional symbols of justice.

20 *So . . . fatal.* A most pregnant compression. *fatal*, deadly; or perhaps, threatening mischief.

21 *cruel.* Ambiguous. Perhaps the word means 'associated with an act of cruelty'.

21-2 *This . . . love.* Othello is saying that because his grief arises from punishing someone he loves it is of a heavenly kind. The use of 'heavenly' may perhaps be explained by the text of *Hebrews*, ch.12 v.4. Possibly Shakespeare deliberately intends Othello to blaspheme—to commit the error of identifying himself with God.

28 *solicit*, pray.

32 *forfend*, forbid.

35 *If*, even if.

37 *fatal.* See the previous gloss on l.20.

38 *When . . . so.* Though Othello is certainly beginning to lose his initial control, we should be careful of exaggerating the impression conveyed by these words (and those in l.43). Elizabethan and Jacobean acting favoured what we should now consider strong—perhaps melodramatic—expressions and gestures.

I can again thy former light restore
Should I repent me; but once put out thy light,   10
Thou cunning'st pattern of excelling nature,
I know not where is that Promethean heat
That can thy light relume. When I have plucked thy rose,
I cannot give it vital growth again—
It needs must wither. I'll smell it on the tree. [*kissing her*]   15
O balmy breath, that doth almost persuade
Justice to break her sword! One more, one more.
Be thus when thou art dead, and I will kill thee
And love thee after. One more, and this the last.
So sweet was ne'er so fatal. I must weep,   20
But they are cruel tears. This sorrow's heavenly—
It strikes where it doth love . . . She wakes.

DESDEMONA Who's there? Othello?

OTHELLO   Ay, Desdemona.

DESDEMONA Will you come to bed, my lord?

OTHELLO Have you prayed tonight, Desdemona?

DESDEMONA   Ay, my lord.   25

OTHELLO If you bethink yourself of any crime
Unreconciled as yet to heaven and grace,
Solicit for it straight.

DESDEMONA Alas, my lord, what may you mean by that?

OTHELLO Well, do it, and be brief; I will walk by.   30
I would not kill thy unprepared spirit;
No, heaven forfend! I would not kill thy soul.

DESDEMONA Talk you of killing?

OTHELLO   Ay, I do.

DESDEMONA   Then heaven
Have mercy on me!

OTHELLO   Amen, with all my heart!

DESDEMONA If you say so, I hope you will not kill me.   35

OTHELLO Hum!

DESDEMONA And yet I fear you, for you are fatal then
When your eyes roll so. Why I should fear I know not,
Since guiltiness I know not; but yet I feel I fear.

OTHELLO Think on thy sins.

40   *They ... you*, any sins I may have committed are in (and excused by) my love for you. Possibly Desdemona is thinking of her deception of her father.

42   *That ... loving.* This line may sound a little odd to modern ears but the meaning is clear enough: 'death when it involves a killing out of feelings of love is unnatural'.

47   *What's the matter?* Not our casual idiom but something like 'What are you really alleging?'

48   *That handkerchief.* Whatever we may think of the crudity of the handkerchief incident in the plot mechanism, it is this trifle, 'light as air', that Othello chiefly harps on before killing Desdemona.

52   *presently*, at once.

54   *article.* An item or head in an accusation.

55   *remove nor choke.* An interesting, though not admirable, example of a common feature of Shakespeare's style: the supporting of an abstract word by a synonymous but concrete one. *conceit*, idea, or even belief—without the frequent sense of something imagined.

56   *withal.* Here simply 'with'.

59   *Offend*, wrong. (Stronger than the modern sense.)

60-1   *But ... love*, but in the way God tells us to love all our fellow men.

63-5   *Thou ... sacrifice.* In view of the problem raised in the previous note on l.1 it is a pity that these lines are more complex and uncertain than they may at first appear. What is clear is that the centre of them is Desdemona's apparent obduracy and Othello's frustrated hope that she would confess her sin. But even in the terms of the opening soliloquy it is not easy to see how Othello, represented in the play as a Christian believer, could regard the killing as a 'sacrifice'.

      Even at this stage Othello would never regard the deed as murder, and because he would not want to harden ('stone') *his* heart to commit a murder it seems that the Quarto 'thy' is preferable to the Folio 'my' in l.63. The sense behind 'mak'st ... murder' is not that Othello does in fact intend to call the deed murder but rather a protest that Desdemona's pretence of innocence is compelling the deed to take on a murderous complexion.

DESDEMONA   They are loves I bear to you.   40

OTHELLO   Ay, and for that thou diest.

DESDEMONA   That death's unnatural that kills for loving.
Alas, why gnaw you so your nether lip?
Some bloody passion shakes your very frame—
These are portents. But yet I hope, I hope   45
They do not point on me.

OTHELLO   Peace, and be still!

DESDEMONA   I will so. What's the matter?

OTHELLO   That handkerchief which I so loved and gave thee
Thou gav'st to Cassio.

DESDEMONA   No, by my life and soul!
Send for the man and ask him.

OTHELLO   Sweet soul, take heed,   50
Take heed of perjury. Thou art on thy death-bed.

DESDEMONA   Ay, but not yet to die.

OTHELLO   Yes, presently.
Therefore confess thee freely of thy sin,
For to deny each article with oath
Cannot remove nor choke the strong conceit   55
That I do groan withal. Thou art to die.

DESDEMONA   Then Lord have mercy on me!

OTHELLO   I say, amen.

DESDEMONA   And have you mercy too! I never did
Offend you in my life; never loved Cassio
But with such general warranty of heaven   60
As I might love. I never gave him token.

OTHELLO   By heaven, I saw my handkerchief in his hand!
O perjured woman! Thou dost stone thy heart,
And mak'st me call what I intend to do
A murder, which I thought a sacrifice.   65
I saw the handkerchief.

DESDEMONA   He found it then.
I never gave it him. Send for him hither.
Let him confess a truth.

OTHELLO   He has confessed.

DESDEMONA   What, my lord?

73   *ta'en . . . for't,* taken steps to do that; or, simply, seen to it.

74   *my fear interprets!* Not an easy phrase. Perhaps, taking it in conjunction with l.77, Desdemona means that her interpretation (or understanding) of Cassio's death is the fearful one that he will not now be able to testify to her innocence. Or, alternatively, 'interprets' may be used reflexively, and Desdemona may be saying that all her fears are now illuminated because she at last knows the reason for Othello's recent attitude towards her.

75   *Had . . . lives,* had he as many lives as hairs on his head. More Elizabethan hyperbole.

78   *Out . . . face?* It is of course Desdemona's undisguised distress at the report of Cassio's death that finally shatters the control Othello had displayed at the beginning of the scene. One consequence of this is that Othello breaks his earlier promise that Desdemona will be given time to pray. In some sense it is Desdemona's tender compassionate nature that finally destroys her.

83   *Being . . . pause.* In very pedestrian paraphrase: 'now the action is started, there's no stopping it'. These words are not in the Quarto.

85   *O . . . Lord!* These words are not in the Folio, but see Granville-Barker's excellent comment: 'Imagine it: Desdemona's agonized cry to God, and as the sharp sound of it is slowly stifled, Emilia's voice at the door rising through it, using the same words in another sense. A macabre duet . . .' (*op. cit.,* p. 122).

90   *So, so.* Though there has been some learned argument on the point, it seems clear from the evidence of the text (see especially l.204) that Desdemona is smothered, not stabbed.

93   *By and by.* This is of course a shout to Emilia.

95   *here.* Choice between this word and the Folio 'high' (loud) is complicated by the problem of what the 'noise' refers to. There are several possibilities.

OTHELLO   That he hath . . . used thee.

DESDEMONA   How? Unlawfully?   70

OTHELLO   Ay.

DESDEMONA   He will not say so.

OTHELLO   No, his mouth is stopped.
   Honest Iago hath ta'en order for't.

DESDEMONA   O, my fear interprets! . . . What, is he dead?

OTHELLO   Had all his hairs been lives, my great revenge   75
   Had stomach for them all.

DESDEMONA   Alas, he is betrayed and I undone.

OTHELLO   Out, strumpet! Weep'st thou for him to my face?

DESDEMONA   O banish me, my lord, but kill me not!

OTHELLO   Down, strumpet!   80

DESDEMONA   Kill me tomorrow; let me live tonight!

OTHELLO   Nay, if you strive—

DESDEMONA   But half an hour!

OTHELLO   Being done, there is no pause.

DESDEMONA   But while I say one prayer!

OTHELLO   It is too late.

DESDEMONA   O Lord, Lord, Lord! [*He smothers her*]   85

EMILIA [*within*]   My lord, my lord! What, ho! My lord, my lord!

OTHELLO   What noise is this? Not dead? Not yet quite dead?
   I, that am cruel, am yet merciful—
   I would not have thee linger in thy pain.
   So, so.   90

EMILIA [*within*]   What, ho! My lord, my lord!

OTHELLO   Who's there?

EMILIA [*within*]   O, good my lord, I'd speak a word with you.

OTHELLO   Yes, 'tis Emilia . . . By and by . . . She's dead.
   'Tis like she comes to speak of Cassio's death.
   The noise was here. Ha! No more moving?   95
   Still as the grave. Shall she come in? Were't good?
   I think she stirs again. No. What's best to do?
   If she come in, she'll sure speak to my wife—
   My wife! my wife! What wife? I have no wife.

100–3   *O . . . alteration.* Already—and as early as this—some hint of regret for his action.

103   *yawn,* gape in earthquake. There is evidence of a belief of the time that earthquakes and eclipses were connected. But it is not entirely impossible that ll.101–3 echo the New Testament description of the phenomena at Christ's death. Profane or not, such an allusion would not be out of keeping with Othello's distraction, bold imagination, and fundamental love for Desdemona.

Further, Kott reminds us that 'a simultaneous eclipse of the sun and the moon is a vision of the end of the world found in Baroque painting' (*op. cit.*, p. 84).

alteration, i.e. the change in nature brought about by Desdemona's death.

106   *soft,* stay, stop!   *curtains.* Probably those of the bed, so as to hide Desdemona's body. But since in original production the bed (or only part of it?) was almost certainly inside the back inner stage, these curtains might, just possibly, be those of the inner stage.

110   *But now,* only just now.

111–13   *It . . . mad.* This reference to the belief in 'lunar' madness parallels the allusion in Act2Sc.3,l.164.   *error.* A straying from its proper path.

117–18   *Then . . . harsh.* For the full impact of these lines we must remember the Elizabethan idealization of harmony and music. Othello's tragic inversion of moral values is so complete that murder and revenge are for him the harmony, the failure of them the discord.   *harsh,* discordant.

119   *O . . . murdered!* Any learned medical discussion about Desdemona's revival is pointless and only illustrates our modern obsession with realism. Other Elizabethan and Jacobean plays (e.g. Webster's *Duchess of Malfi*) employ this kind of make-believe, dramatic recovery at the point of death.

123   *Sweet . . . speak!* It is difficult to decide how long our ears retain word-echoes, but Emilia's iterated 'sweet' might ring ironically against Othello's 'sweet revenge' in l.118.

126   *Nobody; I myself.* What do we think of Desdemona's lie? There have been some critics who condemned it.

O, insupportable! O heavy hour!   100
Methinks it should be now a huge eclipse
Of sun and moon, and that the affrighted globe
Should yawn at alteration.

EMILIA [*within*]   I do beseech you
That I may speak with you. O, good my lord!

OTHELLO   I had forgot thee. O, come in, Emilia.   105
Soft; by and by. Let me the curtains draw.
Where art thou? [*unlocks the door*]
                    What's the matter with thee now?

Enter EMILIA

EMILIA   O, my good lord, yonder's foul murder done.

OTHELLO   What, now?

EMILIA   But now, my lord.   110

OTHELLO   It is the very error of the moon.
She comes more nearer earth than she was wont
And makes men mad.

EMILIA   Cassio, my lord, has killed a young Venetian
Called Roderigo.

OTHELLO   Roderigo killed?   115
And Cassio killed?

EMILIA   No, Cassio is not killed.

OTHELLO   Not Cassio killed! Then murder's out of tune,
And sweet revenge grows harsh.

DESDEMONA   O, falsely, falsely murdered!

EMILIA   O Lord! What cry is that?

OTHELLO   That? What?   120

EMILIA   Out and alas, it is my lady's voice! [*She draws back the bed-curtains*]
Help, help, ho, help! O, lady, speak again!
Sweet Desdemona, O sweet mistress, speak!

DESDEMONA   A guiltless death I die.

EMILIA   O, who has done this deed?   125

DESDEMONA   Nobody; I myself. Farewell.
Commend me to my kind lord. O, farewell! [*She dies*]

OTHELLO   Why, how should she be murdered?

EMILIA   Alas, who knows?

131-2   *She's . . . her.* Some ingenious interpretation can be read into these lines. But there seems nothing wrong with their straightforward meaning. From the time of Iago's allegations Othello has held fairly steadily to the belief that Desdemona is a devil who deserves the punishment of damnation. Her final lie—and he is in too distraught a state to weigh its implications—seems further to vindicate his belief. As a wronged husband he has no reason to fear extreme punishment for a love-killing and no need to snatch at an improbable 'cover' story.

132-3   *O . . . devil!* Very important lines. Now these antithetical terms ('angel', 'devil', etc.) are at last being put right. The 'divine' Desdemona is being firmly reinstated, and Othello is to be revealed (especially to himself), as the one who has been beguiled into devilish damnation.

134   *folly,* promiscuous behaviour. (See Act2Sc.1,l.137 and l.236 and notes).

136   *false as water.* Presumably Shakespeare means something like the 'inconstancy' of water, e.g. one can never grasp it firmly. This suggests the natural 'fire' antithesis.   *rash.* Probably 'swiftly and easily kindled'.

140-1   *But . . . extremity.* This is of course the gist of Othello's speech at the opening of the scene.   *But that,* unless, except. *extremity,* i.e. of justice.

146-7   *If . . . chrysolite.* 'Notice the single word "chrysolite" with its outstanding and remote beauty: this is typical of *Othello*' (Wilson Knight, *op. cit.,* p. 98). Othello is imagining a chrysolite (topaz) as big as the world. The chrysolite allusion is probably another echo from Holland's translation of Pliny's *Natural History.*

153   *made mocks with.* Either 'made a mockery of' or 'made a plaything of'. (Cf. Act3Sc.3,l.170.)

159   *fond of,* (foolishly) infatuated by.

OTHELLO   You heard her say herself it was not I.

EMILIA   She said so—I must needs report the truth.   130

OTHELLO   She's like a liar gone to burning hell.
    'Twas I that killed her.

EMILIA   O, the more angel she,
    And you the blacker devil!

OTHELLO   She turned to folly, and she was a whore.

EMILIA   Thou dost belie her, and thou art a devil.   135

OTHELLO   She was false as water.

EMILIA   Thou art rash as fire to say
    That she was false. O, she was heavenly true!

OTHELLO   Cassio did top her—ask thy husband else.
    O, I were damned beneath all depth in hell
    But that I did proceed upon just grounds   140
    To this extremity. Thy husband knew it all.

EMILIA   My husband!

OTHELLO   Thy husband.

EMILIA   That she was false to wedlock?

OTHELLO   Ay, with Cassio. Nay, had she been true,   145
    If heaven would make me such another world
    Of one entire and perfect chrysolite,
    I'd not have sold her for it.

EMILIA   My husband!

OTHELLO   Ay, 'twas he that told me first.
    An honest man he is, and hates the slime   150
    That sticks on filthy deeds.

EMILIA   My husband!

OTHELLO   What needs this iteration, woman? I say thy husband.

EMILIA   O mistress, villainy hath made mocks with love!
    My husband say that she was false?

OTHELLO   He, woman.
    I say thy husband—dost understand the word?   155
    My friend, thy husband, honest, honest Iago.

EMILIA   If he say so, may his pernicious soul
    Rot half a grain a day! He lies to the heart.
    She was too fond of her most filthy bargain.

162–3   *This . . . her.* Presumably Emilia is reminding Othello of his damnation, but the expression, especially 'worthy heaven', is a little odd. Of course Emilia has not overheard Othello's opening soliloquy, but perhaps her words are intended primarily to remind the audience of his false belief that he was acting as the agent of heaven.

163   *Peace . . . best,* silence, if you know what's best for you.

164–5   *Thou . . . hurt,* i.e. nothing that Othello can do to her physically compares in pain with the inner distress she is beginning to feel. 'It is my own inner feelings that really hurt me'.

165   *gull,* dupe.

166   *ignorant as dirt.* Possibly Emilia is twisting the more familiar 'cheap as dirt' to her own needs of expression here.

170   *What . . . matter?* Probably, as in l.47, a little more serious and sharply pointed than our similar expression.

172   *on your neck.* Since Emilia has still to be convinced of Iago's villainy—though she must be near that point—her words may be intended to mean no more than 'to your account'. But for the audience the association of hanging with neck gives these words an ironical ambiguity.

177   *for . . . full.* Presumably Emilia means 'full of conflicting thoughts and emotions'. She wants the truth that will at least end this conflict.

179   *apt,* credible, likely. Cf. Act2Sc.1, l.270.

185   *charm your tongue,* i.e. into silence.

187   *My . . . bed.* All through the latter part of the scene (and particularly at points like this and ll.276–7) we must remember that the stage is to some extent dominated by the sight of Desdemona's body.

188   *forfend,* forbid.

189   *set . . . on,* instigated the murder.

OTHELLO   Ha!   160

EMILIA   Do thy worst.
　This deed of thine is no more worthy heaven
　Than thou wast worthy her.

OTHELLO   Peace, you were best.

EMILIA   Thou hast not half the power to do me harm
　As I have to be hurt. O gull! O dolt!   165
　As ignorant as dirt! Thou hast done a deed . . .
　I care not for thy sword. I'll make thee known
　Though I lost twenty lives. Help! Help, ho! Help!
　The Moor has killed my mistress! Murder! Murder!

Enter MONTANO · GRATIANO · IAGO · *and others*

MONTANO   What is the matter? How now, General?   170

EMILIA   O, are you come, Iago? You have done well
　That men must lay their murders on your neck.

GRATIANO   What is the matter?

EMILIA   Disprove this villain, if thou be'st a man.
　He says thou told'st him that his wife was false.   175
　I know thou didst not; thou art not such a villain.
　Speak, for my heart is full.

IAGO   I told him what I thought, and told no more
　Than what he found himself was apt and true.

EMILIA   But did you ever tell him she was false?   180

IAGO   I did.

EMILIA   You told a lie, an odious damned lie—
　Upon my soul, a lie, a wicked lie!
　She false with Cassio! Did you say with Cassio?

IAGO   With Cassio, mistress! Go to, charm your tongue.   185

EMILIA   I will not charm my tongue; I am bound to speak.
　My mistress here lies murdered in her bed.

ALL   O heavens forfend!

EMILIA   And your reports have set the murder on.

OTHELLO   Nay, stare not masters. It is true indeed.   190

GRATIANO   'Tis a strange truth.

MONTANO   O monstrous act!

193–5   *Villainy . . . villainy!* The difficulty here (perhaps connected with the fact that ll.187–95 are not in the Quarto) is the extent of Emilia's discovery. Her 'then' (l.194) can hardly refer to the time when she gave Iago the handkerchief because (1) she did so without suspicion, and (2) the significance of the stolen handkerchief has still to be revealed. All she now knows for certain is that it was Iago who had informed Othello of Desdemona's infidelity; and it seems most likely that 'then' refers to her earlier guess (Act4Sc.2, ll.131–4) that some 'cozening slave' had been devizing slander.

199   *Perchance . . . home.* Ominous, ironic words—especially for those who know the play.

202   *O . . . foul!* These words, after the falling on the bed, show how Othello is still torn between violently contradictory attitudes towards Desdemona. He has of course no reason yet to suspect Iago's story.

207   *mortal,* fatal.

208   *Shore . . . thread,* cut his old thread of life.

209   *do . . . turn,* do something desperate.

210–11   *Yea . . . reprobation.* Reference to the 'guardian' angel—'better' because of the belief that a man in his path through life is accompanied by a good and bad angel. (See Marlowe's *Dr. Faustus*).

     This reference to 'angel' and 'reprobation' (rejection by God that may lead to damnation), coming from a minor character, like Cassio's drunken talk about 'salvation' (Act2Sc.3, ll.95–7), should be carefully noted. The rich cluster of such references may take us to the heart of the play. In fact these two lines of Gratiano are a close description of what has happened to Othello, and even if we deny their central significance, they still remain full of dramatic irony.

214   *A thousand times.* Though time in this play is, in Granville-Barker's words, 'contracted and expanded like a concertina' (*op. cit.*, p. 11), this phrase is pure rhetorical hyperbole.

215   *gratify,* reward.   *amorous works,* love-making.

216   *recognizance,* token (synonymous with 'pledge').

219   *My . . . mother.* Hardly consistent with Othello's previous account (Act3Sc.4, ll.53–4) and almost certainly a slip on Shakespeare's part.   *antique,* ancient.

221   *I.* With 'hold' understood.

222   *liberal,* unrestrained, free. (Cf. Act2Sc.1, l.162.)   *north.* This word is retained because the rest of the line is also given in the Folio version, which differs slightly from the Quarto one; but perhaps the Quarto 'air' is to be preferred. However, the north wind (if that is the meaning) could signify a particularly cutting, icy and exposing, sort of wind, in keeping with what Emilia is about to unfold.

223   *heaven, devils.* Note these words.

EMILIA   Villainy, villainy, villainy!
    I think upon't, I think—I smell't! O villainy!
    I thought so then. I'll kill myself for grief.   195
    O villainy, villainy!

IAGO What, are you mad? I charge you get you home.

EMILIA Good gentlemen, let me have leave to speak.
    'Tis proper I obey him, but not now.
    Perchance, Iago, I will ne'er go home.

OTHELLO [*falling on the bed*] O! O! O!

EMILIA   Nay, lay thee down and roar,   200
    For thou hast killed the sweetest innocent
    That e'er did lift up eye.

OTHELLO [*rising*]   O, she was foul! . . .
    I scarce did know you, uncle. There lies your niece,
    Whose breath indeed these hands have newly stopped.
    I know this act shows horrible and grim.   205

GRATIANO Poor Desdemona, I am glad thy father's dead.
    Thy match was mortal to him, and pure grief
    Shore his old thread in twain. Did he live now,
    This sight would make him do a desperate turn,
    Yea, curse his better angel from his side   210
    And fall to reprobation.

OTHELLO 'Tis pitiful; but yet Iago knows
    That she with Cassio hath the act of shame
    A thousand times committed. Cassio confessed it.
    And she did gratify his amorous works   215
    With that recognizance and pledge of love
    Which I first gave her. I saw it in his hand—
    It was a handkerchief, an antique token
    My father gave my mother.

EMILIA O God! O heavenly God!   220

IAGO Zounds, hold your peace!

EMILIA   'Twill out, 'twill out. I peace?
    No, I will speak as liberal as the north.
    Let heaven and men and devils, let them all,
    All, all cry shame against me, yet I'll speak.

IAGO Be wise, and get you home.

229   *solemn.* Perhaps in the sense of 'making a strong impression'.

235   *coxcomb,* fool.

236–7   *Are . . . thunder?* i.e. are there not also thunderbolts ('stones') in heaven for striking villains?

237   *precious.* A colloquial intensive in abuse.

241   *notorious.* Not 'of well-known infamy' but 'outstanding', 'utter'.   *you this.* This Folio reading would mean that Othello used his own sword in his own onslaught on Iago, and this is consistent with Emilia's remark in l.166. The Quarto reading 'your' would mean that Othello had snatched Gratiano's sword.

242   *recovered from,* taken away from.

246   *whipster.* A term of contempt, of uncertain origin, denoting an insignificant person.

247   *But . . . honesty?* 'Honour' and 'honesty' can be near synonyms in Shakespearean English. With 'honour' Othello is referring to honour in its more superficial sense—'reputation': he is dishonoured by having his sword taken away. 'Honesty' is a more essential, internal quality of virtue, integrity, etc.

249–50   *I . . . music.* An old belief that the swan sings before its death. The snatch of the 'Willow' song, better than any explanatory words, rightly re-unites Emilia with Desdemona in her death. Bradley has an interesting comment on Emilia: 'Few of Shakespeare's minor characters are more distinct than Emilia, and towards few do our feelings change so much within the course of a play. Till close to the end she frequently sets one's teeth on edge; and at the end one is ready to worship her'. (*op. cit.*, p. 239.)

252   *So . . . bliss.* Another 'salvation' reference.

EMILIA   I will not. [IAGO *draws his sword*]

GRATIANO   Fie!   225
   Your sword upon a woman!

EMILIA   O thou dull Moor, that handkerchief thou speak'st of
   I found by fortune and did give my husband,
   For often with a solemn earnestness,
   More than indeed belonged to such a trifle,   230
   He begged of me to steal it.

IAGO   Villainous whore!

EMILIA   She gave it Cassio? No, alas, I found it
   And I did give't my husband.

IAGO   Filth, thou liest!

EMILIA   By heaven I do not, I do not, gentlemen.
   O murderous coxcomb, what should such a fool   235
   Do with so good a wife?

OTHELLO   Are there no stones in heaven
   But what serve for the thunder? Precious villain!
   [*He runs at* IAGO. IAGO *stabs* EMILIA *from behind and escapes.* MONTANO *disarms*
   OTHELLO]

GRATIANO   The woman falls. Sure he hath killed his wife.

EMILIA   Ay, ay. O, lay me by my mistress' side.

GRATIANO   He's gone, but his wife's killed.   240

MONTANO   'Tis a notorious villain. Take you this weapon,
   Which I have here recovered from the Moor.
   Come, guard the door without; let him not pass,
   But kill him rather. I'll after that same villain,
   For 'tis a damned slave.   [*Exeunt* MONTANO *and* GRATIANO

OTHELLO   I am not valiant neither,   245
   But every puny whipster gets my sword.
   But why should honour outlive honesty?
   Let it go all.

EMILIA   What did thy song bode, lady?
   Hark, canst thou hear me? I will play the swan
   And die in music. [*sings*] Willow, willow, willow . . .   250
   Moor, she was chaste. She loved thee, cruel Moor,
   So come my soul to bliss, as I speak true.
   So speaking as I think, I die, I die. [*She dies*]

255   *ice-brook's temper,* tempered, during manufacture, by being plunged into an ice-cold stream.

256   *Uncle.* Gratiano was Brabantio's brother.

258   *perforce,* of necessity, inevitably.

260   *naked,* unarmed.

261–84 *Behold . . . oh!* A central point of Wilson Knight's acute analysis of the play is that the beauty of Othello's speech, 'the exquisitely moulded language, the noble cadence and chiselled phrase' (*op. cit.,* p. 106) degenerates, under extremes of anguish, into an 'inartistic ugliness' (p. 105). Othello's bombast and hyperbole are forms of this ugliness, and Knight cites the last six lines of this speech as an example. For Knight this stylistic degeneration reflects the essence of the play: Iago's corruption of all the nobility and idealism, poetry and romance, that are embodied in Othello. Iago is an 'acid eating into bright metal' (p. 103). This interpretation of Othello's speech is interesting and attractive, but, unqualified, it is open to several objections.

261   *Behold . . . weapon.* A grimly triumphant rejoinder to Gratiano's confident 'Thou hast no weapon'.

266   *Than . . . stop,* twenty times stronger than your power to hinder me. 'Impediments' and 'stop' are synonyms.

268–74 *Be . . . wench!* Not in the Quarto.

269   *butt,* goal.

270   *sea-mark,* beacon; or some sign of landfall.   *utmost sail,* furthest sailing.

271   *lost,* vain, groundless.

272   *Man . . . rush.* 'Man' is an odd word, but the meaning is probably 'advance but a spear of rush'.

275   *smock* woman's undergarment.

275–7   *When . . . it* Othello clearly realizes his damnation, and unless Leavis was thinking purely in psychological terms of the most limited sort, it is difficult to understand how he could write of this speech: 'there is no tragic self-discovery' (*op. cit.,* p. 150). *compt,* Judgment Day.

278   *chastity.* At last the fundamental admission, but too late now—'cold'.

279   *slave.* Almost certainly refers to Othello himself, though it might, just possibly, mean Iago.

279–82 *Whip . . . fire!* Conventional pictures of hell-torment. Othello is now calling down on himself immediate damnation. Note the 'heavenly' for Desdemona and her love.

282   *steep-down,* precipitous.

285   *Where . . . man?* For the moment, to give full effect to Othello's final speech, the stage is dominated by Lodovico conducting a kind of judicial inquest, not by Othello.

286   *That's . . . Othello.* Most simple but most pregnant words—very Shakespearean.

OTHELLO   I have another weapon in this chamber;
    It was a sword of Spain, the ice-brook's temper.   255
    O, here it is. [*aloud*] Uncle, I must come forth.

GRATIANO [*within*]   If thou attempt it, it will cost thee dear.
    Thou hast no weapon, and perforce must suffer.

OTHELLO   Look in' upon me then and speak with me,
    Or naked as I am I will assault thee.   260

Re-enter GRATIANO

GRATIANO   What is the matter?

OTHELLO   Behold, I have a weapon—
    A better never did itself sustain
    Upon a soldier's thigh. I have seen the day
    That with this little arm and this good sword
    I have made my way through more impediments   265
    Than twenty times your stop. But, O vain boast!
    Who can control his fate? 'Tis not so now.
    Be not afraid, though you do see me weaponed.
    Here is my journey's end, here is my butt
    And very sea-mark of my utmost sail.   270
    Do you go back dismayed? 'Tis a lost fear.
    Man but a rush against Othello's breast,
    And he retires. Where should Othello go?
    Now, how dost thou look now? O ill-starred wench!
    Pale as thy smock! When we shall meet at compt   275
    This look of thine will hurl my soul from heaven
    And fiends will snatch at it. Cold, cold, my girl,
    Even like thy chastity.
    O cursed, cursed slave! Whip me, ye devils,
    From the possession of this heavenly sight!   280
    Blow me about in winds! Roast me in sulphur!
    Wash me in steep-down gulfs of liquid fire!
    O Desdemona! Desdemona! dead!
    Oh, oh, oh!

Enter LODOVICO · MONTANO · *Soldiers with* IAGO *prisoner and* CASSIO *in a chair*

LODOVICO   Where is this rash and most unfortunate man?   285

OTHELLO   That's he that was Othello. Here I am.

LODOVICO   Where is that viper? Bring the villain forth.

288–9   *I . . . thee.* The significance of these grimly ironical words (to be contrasted with Lodovico's conventional and superficial 'viper' and 'villain') is that Othello at last identifies Iago not simply as an evil-doer but as what he essentially is: a devil who has tempted him to damnation. The two conventional devil references are to the cloven feet and the fiend's ultimate invulnerability to physical destruction.

292   *in my sense,* in the way I feel.

294   *Fallen.* This word may, just possibly, carry some religious overtone, i.e. 'damned'.   *practice,* plotting.

295–7   *Why . . . honour.* These words are obviously important for our interpretation of Othello, but they raise problems. The force of 'Why, anything' seems to be 'I do not care how *others* regard my action'; and he continues 'you can call me an "honourable murderer" if you like'. But then in the next line, in apparent self-justification, he appears to identify himself with this point of view. Can this be reconciled with his earlier realization that he has committed an act of damnation? Or is Othello, even at this stage, still in spiritual confusion?

299   *consent,* agree.

301   *Dear . . . cause.* We never admire Cassio more than when he utters these generous, simple words.

303–4   *Well . . . body?* Again Othello's realization that his very soul has been lost to a 'demi-devil'.

305–6   *Demand . . . word.* For all Iago's evil, there is a certain impressiveness in these laconic words. And he makes a promise that he keeps. Though it is usually futile to think of characters in an existence outside the play, Swinburne adds a suggestive postscript to his comments on Iago when he writes: 'we might conceive something of Iago's attitude in hell—of his unalterable and indomitable posture for all eternity'. *(op. cit.).*

308   *Well . . . best.* This refers to Iago's determination to say no more.

312   *imports,* signifies, informs of.

315   *gross.* Something like 'flagrant' or 'monstrous'.

316   *discontented,* expressing discontent, dissatisfaction (of how things were going).

319   *nick,* of time. The Folio has the less colloquial 'interim'.

OTHELLO I look down towards his feet; but that's a fable.
    If that thou be'st a devil, I cannot kill thee. [*wounds* IAGO]

LODOVICO Wrench his sword from him.

IAGO   I bleed, sir, but not killed. 290

OTHELLO I am not sorry neither. I'd have thee live,
    For in my sense 'tis happiness to die.

LODOVICO O, thou Othello, that wert once so good,
    Fallen in the practice of a damned slave,
    What shall be said to thee?

OTHELLO   Why, anything—   295
    An honourable murderer, if you will,
    For naught did I in hate but all in honour.

LODOVICO This wretch hath part confessed his villainy.
    Did you and he consent in Cassio's death?

OTHELLO Ay.   300

CASSIO Dear General, I never gave you cause.

OTHELLO I do believe it, and I ask you pardon.
    Will you, I pray, demand that demi-devil
    Why he hath thus ensnared my soul and body?

IAGO Demand me nothing. What you know, you know.   305
    From this time forth I never will speak word.

LODOVICO What, not to pray?

GRATIANO   Torments will ope your lips.

OTHELLO Well, thou dost best.

LODOVICO Sir, you shall understand what hath befallen,
    Which, as I think, you know not. Here is a letter   310
    Found in the pocket of the slain Roderigo,
    And here another. The one of them imports
    The death of Cassio, to be undertook
    By Roderigo.

OTHELLO O villain!

CASSIO   Most heathenish and most gross!   315

LODOVICO Now here's another discontented paper
    Found in his pocket too; and this, it seems,
    Roderigo meant to have sent this damned villain,
    But that, belike, Iago in the nick
    Came in and satisfied him.

320   *caitiff*, wretch, miscreant, etc.

325   *Which . . . desire*. A possible paraphrase might be: 'which furthered his general plans (or intentions)'.

328   *Brave*, treat with bravado, provoke.   *came*, ensued.

329–31   *And . . . on.* As punctuated here, 'Iago hurt him' and 'Iago set him on', preceded by 'that' understood, are both objects of 'spake'. But 'Iago hurt him' could be a parenthesis added to 'seeming dead', with 'Iago set him on' as the single object of 'spake'.

335   *cunning cruelty*, ingenious form of torture.

336   *and . . . long*, and (yet) keep him long alive.

340–58   *Soft . . . thus.* Most are likely to accept the poetic eloquence of this speech. What has to be settled—and the question involves the whole play—is whether the speech is to be taken as a valid, entirely sincere, and to some extent admirable utterance of an essentially 'noble' Othello, or whether, as Leavis would have it, 'a habit of self-approving, self-dramatization is an essential element in Othello's make-up, and remains so at the very end' (*op. cit.*, p. 142). T. S. Eliot presents a point of view similar to that of Leavis in his essay, 'Shakespeare and the Stoicism of Senaca'. In any discussion it should be remembered that nobility, even some degree of self-defence, are not necessarily inconsistent with Othello's earlier acceptance of soul-damnation. As Granville-Barker says, 'Othello—even though no spiritual salvation will dawn for him—is not to be left in "mere chaos" ' (*op. cit.*, p. 128). To this might be added Wilson Knight's comment: 'The beauties of the *Othello* world are not finally disintegrated: they make "a swan-like end, fading in music" ' (*op. cit.*, p. 119).

340   *Soft you.* As in l.106.

343   *unlucky*, ill-fated, disastrous.

344   *extenuate*, minimize, tone down.

345–8   *Then . . . extreme.* For many (most?) these will be true and revealing words about Othello's basic attitudes and situation in the play. In particular, 'too well' may point to a realization that his life and world have been too excessively based on his love for Desdemona.

348   *Perplexed.* More in the sense of 'distracted', 'bewildered'.

349   *base*, uncivilized, degraded; even perhaps, ignorant.   *Indian*. Some editors have been attracted by the enigmatic variant in the Folio, 'Iudean', which might have some connection with Judas.

350   *subdued*, i.e. by tears, grief.

351   *melting mood*, weeping, or tender mood.

353   *medicinal gum*, myrrh. (Perhaps referred to for its religious associations.)

355   *malignant.* A pejorative word, possibly in the sense of 'infidel'.

OTHELLO   O the pernicious caitiff!   320
  How came you, Cassio, by that handkerchief
  That was my wife's?

CASSIO   I found it in my chamber,
  And he himself confessed but even now
  That there he dropped it for a special purpose
  Which wrought to his desire.

OTHELLO   O fool, fool, fool!   325

CASSIO   There is besides in Roderigo's letter
  How he upbraids Iago, that he made him
  Brave me upon the watch, whereon it came
  That I was cast. And even but now he spake,
  After long seeming dead, Iago hurt him,   330
  Iago set him on.

LODOVICO   You must forsake this room and go with us.
  Your power and your command is taken off,
  And Cassio rules in Cyprus. For this slave,
  If there be any cunning cruelty   335
  That can torment him much and hold him long,
  It shall be his. You shall close prisoner rest
  Till that the nature of your fault be known
  To the Venetian state. Come, bring him away.

OTHELLO   Soft you—a word or two before you go.   340
  I have done the state some service and they know't.
  No more of that. I pray you in your letters
  When you shall these unlucky deeds relate
  Speak of them as they are. Nothing extenuate,
  Nor set down aught in malice. Then must you speak   345
  Of one that loved not wisely, but too well;
  Of one not easily jealous, but, being wrought,
  Perplexed in the extreme; of one whose hand,
  Like the base Indian, threw a pearl away
  Richer than all his tribe; of one whose subdued eyes, 350
  Albeit unused to the melting mood,
  Drops tears as fast as the Arabian trees
  Their medicinal gum. Set you down this;
  And say besides that in Aleppo once
  Where a malignant and a turbaned Turk   355
  Beat a Venetian and traduced the state,

359   *period*, ending.

360-1   *I . . . kiss.* Helen Gardner comments on these lines: 'His sense
of eternal separation when he and Desdemona will "meet at
compt" comes earlier, when he sees himself as the murderer
and her as martyred victim. But in the last speech this sense
of separation is lost in the final sense of reunion'. (*Shakespeare Survey*, 21 (*Othello*), p. 6.) But this creates an unwarranted
inconsistency, for nothing has happened since Othello last
spoke of the ensnarement of his 'soul'—and therefore his
damned separation from Desdemona (ll.303-4)—except some
further information on Iago's plotting. The fact that Othello's
final speech to some extent 'saves' the values he stands for
does not mean that he is himself 'saved'. The issue here is of
crucial importance for the final effect of the tragedy. Miss
Gardner offers us a comfort that, alas, does not seem justified.

362   *thought . . . weapon.* It may seem a little odd that in the previous
double disarming of Othello no attention had been paid to
his dagger. However this detail is of no importance.

363   *Spartan.* Hanmer stated that Spartan dogs were noted for their
fierceness and savageness. But there is no certainty about the
allusion.

364   *fell.* dire, cruel, etc.   *anguish,* the most excruciating pain or
suffering.

365   *loading.* In the Arden edition Ridley argues strongly for the
Quarto variant 'lodging'—a country word describing the
action of storm, etc., beating down crops.

366   *object.* Perhaps a fine shade of difference from the modern
word—'what we see', 'spectacle'.

367   *keep.* Probably in the sense of 'live in'.

368   *seize upon,* (legal) take possession of.

369   *they . . . you,* you inherit them.   *Lord Governor,* i.e. Cassio.

370   *censure,* judgment, or trial.

371   *it,* i.e. the torture. A reminder of what Lodovico said in
ll.334-7.

I took by the throat the circumcised dog—
And smote him thus. [*stabs himself*]

LODOVICO O bloody period!

GRATIANO   All that's spoke is marred!

OTHELLO I kissed thee ere I killed thee. No way but this,   360
    Killing myself, to die upon a kiss. [*falls on the bed and dies*]

CASSIO This did I fear, but thought he had no weapon,
    For he was great of heart.

LODOVICO   O, Spartan dog,
    More fell than anguish, hunger, or the sea,
    Look on the tragic loading of this bed: 365
    This is thy work. The object poisons sight;
    Let it be hid. Gratiano, keep the house
    And seize upon the fortunes of the Moor,
    For they succeed on you. To you, Lord Governor,
    Remains the censure of this hellish villain.   370
    The time, the place, the torture—O, enforce it!
    Myself will straight aboard, and to the state
    This heavy act with heavy heart relate.   [*Exeunt*